Play It Again....

...SAM

Play It Again....

...SAM

In front and behind the
scenes in show business

with

SAM SHROUDER

Bookaholics Publishing, 2017.

Published by Bookaholics Publishing
19, Carters Garth Close, Grainthorpe, Louth,
Lincolnshire, LN11 7HT

ISBN: 978-1-5272-1025-7

Printed and bound in Great Britain
by T.J.International Ltd., Padstow, Cornwall.

CONTENTS

DEDICATION

This book is a dedication to Linda and Ben,
the two most important people in my life.

FOREWORD

What a lovely day! What a lovely day for being first in Sam Shrouder's book!

It is a great pleasure to be able to provide the foreword for Sam's story. Now, what shall I say? I know....hmmm, better not say that....Perhaps?... no, better not say that either.

Seriously, Sam Shrouder is one of the real gentlemen of the entertainments and leisure industry and I am delighted to be in his excellent book.

We have known each other for longer than he cares to remember and I have always found him one of the better people to work with. His theatre management was always excellent. Nothing was too much trouble at any time and Sam has earned himself a very fine reputation among performers as well as his fellow theatre professionals.

Sam is always cheerful too and never seems to panic. A crisis soon became a simple problem when Sam Shrouder has been in charge and he is one of those wonderful people who dwells on solutions rather than causes. Never fear, Sam is here!

It helps that Sam has also been a performer. He was one of the most popular DJs at the Labour Exchange! No, really, Sam had his own following during his exciting days as a DJ and all that experience of being in front of audiences clearly showed in his empathy towards the many performers who appeared in his theatres.

There is no end to his talents as I know for a fact that he came close to a career as a professional cricketer and he almost achieved fame as a football star. He told me himself about that.

Throughout the years he has played host to many star performers from all over the world and they all remember Sam Shrouder for his kindness and his enthusiasm to make things work.

He and I have sat in the dressing room together many times haggling over who would pour the tea and I hope that we shall again.

In the meantime, enjoy Sam's book – it is like the man himself – honest and entertaining.

Ken Dodd

PREFACE

In 1999 I was a guest on a panel of "experts" at a theatre industry Conference. The lady chairing it stood up to introduce us and said, "Our first member, as Chief Executive, runs the second largest theatre company in the world." For a few seconds I looked at my fellow guests to see who this important person was – only to hear my name!

Her facts proved to be correct as Apollo, with 26 theatres and concert halls was second only in size to American theatre owners the Schubert Organisation. When it came to Question Time I was asked what I put my career down to. I answered, "Luck, more luck and even more luck!"

This book is about my journey from being an unemployable Time Study Engineer to being a part of the team that created the greatest British Theatre success story of its time. It is also about the people I met along the way which included Royalty, International Stars but also, more importantly the people who helped me along this path and witrhout whom there would be no story to tell.

Should you survive this journey I am certain that you will then close this book saying, "He was one lucky boy!"

Chapter 1

I MUST BE GOOD AT SOMETHING!

I remember it distinctly. It was on July 18th, 1964 and I was standing outside Denstone College on my 19th birthday waiting to be collected by my father. It would be nice to say that I was in a happy frame of mind but I'm not sure that would be totally true.

Denstone was a second rate, slightly unpleasant boys' boarding school on a hill in Staffordshire. In my last two years there I had failed every single exam that I had taken, be it A levels, AS levels or retaken 0 levels. As I stood there being ignored by members of staff hurrying by, I mused that this had been a major waste of my parents' money. Indeed I departed with only two benefits – a lifelong friend in Martin Raybould and that I was a much improved cricketer.

Martin had been my fellow pub goer and instead of studying we had concentrated on the delights of Lonnie Donegan and Joe Brown. Indeed had there been an extra exam on the lyrics of all their songs we would both have got 100%! When in class we were disruptive and giggled a lot. This was obviously the reason for my academic disaster but somehow it did not have the same effect on Martin as he ended up the school's finest scholar with 6 A levels at the highest grade. I used to think that he could have given me three of his A levels as he had played a major part in me not reaching my true potential. Anyway three A levels is enough for anybody. '

The cricket at Denstone was its only saving grace with quality fixtures including the MCC and Derbyshire Club and Ground and coaches that included ex-England player Jack Ikin and a first team that was coached and managed by David Green. He also played for Derbyshire and was one of the few members of staff that I really liked and respected.

In my final year I had had a good season, culminating in my last game against Trent College when I got 122 not out and 5 for 28. This would seem to have been a fine way to bow out but unfortunately it was not meant to have been the last match as we traditionally finished with a two-day match against Stoneyhurst. This was a very important game for the school as lots of parents used to come and watch and it was even reported on by the Daily Telegraph.

When Stoneyhurst came to Denstone the night before the game it was taken for granted that we would all go to the pub. However on this occasion the Headmaster informed us that there would be serious consequences if any of us left the school grounds. So we hung around the school until 11 pm. I was then caught with three Stoneyhurst players having a cigarette in the Pavilion. The absurd result of this dreadful act was that the match was cancelled and the Stoneyhurst team sent home. So even the one thing that I had succeeded in at school ended in disgrace!

As we drove back to Lancashire, my Dad asked me what I intended to do for a job. I had not really given this much thought so I told him that I intended to be a professional cricketer. This was greeted with an incredulous look and a shake of the head. This ambition did have some substance in that I had been written to by Tom Reddick, who ran Lancashire's youth cricket, suggesting that I make contact with him on my return from school. This sounded promising but the fact that he suggested that I found him during one of the days of the forthcoming Test Match amongst 25,000 people less so! Due to perseverance rather than ability he did select me for Lancashire Under 21s v Central Lancashire League Under 21s at Old Trafford.

It was a dream come true when I walked out to bat at this most iconic of grounds. However walking back having been run out for 3 was not the continuation of the dream! Despite that Tom obviously saw enough in that little cameo to select me for Lancashire Colts against Staffordshire. In this game I opened and scored a classy seven and did not get a bowl. Our best player batted at No. 7 and bowled some excellent left arm spin – a certain David Lloyd! I never heard from Tom Reddick again, which was a tad disappointing as this was my chosen career!

The only way to progress things was to be so outstanding for my club side, Ormskirk that I could not be ignored. It was with this mind-set that I approached our game against St Helens Rec. The night before I went, with my oldest friend Nick Hall, to a dance in a quarry in Aughton, where I lived

(Aughton, not the quarry!) Being the dedicated sportsman that I was I told Nick I was leaving when midnight arrived. He said I was mad as we had a chance with two rather attractive girls. I might add that given our track record we had no chance so I duly departed.

The game did not quite start as well as I might have hoped as I dropped an easy chance off their star batsman, Mike Beddows (later to play for Lancashire) when he was on nought. I think that this lapse slightly upset our fiery opening bowler Tommy Wheble judging from his language to me! This was not helped by the batsman going on to score a mighty 122.

When I went out to bat, the Ormskirk team, including my friend Sandy Tittershill, made it very clear to me that I would have to score 123 to register my first positive run. I went out to face their fearsome fast bowler Ken Shutterworth, who later played for Lancashire and England, and the second ball he bowled at me was coming towards my unhelmeted head. In terms of self-preservation I luckily managed to deflect it with my glove on the way to being caught behind by John Lyons, who also went on to play for Lancashire, for nought. As I trudged back, facing certain ridicule from the crowd (all 10 of them) and my team mates, I realised that I would have to reassess my career options.

My parents, Grace and John, now became even more concerned that not only did I not have a job but I did not appear to be very keen about looking for one. I was already well on the way to being the intellectual black sheep of the family.

My mother was an academic who got an honours degree at Oxford University and went on to be a lecturer and she had trouble coming to terms with having a son who was proving to be a complete failure. My father was a chartered engineer and my sister Mary was a psychologist. Just to ensure that I was academically marooned, my brother Stephen had a degree in Radiology and my other brother, Simon, obtained one in Urban Planning, whilst sister Sarah has had a distinguished nursing career. So I was an increasingly big disappointment and things were not about to improve!

Through some family connection I was given employment by Pilkington Glass Works in St Helens for the princely sum of £365 a year. Ten years later I met somebody I had worked with and I was pleased to find that I had legendary status as the worst Time Study Engineer they had ever employed. I think that I followed the Eddie the Eagle principle of if you cannot be the best then be the worst! A few years ago I compered a charity dinner with

Eddie who was an excellent speaker as well as being fun company. However it did occur to me that he would have had no fame if he had come second last in the Olympics Ski Jumping rather than last.

However I digress from the joys of Pilkington, who had four factories in St. Helens – all of which had the benefit of my employment! I did not last very long at the first factory as a result of a bit of a misunderstanding in the Packing Dept. This was a very warm area and the ladies, who worked there, were inclined to wear not much else apart from their overall. I was sent with my stop watch to time their packing but it took no time for them to realise that I was a naive young lad. Early in the proceedings a young lady asked if she could look at my stop watch and being the ever-obliging soul, I duly handed it over. Once she had it she placed it in her breast pocket and told me to come and get it, which seemed like a reasonably pleasant task to me! Unfortunately the works manager appeared at the moment of impact, which very unfairly resulted in me being banned from timing women and being moved to another factory. At the next place of work I had a slight problem with my own time keeping, mainly as a result of Nick's and my ambition to become professional gamblers. We used to go to the Cabaret Club in Liverpool.

I had first visited the Cabaret Club with Dad when we went to see Elaine Delmar. He was a massive jazz fan and one of his friends had been the trumpeter Leslie 'Jiver' Hutchinson. We often used to see Leslie on our annual holiday to St Anne's On Sea (Don't ask!) as he would be appearing in Blackpool in Geraldo's Band. He always gave me a ten bob note when he saw me, which, considering my pocket money was about sixpence at the time, made me a big fan. Leslie was sadly killed in an accident and my Dad tried to help Elaine, who was Leslie's daughter, when he could. Every time she appeared on radio or TV he would write to the BBC and ask why we didn't hear more of this talented singer.

I hope he used a different name otherwise they might have got fed up with him. On this occasion Elaine was having trouble with her digs so he brought her back to stay for the week with us, which resulted in her sleeping in my bed (sadly not with me as I had been moved to the spare room!) All of which has got nothing to do with my future gambling career!

On a good day we could win as much as we earned in a week, obviously on a bad day we could lose the same amount! The problem was that we did not get back until about 4am, with the result that I often missed my 6.30am train at Town Green, which enabled me to catch a bus that got me to work. The manager, who I do not think liked me, gave me a number of warnings. This culminated in me being moved on to the next factory after I reported for work at 3pm. "Sorry I am seven hours late" might have caused mass laughter in the ranks, but it did not go down well with him. I had been to see a girl in Stoke and somehow missed the last train home hence the late arrival. To make matters worse the young lady in question had suggested that we should not meet again as it was upsetting her boyfriend!

Surprisingly things did not go too well at the next factory, although it was more fun as I got into a horse racing syndicate and we used to make our betting decisions in the pub at lunch time. The manager even seemed to have a sense of humour. When I arrived late and explained that I had overslept his response was "What? You sleep at home as well as at work?!" Not quite sure why he got rid of me to the fourth factory.

If my experiences at the other three factories could be fairly described as disappointing, the last one proved to be a disaster. The manager was called Mr Roberts and for some reason that I could not understand he took an instant dislike to me. He was a mild, non-drinking man, who explained that the only time that he swore was at me! Now that is hardly my fault.

For those readers who are not experts on the intricacies of Time Study a watch is crucial to do the job! Each factory had four pristine stop watches that were kept in velvet and locked away. On one unfortunate day I managed to incapacitate the department's complete supply of watches. This was the result of a number of slight accidents that just happened to take place on the same day. By now I was being allowed to time women again and I had been sent to my Bete Noire – the Packing Dept. In preparation for this important task I wound the watch up in readiness, however sadly I appeared to have over wound it (how is that possible?) and it stopped working. This meant that I had to return to Mr Roberts to get a replacement. He seemed to be quite annoyed and said some quite unpleasant things to me before carefully unwrapping another watch to send me back to the job in hand.

I had developed a bit of a flamboyant style. The watch had a string on it to put round your wrist to ensure that you did not drop it. However I had developed a bit of a unique style where every time I clicked the watch at the end of a working phase I would put the string on my finger and whirl the watch around before clicking it again. I found that this seemed to mildly amuse the lady packers and made me stand out as different from my colleagues. On this occasion I got slightly carried away with the reaction I was receiving so I decided to do it even faster. Tragically the inevitable happened and it left my finger at a great rate of knots and smashed against the wall with bits flying everywhere! Somewhat crestfallen I collected all the bits and trudged back to see Mr Roberts.

He went apoplectic and said some even more unpleasant words to me but quite rightly insisted that the job still had to be done. So he lovingly unwrapped watch number three. The demise of this watch was a bit of an anti-climax. As I carefully timed the packaging we stopped for PLT (for those not in the Time Study industry this stands for Personal Lost Time meaning that you can go to the loo!) As I departed for a wee I made the grave error of leaving my board and watch on the table only to return to no watch. I initially hoped that it would reappear in somebody's breast pocket but this was not to be. It had been nicked by person or persons unknown and I was now watchless again. After unsuccessfully pleading for a little help in this matter, I returned with foreboding to the somewhat intolerant Mr Roberts.

As I explained that this latest problem was not of my making he completely lost the plot. He added a number of swear words to his diatribe and indulged in a bit of name calling. By now my colleagues were doubled up with laugher behind their desk lids (think school) and it might have been best to abandon the project at this stage. But no, the fourth and final watch was ceremoniously unwrapped. Sadly something went wrong with the handover and there was a bit of a fumble and the watch fell to ground destined never to work again. For the sake of posterity I would like to emphasize that this latest mishap was entirely Mr Roberts' fault, however he refused to take any responsibility. Having run out of invective he returned, red-faced, to his office and slammed the door to the sound of hysterical laughter from my colleagues. Disappointingly this seemed to harm Mr Robert's relationship with me. I slowly realised this as he never spoke to me again – well he did once but that will come later – and never gave me another assignment!

It was time to make the major decision to forego my promising career in Time Study for another yet to be decided career. The rest of my life was fine with many enjoyable hours spent playing cricket and even more spent drinking at Ormskirk Cricket Club, which was my spiritual home. I had grown up with Sandy and Geoff Tittershall, Derek Anderton and John Summer and we were the new boys on the block in the first team in what was a very lively dressing room. I also played football for Maghull (It was the reserves actually but I never tell anybody that!) When Maghull (Reserves!) played Kirkby Town I was very excited to find that they included three players, who had played for my beloved Southport. When we were 6–0 down I scored our only goal in what ended in an 8–1 defeat. On the way home with my father, who had watched the game, he spent the whole journey saying how embarrassed he had been to see me celebrate as though I had scored the winner at Wembley. He also pointed out that it was a one-yard tap-in that even he could have scored! But despite these enjoyments the facts had to be faced that I had been a failure at Pilkingtons and four managers could not be wrong.

With a heavy heart I approached Mr Roberts with the sad news that I was leaving. I knocked on his door but before I even spoke he told me to go away as he had not had a good week and I could only make it worse. I replied that I really needed to speak to him but he just said that he really did not need to speak to me. However when I insisted that I had to give in my notice his whole demeanour changed. He smiled (I think!), invited me in and said that this was fantastic news, indeed the best news that he had had for some time. Indeed he was so thrilled that he was going to ring Mrs Roberts to arrange to take her out to celebrate. For some reason I had expected a reaction more on the lines of "are you sure?" and you could be making a big mistake leaving a promising career with Pilkingtons". He went on to say that I was on a week's notice but as he personally never wanted to see me again, not to bother coming in for my final week. Slightly disappointed with his attitude I told him that he would never see me again as St Helens was the armpit of Europe (I was qualified to say this as I had been to Rhyl!) and that I would never ever come here again. In the unlikely event that somebody from St Helens is reading this book I apologise unreservedly for that slur on their fine town. I was a bit emotional at the time and they should remember that it was their cricket team that put the final nail in the coffin for my last career. My colleagues were much kinder and had a quick whip round, bought me a Joan Baez LP and took me to the pub.

Life was much different in those days and when I got home I had eight pages of jobs in the Liverpool Echo to peruse. After considering a few I decided to apply to be a Trainee Manager with ABC Cinemas. I rang to apply for the job on the Monday, was interviewed by the Area Manager Mr Evans on the Tuesday and was offered the job. I was told to get measured for my dress suit and to return on Monday to pick it up and to be told which exciting city or town in the North West I was being sent to. Which is how I ended up on the Monday night standing on the steps of the Capitol Cinema – St Helens! As I stood there who should I see approaching but Mr Roberts and his wife, no doubt on the night out to celebrate my departure. He looked at me, took a second take, walked ten yards past me and then came back and just said "Shrouder you are fucking haunting me"!

The Capitol Cinema was managed by a Scotsman who I liked and got on with (so that was a change). His major achievement was scheduling the films to finish quarter of an hour earlier than anyone else on the circuit. This was done with the sole aim of having longer in the Cambridge Pub and to share a few pints whilst I listened to his stories on the joys of being a cinema manager.

These joys did not include the Minors Matinee, which in St Helens was riotous. The first one I did he asked me to go on stage as Uncle Sam to make an announcement. This was his little joke and a big mistake as anyone who went on stage got pelted with boiled sweets etc. Another favourite trick of our young clientele was to set fire to newspapers and lob them over the balcony. It goes without saying that we had to go to the pub on Saturday lunch time to recover!

I did a couple of days as relief manager at the Futurist Cinema in Liverpool and was somewhat surprised when the manager from the restaurant next door popped in on my first evening to ask what I wanted for dinner. It transpired that the cinema's manager allowed him to put his takings in our safe in return for a free dinner. It was a slightly more clever ruse than my friend at St Helens, who was later caught selling his own orange juice! The job was fun and I quite enjoyed being front of house in my dress suit and appearing vaguely important. However the job was not for the ambitious as it was very much a case of dead man's shoes and there were many Assistant Managers in their 40s still awaiting their opportunity to be a Manager. I was also missing my mates and sport.

My digs were a terraced house with an outside loo, which as a result of our visits to the pub after work I always had to visit in the early hours. I had to go downstairs in the dark as I did not want to disturb the very nice couple, whose house it was. Once I got out it was invariably cold and raining. After three months I came to the conclusion that this was another career that was not for me and was about to give my notice in when I got a huge slice of luck.

I was visited by a very apologetic Mr Evans to inform me that I would have to go and do two months as Relief Assistant Manager at the Tuebrook Bowling Alley in Liverpool. In general, cinema managers hated being made to work in a Bowling Alley but for me it was a superb move and I loved every moment of my time there. A licensed bar, girls, music, famous footballers and artistes frequenting it – what was there not to like about it?! Above everything it had Graham Schofield as manager.

Graham was a fantastic character, a great showman, loved by his team and very funny. It was a joy to have the chance to learn from him. He was very much into Winston Churchill's war time speeches and he would adapt them to any missive from head Office. Following one about reducing our usage of postage stamps he came up with a comic master piece which included "we will fight them in the Post Office and will never ever again in human history use another stamp"! He had won the ABC gold star for showmanship and he would wander out from time to time and return having persuaded some poor shopkeeper to move his entire window display and allow Graham to replace it with one advertising our Bowling Alley!

ABC had ten Bowling Alleys, which were overseen by Douglas Ewin, who was a character in his own right. So when Graham had suggested that he turn Monday nights (the worse night for business) into a teenage Beat and Bowl session he was most encouraging and promised to be there for the first one. He also arranged for ABC News (the in-house magazine) to be there.

In advance of the great night Graham had a Disco Booth built and arranged with Liverpool music store Rushworth and Drapers to lend us the records each week. On the morning of the first session we were both looking lovingly down from the balcony at the Booth and the decorations when Graham somewhat surprised me by suggesting that I pop down play a few records and test the mike. When I suggested that it might be better if the DJ did that he responded very simply with "You are the DJ" I felt a certain level of panic and just as I was about to decline he added the sweetener that he had arranged for Miss UK Industry 1966 and Miss Bootle (not quite as impressive) Margaret Stephens to assist me by handing me the records. This added a very pleasant extra dimension to the task and I happily agreed. Margaret had recently joined host Hughie Green in Opportunity Knocks and regularly popped in to the Bowl to pick up publicity photos and her visits certainly brightened up a young lad's day!

So the great day arrived. The teenagers flocked in, Margaret passed me the records and I babbled away on the mike. The youngsters gathered round the Booth with their requests, most of which I had never heard of and incompetent though I was, I really enjoyed myself. The evening was deemed a great success, Douglas Ewin was impressed and Graham, Miss UK Industry 1966 and myself appeared on the front cover of the ABC News! There were people who had worked for ABC for over 100 years, who had never been mentioned in this important journal. So the front page after four weeks at Tuebrook undoubtedly meant that my career could only go downhill.

Life was blissful, I lived off oranges and marmite sandwiches in a bedsit at 3, Radstock Rd, off Shiel Rd and walked to work every day through Newsham Park full of joy and anticipation. The people who worked there were great fun and always looked after me. Arthur and Elsie, who managed the bar, would survey all around them and give me hints of things that needed doing. Nellie was the queen of the venue. Nominally head cleaner she could turn to every aspect of operating the Bowl, including manning the shoe and booking console, running the cafe and mending the machines. She mothered me and solved every problem including finding me a dentist. She also was always ready for a cup of tea and a chat. When anyone interesting came in, particularly the Liverpool footballers, she would buzz up to let me know. I would then find an excuse to pop into the bar and stare at the likes of Ian St John and Roger Hunt.

But Monday was my day. I would get behind the turntables, talk nonsense and have lots of girls gathered round. My image even survived my mother, who lectured at nearby Millbrook College, popping in with my washing and telling everybody that I appeared to be short of underpants!

Graham arranged for the legendary Bob Wooler of The Cavern and Radio Luxembourg fame to make a guest appearance. He brought The Orions, who were playing The Cavern with him and at the reception in the office suggested that we turn the lights down and make it nice and moody! I was living the dream and enjoying every moment. Well almost every moment. Because of the area we were in we did attract a certain amount of trouble. On one occasion I was advised to check the Gents and I found a young boy, who had been stabbed, apparently by Irish Terry. The local boys very reluctantly gave the police evidence under the encouragement that if Terry was locked up he could not come after them. On the day of the trial they took to fright and failed to appear, which was how a 'Not Guilty' Terry came to reappear at the Bowling Alley.

It was like a scene from a Western with everybody backing away as he came up the stairs. I was having a coffee with Graham, who looked at his watch and said that as I was still the Manager on duty I would have to tell him he was banned! With trepidation I gingerly approached Terry to say how delighted I was that he had been released but I wondered if he would do me a big favour and not come into the Bowl for a couple of weeks. I explained that, completely against my wishes, Head Office had banned him but I would ensure that this was reversed. He patted me on the shoulder and said "No problem" and left. I went back to the cafe like a returning hero. Graham wanted to know what had been said. So I explained that I had told him it was Graham who had banned him for life but was not on duty at present so Terry was going to come back when he was. Not often that Graham was lost for words.

Apart from such incidents the place was buzzing and business was going up but then Graham was poached to go and manage Allisons Night Club. He had totally inspired me, and for the first time in my working life I was really motivated. I also owe him a lasting debt for forcing me behind the turntables. I have done it from time to time ever since although nowadays the demand for Smiling Sam's Sounds of the 60's does appear to be somewhat limited!

Graham's replacement was not of the same ilk, being a Cinema Manager forced into the life of bowling. The Monday night was cancelled in favour of getting a league in and the happy friendly team including me were sullen and rebellious.

It was not the same place any more so I contacted Douglas Ewin and asked if I could be moved to another Bowl. I respected him and I think he knew what Tuebrook had lost with Graham's departure. So I was sent to work at Wylde green Bowl in Sutton Coldfield.

This was just as bad with a staid manager who never worked nights. So I left.

Chapter 2

STRICTLY CONFIDENTIAL

For everybody that ever employed me, what comes next did not happen and was most certainly not on my CV.

I decided to join Legalite Bingo and Casino Company as a trainee manager but was mostly used as a Bingo caller. My father took some comfort from this as he said that I had reached rock bottom and could not go any lower than taking money off little old ladies!

With that encouraging endorsement I went to Stourbridge for training and then moved to Wod green in London. After a couple of weeks I was picked up following the evening session and taken to work at their Cheltenham venue.

In those days there were two sorts of Bingo calling. There was straight calling of just the numbers and there was fancy calling such as Legs Eleven and so on. Woe betide you if you adopted the wrong style at the wrong venue! One of my colleagues who had been sent down from Cambridge tried to treat the players at Bethnal Green to some fancy callng. Ignoring the outraged murmuring from the players he ploughed on regardless until he cheerfully got to "5 and 9 – the Brighton Line" which brought forth an outburst of "Get on with the fucker!" from some of the women in the audience followed by a chorus of booing. He had to be replaced mid-game!

Luckily Cheltenham prefered the fancy calling which suited me as I tried to be a bit of a performer – of course.

It was hard work as we had to do two sessions, run games such as Golden Nine, in between and then at night we had to be croupiers for the card games.

Cheltenham, where I now live permanently, is an attractive town and I enjoy life there as I did in those earlier days when I was a bingo caller virtually living at the venue.

Before the evening sessions I used to go into the pub opposite and always ended up singing Danny Boy which was particularly odd as I not only sang out of tune – every time – but I also didn't really know the words! The pub is closed now but I like to think that the two events are not connected!

Every night the manager of our bingo establishment had to ring the owner with the figures we had taken but because he would get angry if we lost money with the cards, our manager would always report a profit. So on a bad day he would use some of the float to make the banking up to the announced figure. Then on a good day he would report a smaller profit and restore the float to the correct amount. It was better than having his ears chewed from a distance voice at the other end of the telephone. Seemed reasonable to me!

Unfortunately, on one of the days the float was down we heard that the owner was on his way to Cheltenham. In the knowledge that he was certain to check the float our manager decided to withdraw a bit more of the float and invest it on a horse running in the two o'clock at Ascot. It does not seem the perfect solution now but at the time it seemed a pretty safe bet and it would enable the float to be restored from our potential winnings.

Sadly this all became irrelevant as the owner arrived early and sacked the manager, the assistant manager and – somewhat surprisingly – me!

We had lost two jackpots in a week so he decided that we all must be on the fiddle. I did explain that I just called the numbers but he was having none of it and we were escorted off the premises with our wordly possessions.

We had no money so the landlord of the pub said we could sleep in the bar. We then remembered our racing bet and the day was marginally improved when we found out that we had won and were able to divvy up our winnings between the three of us. Next morning I was at Cheltenham Station to catch a train to Liverpool and to return to live with my delighted parents!

Things were not going very well. How's that for an understatement? Still, all was not lost as I quickly got a commission-only job selling encyclopaedias. In fairness to my Father he quickly apologised for having said I could not go any lower as I now had!

As I tramped the streets of St Helens (of course!) on behalf of the Caxton Press I failed spectacularly making only one sale, which was reversed as they felt they had been pressurised into buying the set of 23 books! We had to knock on doors of houses with children. You were meant to check the washing line to see if they had children's clothes on – not sure what we were meant to do if it was raining! We would then tell the lady of the house that we were running a survey for Caxton Press and wondered if she had any children and when she answered in the affirmative, we would say, whatever the ages, that they were perfect for the survey. We would then ask if we could pop back in the evening to do the survey with her and her husband. I quickly lost any ambition to sell the books and was just grateful if I got the chance to talk to people. So another job bit the dust!

On my return to home I reappeared at Ormskirk Cricket Club, where amongst much mirth I was advised to sign on the dole. Luckily Peter Guy, an outstanding batsman and mickey taker, had lovely Rhona as a wife and she worked for Social Security. She promised to look after me and was as good as her word as she filled in my forms and enabled me to pick up my £4 a week. This was the last straw for my Mum and Dad and I was directed to somebody they knew in Social Services and bewilderingly I ended up as a house father at a home for young boys in Leyland.

I actually entered into the latest career with considerable enthusiasm. In the main the boys had been to Approved Schools or Borstals and had been released but sent here because the authorities deemed their homes an unsuitable environment for them to return to. They were at the home to be looked after and nurtured. On my first day I met up with the Superintendent, who ran the home. He was very negative and I did not warm to him. When I told him I was interested in football, he informed me that I would never get these boys playing football as they were far too lazy – Challenge number one! I lived in and had to work in the garden when the boys were out.

Shortly after arriving, a boy who had played for Kirby Boys, was sent there. With his help we set up a six-a-side game, which was some feat considering there were only 14 boys in the home. The game started on the home's lawn with snow on the ground and for fifteen minutes they had great fun until the Superintendent arrived with a "What is going on here Mr Shrouder?"

It was self-evident but I humoured him and explained that it was a game of football. He immediately stopped it telling the boys that there were more important things than football – there were drains to be unblocked and potatoes to be peeled.

We had also arranged a table tennis match against the local youth club and three boys and myself went to play with his comment of 'no-hopers' ringing in our ears. The boys were thrilled to win and had a real spring in their step as we walked the mile home. The euphoria vanished as soon as we got back when they were sent straight to bed without their usual cocoa and a biscuit because we had got back late. One boy ran away and confided in a Catholic priest, who used to visit us, telling him where he was. The priest refused to divulge where the boy was which resulted in the police and then the Bishop insisting that he tells them. He still refused, saying that the boy was better off where he was, and whilst he would encourage him to return he would not breach his confidence. It later transpired that the boy had run off with a girl so he was certainly in a better place!

I liked the priest enormously and when he was banned from the house I lost my only adult ally. During a Home Office visit I complained bitterly about the way it was run, but I was told that the books always balanced and that our residents committed very little crime.

It was time for another change!

I had met a girl called Sandy from Birkenhead and we decided to respond to an advert inviting young people to go to Africa to build a trade centre. Whilst we were planning this we went to the ABC Lime Street Cinema in Liverpool. By this stage I was beginning to look a bit odd with long hair and a green satin shirt. To my horror I saw my old divisional manager, Mr Evans heading toward me. However it was impossible to avoid him and I just hoped that he did not realise that we were there on passes that I should have returned when I left the company. He was very friendly and on finding out what I was doing commented that it did not seem like me and if l ever wanted to return to ABC to just drop him a line. I did this, left Sandy to build trade centres in Africa and re-joined ABC. Hence the gap in my CV between other jobs never officially happened so it is yours and my secret!

Having followed Mr Evans' invitation to contact him about my return to ABC, I was surprised to receive a two line letter in response to mine informing me there were no vacancies! Luckily he passed my letter on to Douglas Ewin, who immediately responded by offering me the Assistant Manager's job at the ABC Hanley Bowl. The venue was a CineBowl with Douglas Ewin's younger brother Tony as General Manager in charge of both the Cinema and the Bowl. He was a great help to me and gave me a number of projects including starting a Tuebrook style Beat and Bowl session with me as the DJ and also to set up a different promotion for every week.

Bowling was really fun again and I entered into the challenge of getting companies to do a week's promotion with great gusto. As Tony had advised me, the art was to write loads of letters, most of which will be ignored, but by the laws of average the more I sent the more success I would have. In no time I had more than 20 weeks' worth of offers such as Timex giving us 12 watches, Monte Cristo 24 bottles of Sherry, Peter England 10 shirts and Jacobs Biscuits 24 tins. In return for their largesse we gave them a window display space and promised regular mentions over the mike.

As the stock room got fuller and fuller, the next problem was how to get rid of the stuff! Fortunately the problem was solved by Trevor Tatton, who along with his wife Christine had quickly become firm friends. Trevor invented Bango, which involved me stopping everybody's game to announce that it was Bango time sponsored by the promotion company of the week. The players would add up their score and we would get three volunteers to spin the arrows on the big boards made by Trevor and if anybody had this score they won whatever we were giving away. On the last game we would give a prize to the person who was nearest to encourage people to keep bowling (I hope you have followed this as I am a bit confused myself!) As a result of prancing about every night doing this as well as the Disco I got a number of other opportunities including being the DJ at The Penny Farthing Club from midnight every Thursday night as well as regularly compering fashion shows for a local entrepreneur.

The Queen Bee of the Bowl was a lovely lady called Christine Blundred, who was nominally the secretary but actually knew more about running the Bowl than anybody. I think that she saw me as a lost soul, so helped me to cover up my deficiencies such as filling in the stock-taking reports, which she did for me knowing that I did not have a clue how to do them. One night she invited me to dinner with her and her husband Harold at their house near Leek. Opposite the house was Ashcombe Park Cricket Ground, which caused me to say how much I missed playing. She then made it her life's work to enable me to play. A week later she asked me that if I could play cricket on a Saturday would I be happy to work both shifts on a Sunday. Would I ever!

Christine persuaded the other Assistant Manager to do every Saturday evening with the incentive of every Sunday off and she would do every Saturday day shift, which was never in her remit. She also made contact with Ashcombe Park to arrange for me to go to nets there. As a result of this on the first Saturday of the season I strode out in their first team to play in the North Staffs league. This proved to be a bit of a culture shock as it was the most competitive environment that I was ever to play in. This was epitomised by our pro Jack Shaw, who saw his job as winning cricket matches any which way he could. I was very fond of Jack and his wife, who would give me a lift to every match. She was a perfect foil to Jack, he would mention a game and she would say Is that the game you got 147 not out and he would respond that that was the previous season this was the one when he got 8 for 32 and 74!"

All went well until we played Burslem, who had an equally competitive pro in Terry Harrison. The games had no allocation of overs and no amount that had to be bowled in the last hour. They were batting second and seemed to be on their way to an easy win, when Jack put on a master class of time wasting. He managed to make one over last 12 minutes with field changes (moving long on to 3rd man was one!), his laces coming undone, running in to bowl, stopping and then deciding to go round the wicket and then again stopping just as he was about to bowl to make another fielding change. I was loving it and as their pro got more and more angry the funnier it got. The two pros nearly came to blows in a mid-wicket confrontation and the crowd joined in by not returning the ball when it went to the boundary. The Umpires issued warnings all over the place and sadly Burslem still won. To make matters worse Jack was given a warning by our Chairman over his future conduct.

The scene was set for a bitter return fixture at Burslem. When we arrived it was obvious that the wicket was terrible and that it would be a very low scoring game and so it proved. Bursiem batted first and were 52 for 9 but we could not get the last wicket. By the time that they had got to 80 Jack had lost it completely, he ran in to bowl, turned his arm over, did not release the ball and ran out the batsman backing up! The crowd went crazy (there was a crowd because the pubs closed at 2.30 pm whilst the cricket club bar was open all afternoon) they booed and said some quite rude things to Jack, who then wasn't given any tea! So when I opened the batting with Jack it was the most hostile atmosphere I had ever encountered. It soon boiled over and Jack and Terry Harrison started fighting, this was quickly broken up with the Umpires threatening to send us all off! Jack was soon out, but I batted for 80 minutes, got hit all over the body and was out when the score was 37 for 8 having scored 4!

The Ashcombe Park team refused to stay for a drink, which left me in a dilemma as Burslem's ground was near the Bowling Alley and I fancied a drink before going into do the Bango promotion. So I elected to stay and have a drink with their more reasonable players whilst avoiding their pro who, as well as being the cause of much of the trouble, had also said some quite unpleasant things to me during my marathon innings of four. Eventually he came over, put his hand out and said "well batted". He then fell about laughing as he pointed out that I had batted all that time, had been hit regularly and had scored four and did I realise that the next batsman in snicked his first ball for 4 and then had his middle stump up rooted with the next. He then helpfully pointed out that in the Evening Sentinel scoreboard his innings would look as good as mine! We then chatted and I left with a new best friend and having agreed to sign for Burslem the following season!

To add to my sporting pleasure my friend Trevor, of Bango game, ran the ABC Hanley football team and I became their leading goal scorer (Modesty has always been a fault of mine!)

Everything was now going well. I moved into a great flat on the edge of Hanley Park (the lady who owned it later went to prison for embezzling a fortune from the Staffordshire Building Society) and was having a great social life. At work Tony Ewin was promoted to be an Area Manager resulting in them splitting the Bowl and Cinema and I was appointed as Manager of the Bowl. At 22 I was the youngest Bowling Alley Manager in the country and was really proud of that.

If I worked hard before, it was now even more the case as I was determined to show that Douglas Ewin's faith in me was well founded. I was part of a great team in which Christine continued to run things, whilst I enjoyed being the front man. I was also given a quality Deputy Manager in Dennis Mountford. Dennis was 10 years older than me and a really bright guy, who had been a student at the London School of Economics. We hit it off immediately as he did with Terry Harrison, who by now spent most of his time in the Bowl chatting up ladies. When we met, Terry was engaged but once that was broken off he just became a magnet to ladies. He and I would go to The Place nightclub and find a couple of girls to chat to, but the problem was that they would both want to go out with Terry!

The rest of the team were great with me, particularly the two mechanics Ron Parry and Mike Smith, who spent less on spare parts than any other Bowl, which rightly meant that they were regarded as the best on the circuit.

The secret of their success was that Ron would be sent to work overnight at Bowls that had major technical problems. The first time that he did this when I was in charge; he popped his head round the door to check if there was anything we were short of. As always we were down on bowling shoes size 7 and 8 (for some reason nobody ever stole our size 11 shoes) and when he returned he would drop some shoes into the shoe desk, whilst obviously returning with any spares that he needed. Hence the myth that we spent less than other Bowls was self-perpetuating.

Dennis, Terry and I even discussed taking over a Bowl to run ourselves but I put this down to alcohol! I was then contacted by Douglas Ewin and asked to take over as Manager of Tuebrook and of course the pull of returning to Liverpool was irresistible. I had loved my time at Hanley and was particularly indebted to Tony Ewin and Christine for their guidance and friendship. Not long after I moved to Liverpool, they left their respective partners and went on to get married. They were both people who would have found this step very difficult, particularly Christine, who was a devout Roman Catholic.

Many years later Christine saw me doing a TV interview regarding Apollo taking over The Bristol Hippodrome and got in touch. She had terminal cancer and we both met and chatted on the phone. She was determined to fight it but in the end it was sadly to no avail and it was with a heavy heart that Terry and I attended her funeral. When we had chatted she did tell me that she had a great marriage with Tony and never regretted taking that giant step.

Returning to Tuebrook was like coming home again. Nearly all the team were still there and there was also a very important addition in Roz Johnston, who, like Christine, was much more than a secretary. Every competition that Head Office came up with we were determined to win. One was to raise money for Shelter and Roz drew a house divided into bricks that could be sponsored for the charity. This was put in the bar and Arthur and Elsie did the rest, cajoling the members to get involved. We also arranged a Midnight Bowl between the Christmas Shows at The Empire Theatre and The Royal Court. This was intended to be a relaxed social fund raising event, but not for Frankie Vaughan, who took it very seriously and regularly came to practice. It was excellent to have a star of his magnitude in the Bowl and he was always charming to everybody he encountered. With all this practice he became a very proficient bowler. This proved not to be very important as the evening proved more of a show case for the comedy of Mike Yarwood and Billy Dainty. Many years later I had dinner with Frankie and when remembering this event he still seemed to be a bit miffed that he was the only one who took it seriously! His manager was John Redgrave and while Frankie practiced he regaled me with his show business stories. As it transpired we were to meet many times more with his shows going into our theatres, including an ill-fated Black and White Minstrels Show he toured, which resulted in all sorts of race relations problems!

As previously mentioned, many of the Liverpool players frequented the bar and I got quite friendly with their latest signing Emlyn Hughes. He so enjoyed coming with Peter Wall, another new signing, that he asked to become a member of the Club. We filled the form in and I seconded his application. When I handed it to Arthur with the required half-crown he nearly blew his top. He told me he could not possibly accept this as Emlyn had signed that he was over 21 and he wasn't. I protested that as long as he had signed he was over 21 did it matter? Arthur was having none of it as he correctly pointed out that every paper in the country had run the story about Bill Shankly signing 19-year-old Hughes from Blackpool for £65,000. In the end I had to tell the future captain of England that he could not be a member of the ABC Tuebrook Bowl Club! So I had to sign him in and enjoy our chats whilst I had my pint and Emlyn had his half of shandy.

I was having a great time at Tuebrook when I received the call from Douglas Ewin that he wanted me to move to Aberdeen and take over the Bowl there. It was a good move for me as Aberdeen was regarded as ABC's number two Bowl.

Terry took a week off work and drove me up to Aberdeen and I quickly found a small flat within walking distance of the Bowl. When I turned up for work I realised that I had been sent there because the opposition Magnet Bowl was closing and we needed to persuade as many of their bowlers as possible to swap allegiance. They were having a closing down party and I promised to attend it once I finished work. Terry went ahead of me to start a charm offensive. However this did not go as well as planned as I arrived to find him about to be involved in a fight with one of their members!

Despite this hiccup things went well with many of their leagues moving to us (In reality they had nowhere else to go!) This resulted in Aberdeen having a different mix from most Bowls with a heavy dependence on league bowling. We had some fabulous bowlers, which was borne out when I went with them to the Scottish trials and we ended up with more than half the International team. I really took to the lovely pre-oil City of Aberdeen even with all bars closing at 9.30pm!

I had joined Aberdeen Cricket Club and was looking forward to at last seeing the snow and ice disappear when I got a phone call that was to change everything.

The phone call was from Dennis Mountford and Terry Harrison and they excitedly told me that they had found a venue for us to run. It was a function suite, which we could turn into a night club in Newport, Shropshire. The story behind it was that it had been created by a millionaire builder for his daughter but she had tired of it and he was now anxious to get it off his hands. Knowing that we did not have much money he had told them that we could have it for £75 a week and that he would leave all the bar stock and we would just pay him as we used it. His only proviso was that we had to honour the pre-booked functions and to carry on doing lunches. The plan was that Dennis would be Company Secretary and do all the sensible things like setting up our new company, dealing with the bank, being the licensee, dealing with solicitors and other people who needed to deal with an intelligent, suit wearing person. Terry would run the bars and I would book all the entertainment, do all the marketing and be the compere and DJ. Being devoid of all common sense I did not even bother to go and visit the venue nor indeed give it a great deal of thought, but just agreed there and then to give up my job and be part of this bizarre adventure. I rang Douglas Ewin immediately to give my notice in and he was very generous in saying that if it did not work out there would always be a job for me back at ABC. So there I was at the age of 24 sat on a train making that beautiful journey down the east coast of Scotland heading for Newport and the new world of The Vine Club. I also reflected for the first time that I did not have a clue how I was going to programme this unseen night club and also that as a DJ I didn't have any records, which was an obvious weak link!

Chapter 3

HOW I BECAME A SAINT

As we planned for the opening of the Vine Club we were based in Dennis' small flat in Hanley using newspapers for blankets and each day he would drive us over to Newport. On my first visit I realised that this was madness. The venue was great with an entrance at ground level, stage, dance floor, kitchens and bar on the first level and then a mezzanine with balcony bar, office, changing room and storage. However Newport was a lovely market town with a population of approximately 4000 people. It was self-evident that there were not enough people in the area to support a night club, but of course there was no turning back and it was all very exciting. We found a house to rent just outside Newport and had added a fourth director in Trevor Buckley, the editor of a Potteries newspaper. It was agreed that the three of us working the club would be paid £5 a week with 11p deducted to cover our self-employment stamp. Dennis was able to take over the licence for the premises, which was a supper licence until 2.OO am with alcohol to be supplementary to food and entertainment. This wording was to come back and haunt us. With our limited finance we managed to build a DJ stage next to the main stage and to install a decent sound system with speakers all round the club. There were also a lot of windows, which we had to black out and due to diminishing funds we could only put up black polystyrene sheets – so you will gather not very elegant!

The editor of the Newport Advertiser was a kind man called Doug Watts and he was really supportive throughout our time there. He ran the story of us opening The Vine Club as his front page headline. As well as telling his readership of our plans to provide entertainment for all age groups he also drew attention to Terry's sporting ability as a pro-cricketer and semi-pro footballer (Congleton Town), whilst not mentioning my somewhat lesser skills! As a result of this publicity Richard Butter, as captain of Newport

Cricket Club and his friend Brian Ferriday came to find Terry to persuade him to play for the club. We had already agreed that we would play for the local team to enable us to influence people to come to The Vine, so they were pushing at an open door.

As they courted Terry and asked him to play in a friendly against Lilleshall before the Shropshire League started he casually mentioned that I also played. This was greeted with a "well I suppose he can come along if he wants", before returning their attention to Terry. They told him that he would obviously take the new ball with a choice of ends but where would he like to bat and Terry, not one to miss an opportunity told them he would bat at 3. He valiantly pushed my claims as a leg spinning opener and to keep him happy they agreed I could do this in the friendly game but the league team already had two openers. So it was that I marched out to open the batting with Jimmy Lawton against the might of Lilleshall. To my eternal joy Terry never got in to bat at 3 with Newport declaring at well over 200 without loss and a century to my name. Terry took a few wickets and after a few post-match beers the guys at the cricket club were our newest best friends. They also rallied round to support The Vine Club and although we offered them free admission they insisted on paying in the knowledge that we were really struggling. I had five happy years playing for Newport and was always grateful to the players for their initial support.

My biggest problems were deciding what to put on to attract a decent audience and to find enough records to DJ (this was helped by Terry stealing a lot of his sister's records as well as mass purchasing). The first week's entertainment resulted from me studying what the local Civic Halls were putting on. The posters were done and Trevor of Bango fame came to our rescue in doing lots of Day Glo posters around the club with such messages as "The Vine Club The Scene to be Seen In"! He also promised that he and Christine would help with the bar.

So the opening week arrived and we proudly commenced on the Monday with a Disco hosted by St Sam – Your heavenly Disc Jockey softly, souly, socking it to you"! The attraction of this outstanding event – plus free admission – resulted in a massive attendance of 37 discerning people (mainly loyal friends and cricketers). Tuesday night was Modern Dancing with a 20-piece orchestra – think Joe Loss/Syd Lawrence but obviously not as good! This resulted in three customers and to add insult to injury one of the band stole some Christmas puddings from our store room. As the stolen goods were worth more than the money received in admission the night could be truly described as a disaster!

We were now a bit desperate and Dennis, who ran the door, was approaching any person walking by to see if they would like to come in as a guest. But even this totally failed, although one man said he might come in if he had not been walking his dog!

Wednesday night was Cabaret Night, which was attended by 19 blokes, who were working in the area laying a pipe line. Luckily they were very thirsty but there was obviously not a lot of dancing to the sounds of St Sam, who also had to compere the Cabaret and to fill time in between acts, had to tell jokes!

On Thursday we hit a new low with our Olde Tyme Dancing Night for which we sold two tickets, but unfortunately they had got their days confused and had come on the wrong night and we had to give them a refund!

Friday night was a glimpse of the future when we had a local band Eddie Maiden and the Biancos supported by St Sam (I was certainly earning my 4 pound, 19 shillings and a penny!) For this we had 139 customers and a good bar take.

Saturday was our most challenging event as we honoured a previous booking for Newport Rugby Club's Dinner and Dance. The night could have been a disaster with unservable frothy beer, which Terry was trying to solve whilst at the same time acting as the wine waiter. Luckily Richard Butter and Brian Ferriday were also stalwarts of the Rugby Club and they sorted out the beer and generally helped. Thanks to them and some general good fortune we survived this ordeal although probably did not impress their special guest the local Conservative MP Tony Trafford.

After one week it was obvious to us all that the entertainment plans needed a drastic revamp! We kept the Cabaret on the Wednesday, introduced Discomania on the Friday and put groups on every Saturday. Slowly things began to improve with Friday being the night you go out with your mates and Saturday proving increasingly popular. Quite early on a vivacious young lady called Sheila Carrol started coming in with her two friends Audrey and Alison and they were collectively known as Virgins Anonymous!

I soon got friendly with Sheila and persuaded her that her destiny was a life behind the turntables and so Dolly DJ She was born. This not only provided a bit of glamour but she was also a natural. We also added a great DJ Y Willie P to the Fridays meaning that we now had Triple Discomania with St Sam,

She and Y Willie P. He would always turn up as someone different being it his sister, a vicar or his mother and I would have to announce that he was unable to do the show, but so as not to let anybody down he had persuaded whoever to do it for him. He was a great act and in the new format Fridays really grew in popularity.

We were also having to do lunches but these were a shambles with the three of us taking it in turns to be the waiter whilst the other two mocked his efforts. In fairness I think I did manage to serve a couple with their soup with both my thumbs and tie in it! We had to cut back on the expense of doing the lunches by hiring a lady, who had been a school cook. She made good basic meals but had a very loud voice and would point out that this was yesterday's pie but the customer would not know because of the gravy. The customer would know because they could hear every word! We then got agreement from the landlord that we could drop the lunches and we left Dennis (of course) to tell her.

We had become an out and out entertainment club and numbers were growing because we got lucky (that word again) in that whilst Newport would never be able to support a nightclub, up the road was Telford New Town. Telford was an overspill from Wolverhampton and in their wisdom the planners had failed to provide any entertainment, so we were the major benefactors.

Then disaster struck as we lost our supper licence as a result of the police and the magistrates deeming that the food we provided was not substantial enough and therefore alcohol could not be described as a subsidiary to it. It would be fair to say that the police never welcomed us into the town, even though they allowed the pubs to serve to the early hours, and we were to cross swords many more times. Although we could not serve alcohol after 10.30pm, astonishingly we still got reasonable audiences dancing through until 2.OOam. We put the matter in the hands of a local solicitor, who told us that we could reapply but we needed to show we were serving substantial food. He agreed that hamburgers and chips would be acceptable so we went to court and the Magistrates agreed between themselves that it was not acceptable! One of the Magistrates also pointed out that Disco Music could also not be regarded as entertainment – she had obviously seen me work! We then started serving TV Dinners which could be beef or chicken and at our next court appearance they were deemed acceptable and our licence was restored.

During our licence restrictions we had announced in an interview with the Newport Advertiser that without the licence we would not be able to keep the club open. This resulted in our young customers organising a protest march through the centre of Newport. Again the paper helped us by making this its front page story and questioning the authority's motives in trying to close down the only establishment that provided entertainment for young people.

The rest of life was fun. The cricket was great as I had a golden start scoring 144 against Dudley and 80 not out against Wem, who had the Shropshire's opening attack. I was also taking wickets and was playing the best cricket of my life. My hair was very long by now and I had to use a red head band to enable me to see. It was mentioned by one member that if I got my hair cut, I might be considered for the county team. However as it turned out the hair got longer and the runs got fewer! In one match at Sutton Goldfield a couple of gentlemen in MCC ties saw me going out to bat and one turned to the other and said "George do look, its fucking Geronimo!" I had a good innings scoring a quick 70 and as I went past them I said "Not bad for a Red Indian". However the name stuck.

All was not sweetness and light at the Cricket Club as Terry and I played our cricket as we would have done in the North Staffs League whereas the Shropshire League was more genteel. It all came to a head when I ran out a Shrewsbury player who was backing up too far. Jack Shaw would have been proud of me but not many others! This ended up with the Chairman, Jimmy Davenport, who was a big friend of mine having to come into the dressing room and warn the team (Well Terry and me!) that this is not how Newport plays its cricket and any player behaving this way in future would be suspended. After this blip we settled back into the pleasure of playing for a successful and friendly cricket club.

The Manager of Newport Town FC, Basil Dooley. also played cricket and he persuaded Terry and me to play for him. He had a very good team that had had to move from the Shropshire League to the stronger Staffordshire County Combination. I knew he was the manager for me when after my debut when I scored as a result of somebody's shot hitting me on the knee and going in he described me in the paper as the natural goal scorer that he had been looking for! I loved playing centre forward for them and because of the quality of players around me was able to score lots of goals. With my long hair and nickname of Geronimo I was a natural target for

supporters (home and away!) and opposition teams. On one occasion two
of the opposition got sent off for assaulting me and their goalkeeper chased
me round the pitch for standing over him and sarcastically applauding after
I scored (Even I would not have liked me then!) I never worked out how
Newport had got so many good players until I found out later that most of
them were being paid – not their leading scorer however!

Back at The Vine Club the audiences continued growing and we had
our first inspired booking (well by the law of averages we were bound to
get one sooner or later!) I booked The Sweet for £25 on a Saturday night
and by the time the gig arrived they were in the top 20 with Funny Funny.
They were great lads and did their 2 x 45 mins, 1 x 30 mins spot with no
complaints and as we had a drink together afterwards we celebrated that this
would be their last ever £25 gig and I drunk to their success, which was to
be considerable.

Our style was still a bit ramshackle but our customers seemed to either
not notice or not care. We were loud, dancy and sweaty and I loved every
minute of it. We were now running out of glasses so we went to an auction
from a club that was closing down. Man of the world Dennis was discreetly
bidding until at last there were no other bidders. Just as the hammer was
about to come down there was a cry from Terry "Hey Mounters we need
these" as he put a bid in against Dennis! It was worth the extra quid for the
laughter on the way back.

The increased number of customers had brought security problems.
Initially we relied on Terry who did karate and had a threatened Fuma Kina,
which would sort out all problems. After a few drinks and under pressure to
show us what he could do, he leapt in the air kicked his legs out missed the
target by two feet and landed on his back injuring himself in the process. It
was time for a security reassessment!

The answer to this problem literally walked through the door. It was like
a western film as word went round that Johnny Harris, whose sister Carole
sometimes helped us, was walking up the stairs – people moved to either
end of the bar. He ordered a coke and everybody glanced at this guy with
rippling muscles, a white T shirt two sizes too small, black hair and a Fu
Manchu moustache. Dennis was in charge of security, as well as all the staff
and as well as just about everything else, and he approached Johnny who
agreed to be our head of security. Indeed for some time we only needed him,
he used to sit in the balcony watching everything that was going on. If he

saw anybody causing problems he would just send a message down that if the person did not stop immediately, Johnny would be coming down. That always did the trick whilst our audiences were predominantly local and his reputation went before him.

When we started attracting people from Wolverhampton and Stoke we had to employ more security but by then Johnny had moved on. He was a lovely guy and a massive help to us in the early days and it was with great sadness that I later learnt that he had taken his own life.

As we became more established we took on John Broome (Brush to all and sundry) as Manager. He was invaluable, getting involved in all aspects of the club. He was also in charge of lighting and sound and around 1.00am when I was on stage he would come and ask if I was ready to blow my mind. This would involve my shirt coming off (not a pretty sight!), manic dancing, the mike being hurled in the air and jumping into the bemused audience. Brush's job was to put an electric fan in front of the spotlight giving us an early version of strobe lighting! No wonder admissions were up! Also in our team of helpers were Sheila's Mum Hilda, who did the food and was known as Cooker and Mary, who cleaned the club and generally looked after us. Her husband Mick or Kelt played football with us and drank at the club and was an expert on one subject — Derby County. We also had a great group of regulars, who would always help us out if we were stuck.

One great character was Eddie Melia, known as Lurker because he once described that as his position on the football field!

Eddie was a massive Wolves fan and when asked what he would do if he won the pools, he said he would buy Derek Dougan and put him on his mantelpiece. When Dennis asked him one day why he hadn't gone to work he said that a little voice inside told him not to go. When Dennis asked him what he would do if the little voice told him not to go to the Wolves, he was in no doubt – "I would tell it to piss off!"

Chapter 4

I'M A RADIO ONE DJ!

From the start we had always got some great bands at the club and this initially was thanks to Keith Fisher, a Stoke-based agent. He and I got on really well and he would pull out all the stops to get them at the best price. The fact that he quite often came to the club did help in cementing our relationship. One night after a few drinks he asked if I would fancy doing a gig for him on a Tuesday night at the 007 Club in Burslem. It was a striptease night and they needed a compere with a few gags.

By now Dennis, Terry and I had agreed that any money earned from outside jobs would go into the company's overall pot. This enabled Terry to go and play pro for Audley Cricket club (and win them the league) with Brush running the bars and his fee coming back to us. So for the good of the company's finances rather than personal pleasure, I took the job!

It was literally an eye-opener as the six girls and myself shared one dressing room. In those days when the G-string came off the lights went out and the girl had a blanket thrown over her and she was taken back to the dressing room whilst I told a joke and then introduced the next act. I would then return to the dressing room and the delights of the semi-naked and totally naked ladies and I got paid!

Keith persuaded me to pay £50 (our normal price was £25 to £40 maximum) for Jimmy Powell and The Dimensions. Life at the Vine Club was never going tobe the same again. Jimmy was a larger-than-life character, both on and off the stage, who should have been a real star. He had quite a lot of record success and at the time had just released an album with Don Fardon – of Indian Reservation fame – on Young Blood Records.

At one stage Jimmy told us that he had a young Rod Stewart playing harmonica with his band but he left because Jimmy wouldn't let him sing! Jimmy's Saturday night show for us was mesmerising and when he sang

Everybody's Talking you could have heard a pin drop. That was something we had not experienced before. I was really overwhelmed by his performance which, when he finished his spot, drew the greatest ovation of any artiste that had appeared with us.

I got on really well with Jimmy and we both agreed to put another date in for a couple of months' time. Word must have got round because when he next appeared we were sold out with people still queuing on a one-out-one-in basis. He again went down a storm and when we were having an after show drink, he told me that he had lots of ideas, and contacts, which would really boost The Vine Club and that he would like to get involved.

I promised to chat with Dennis and Terry and get back to him on his suggestion. Terry was keen to involve him, Dennis was sceptical and I was in love with him -metaphorically speaking – particularly as he had told me that he could get the BBC Radio One Club to come live from The Vine Club and he would ensure I got the guest DJ Spot! I was easily bought!

We arranged to meet at Frankley Service Station and against Dennis' better judgement we agreed to give Jimmy 20% of the Company and as he had no money he would do four free gigs to pay his investment. He rented a flat in Newport, bought a left hand drive Ford Mustang and was ready to change our lives! He particularly focused on our Thursday nights, for which we went from a low key band night with 80–100 custom to big name night. Because of his contacts with groups and agents we widened the circle of whom we dealt with rather than use Keith Fisher exclusively. I was sad about this as he had played a big part in getting the Club started as well as giving me the 007 Club gig! The new agents included Austin Powell a Shrewsbury agent who managed local band Fluff. They were getting a lot of Radio one airplay, were a really big draw in the area and were a really nice bunch of lads as well. Austin was also responsible for giving us one of our best nights when he booked us Thin Lizzy for £75. Phil Lynott had a real aura and it was one of many memorable nights. We also started dealing with the Wolverhampton agency, Astra, who were additonally owners of The Lafayette Club.

At Astra I dealt with Jake Elcock and Alan Clayton both of whom I really liked, and Maurice Jones, who I found slightly difficult – particularly as he would not let me have Slade. In later days I would do a lot of business with Maurice and his partner Tim Parsons, who between them had built MCP into the biggest music promoters in the UK. Maurice was also Harvey Goldsmith's fellow promoter, working on the historical Live Aid Concert with Bob Geldof and Midge Ure. After a drunken night at Glasgow Apollo with Maurice we became good mates! Tim Parsons was a massive part of MCP's success and it was him I mainly dealt with and we were to go on to be close friends.

Astra were able to divert a lot of up and coming bands to us as well as those with big followings in the Wolverhampton area. These included Light Fantastic, whose lead singer was Ian Sludge Lees and Sludge went on to be a top comic after winning New Faces. He always started his show with the same joke "I have just seen this girl crying outside the dressing room and I said what are you crying for cock and she said yes" and he still went on to be a top comedian! They also provided us with rock superstars Judas Priest for £50 and the artiste that was to become our first £100 act, Raymond Froggatt. A couple of years ago I met up with Froggie after a show and he said that he remembered The Vine Club as a posh gig, which really made me worry what the other venues must have been like!

Jimmy was also working his magic and persuaded his friend Geno Washington minus the Ram Jam Band to play a Thursday night. The deal was that for £50 he would be picked up and returned to London with a bottle of vodka each way and Jimmy's Band, The Dimensions would back him. He was a massive draw at the time and of course, we had another night to remember.

About 25 or so years later I popped in to see Geno at Oxford Apollo when he was in a musical "In the Midnight Hour". He recognised me immediately as St Sam from The Vine. I was flattered and the Manager of the theatre who appeared to be astonished had probably primed Geno who otherwise would not have had a clue who I was! Other regular acts at the Club included Shakin Stevens and The Sunsets, who always provided a fabulous show and were really great to work with. It was pleasing to see Shaky's career take off and he played many Apollo dates for us in later years. For no obvious reason he used to have more people in wheel chairs at his shows than any other act (Not a lot of people know that!) Jimmy was also responsible for persuading Dennis to release some cash so we could all buy some clobber. As a result we all went to Carnaby Street and came back looking even more glamorous (hardly seemed possible) in the very latest fashions.

Jimmy then had his finest hour when he persuaded the BBC to bring their Radio One Club to Newport. Jimmy Powell and The Dimensions would play for free (part of the deal to bring the show) as the live band, St Sam would be the guest DJ and Noel Edmonds would host it.

The great day arrived and I met up with Noel who was Mr Cool! He had driven to Newport following a late gig at Swansea and told me he was going to have a kip in his car and I was to wake him up at 11.40am. This was dutifully done and all was primed to broadcast to the nation at midday. This momentous occasion in the life of The Vine Club was heralded in by Jimmy Young "It is now time for Radio One Club. Coming today from Newport, Shropshire and The Vine Club". This was followed by a long silence and then Jimmy Young explained that there was a transmission problem and carried on with his show! Twenty minutes later BT finally cured the fault and we were up and running.

When my great moment arrived I am next to Noel with my headphones on and he introduced me as the guest DJ and resident DJ at The Vine Club and then asked me my name, which he had obviously forgotten! This slightly threw me and when I answered St Sam he said no what is your real name, somewhat flustered I answered St Sam. Not a great start and I ruminated that I bet he would never ask Emperor Rosko what his real name is! However I did get my chance to say "This is St Sam on Radio One Club with a little Motown in our town and the fabulous sound of Marvin Gaye and I Heard It Through The Grapevine". That was it and I was not called on again by Noel. However I have been able to say legitimately – but boringly – that I did DJ on Radio One, in all sorts of conversations!

I was living the dream but so was Terry as the Stud of Newport, which on one occasion had resulted in his mother saying, "Our Terence, the only good thing about having you as my son is that you cannot marry any of my daughters!" Her opinion of me was even lower as for some reason she blamed me for leading this vulnerable Roman Catholic boy astray! But all was to change. In the mornings Terry and I used to meander into the club in various states of hangover, whilst Dennis would have been in for a couple of hours, done the banking, sorted out the staffing rota and by this stage dealt with the new tax of VAT – what would we have done without him?

Terry and I would collapse by a window looking out on to the High Street whilst Mary tried to revive us with coffee and toast. On this occasion I was sorting out my records when Terry was shouting for me to come over and look at a very attractive blonde girl walking down the street. His reaction to seeing her was to say "Shrouder, I am going to marry her!" This initially seemed highly unlikely. He then discovered that she was called

Susan Durose and to his horror was engaged to be married. But Terry was not the sort of man to be put off by such a small obstacle and pursued her relentlessly. He was helped, when he made Jimmy Powell aware that she was a hairdresser. Jimmy had this view that he was a big star in Newport and that I was a minor star and as such we should have our own persona! hairdresser. So the lovely Susan agreed to come to The Vine Club to cut our hair giving Terry even more opportunity to persuade her of his charms. You will no doubt be anxiously waiting to see how the story ended. Well wait no more. Susan broke off her engagement, accepted Terry's proposal and married him in Newport's Catholic Church.

They made a stunning couple and I was delighted to be Terry's best man. When he originally asked me I said that I would love to do it but would not wear a suit. Obviously DJ's who have appeared on Radio One do not wear suits! Terry said that was fine but under family pressure asked if I would do him a great favour and wear a suit. I relented but said it had to be of my choosing and ordered a stars and stripes suit and clogs from Melody Maker. Fortunately they did not arrive in time and I hurriedly bought myself a white suit. On seeing me Terry's Mum, who I think secretly liked me, said something along the lines of "I see that Jesus has turned up!"

Terry and Sue went on to have Nicky, a son that they were rightly very proud of and I was lucky enough to be asked to be his Christian Witness Father (apparently I could not be his Godfather as I was not a Catholic). Only recently I was invited to his stag do in Cheltenham and his wedding to Sarah.

My life was also about to change. I had recently parted from Dolly DJ She with whom I had very happily lived. I moved into an old caravan, owned by Susan's parents, that was in the middle of a field guarded by Fred an arthritic goose! At this time, ever the show-off, I had developed a routine on a Friday night of announcing I was going to do my washing, introducing a record and then running as fast as I could to the Launderette putting my washing in and then running back to introduce the next record! I like to think that the audience all found that mildly amusing although in hindsight I doubt it. This all worked well until the day that I returned to the launderette to find all my washing (bar one sock) had been stolen! The dear old Newport Advertiser made this a news item and it was picked up by the Daily Mirror, who took a photo of me in the Launderette holding up a sock with a headline along the lines of "Disconsolate DJ has his clothes stolen by adoring fans". This was far better for my ego than the likely true story that somebody had listened to me prattling away for long enough and decided that it would be fun to throw my washing away. This story obviously has nothing to do with how my life was about to change!

The advantage of being the DJ was that from my elevated position I could see everybody coming in. This particular Saturday my eye was caught by a group of six people who came in looking slightly different from our regular clientele. The rumours went round that they were from Persia (that's how long ago it was!) and were very rich. One of the group was an older lady, who I took to be their Mother.

Among the group was a very beautiful girl, who I admired from afar. Eventually when she was dancing with her friend Ann round their handbags (only people of a certain vintage will relate to that) I persuaded Brush to come with me to ask for a dance. This is how I met my future wife Linda. It turned out that she was from the tiny South Atlantic Island of St Helena and was not very rich! She had come over to the stately home of Weston Park to work for Lord and Lady Bradford. She was with her brother Campbell who was to marry her friend Ann. Also in the group was Shirley, Laudes (who certainly was not her mother), Graham and Stedson, who is now recognised as one of the leading conservationists in the world for his work on Ascension Island. I was besotted and soon in love and Linda seemed to think that I was ok.

On our first date we went on a walk and Linda asked me where I lived. I pointed at the caravan in the middle of a muddy field but I expect she thought that I meant the house behind it. So when I asked if she would like to see it she was probably somewhat surprised to be taken towards the caravan and even more surprised as she had to run for her life when Fred decided to attack us! I am not sure that she was over impressed.

However despite this our relationship flourished and once I had rented a flat, she left Weston Park to move in with me and got a job working across the road in the office of Woolworths.

Life was perfect and as an added bonus Linda and Sue became great friends. Campbell and Stedson proved to be great characters as well as the best dressed guys in the Club. They appeared to be very successful with the ladies, although their first line was always to check whether the girl had a car so that they would be able to get back to Weston Park. At this time the police and magistrates demanded that as part of our licence all drinks had to be served by a waiter or waitress. Impossible! But clever old Dennis hit on the idea of a person between barriers next to the bar so the customer would give their order to the person, who would then order it from the bar for them. Bizarre as it was this complied with the new requirements. Campbell and Stedson would often volunteer for this job enabling them to charm even more girls and get lots of free drinks!

The Vine Club was still going well and in quick succession we had two bands that were about to be massive in The Bay City Rollers and Mud. As they stormed up the charts it really enhanced our reputation for getting the best up and coming bands. The lead guy in one band spent 2 hours tuning up whilst the customers waited impatiently for "the platters that matter" from St Sam. I frequently gave him the hurry up but he just ignored me as he seemed to be in another world, which he quite possibly was. In hindsight I should have said to everybody forget the Disco and just listen to this guy tuning up, who was the legendary Rock and Blues guitarist Gary Moore.

I also had what looking back was a special moment when I was sat at the bar having a drink before we opened with Eddy Grant who at the time was the lead singer with The Equals. However I am not sure that Eddy Grant goes round telling people that one of the highlights of his career was having a drink with St Sam at Newport's Vine Club,.

One of my favourite bands was Cupids Inspiration, who had a massive hit with "Yesterday Has Gone". As their set was coming to an end they used to let me join them on stage to sing "Keep a Knockin". Hopefully the audience had visited the bar sufficiently not to be offended by the talentless DJ, who decided he could sing. Because their first spot was not until 10.15pm, they used to go round to our flat, 500 yards from the Club to see Linda and watch TV. On one occasion we had a near disaster when our cat Jimmy Fryatt (a female cat named after the great Southport, and about fifteen other clubs, centre forward, who the weekend we got her, had scored 4 goals away at Darlington – so the name was a no brainer!) got entangled in one of the band's Afro Asian hair. In sorting out this problem hair was lost! The cat was a remarkable animal who sometimes would wait outside the Club at 4.00am to walk home with me!

Another Artiste who spent the early evening at our flat was Colin Blunstone, who had insisted that they went somewhere so the band would not have a drink. Other acts that made a big impact when they played the Club were Screaming Lord Sutch and coffin and all, The Real Thing, Mac and Katie Kissoon (one of my favourites) Christie of "Yellow River" fame, The Swinging Blue Jeans and The White Plains.

Trevor Buckley left us after three years, when he got a job promotion and struggled to find time to come to the Club as he had usually done on a Saturday night. He had also probably lost a bit of interest in the dramas of running a nightclub. Jimmy Powell also moved on. His life had always been a bit complicated and he made a fresh start running The Apollo Club in Stoke and keeping his Band on the road. We very much owed Trevor for having faith in us as well as investing in us at the start.

Jimmy had brought a bit of magic to what we did and without him we would never have lasted as long as we did. Jimmy was also great to have around and I learnt lots from him – both good and bad!

Despite quite a few new clubs opening in the area The Vine Club continued to do well, although not at the levels it had been. Back to the three of us again, we all had a fun life in our different ways. Terry and I continued to enjoy Newport Cricket Club, where there were some great characters including the first team Captain Mick Lea, Bill Rooker, Ron Templeton, Tony Blakely and of course Richard Butter. They also had some very good young players with Andrew Watson-Jones, Pete Ranells, Cedric Boynes, who went on to play for Worcestershire and Philip Oliver who played for Warwickshire.

One of my closest friends was Jim Davenport, who along with his wife Kath were two of Bury's finest. Jim formed a table tennis team with Colin Wright and myself and we went from Division 4 of the Telford League to Division 1 in three years. Just to complete the very exciting story of my sporting life I also started playing tennis for Newport. Life was such fun!

Jim was also the Midlands Scout for Bury Football Club and had his finest moment when he discovered a young goalkeeper playing in the Telford Sunday League. He persuaded Bury to sign him and Terry Gennoe went on to have a stellar career with Halifax Town, Southampton and Blackburn Rovers, where he broke the record for the most appearances by a goalkeeper. He was also one of the genuinely nice guys and Linda and I became great friends with him and his wife Angela, when we moved to Rochdale (another very exciting instalment still to come!).

The Vine Club was near The National Sports Centre at Lilleshall and every summer a load of footballers would go there to take their coaching badges. Needless to say the majority very quickly found their way to The

Vine Club and would happily come and boost our bar profits. By far the greatest character among them was Colin Addison, who seemed to return every year and was quick to direct others on the course to us. Colin had a great playing career at Arsenal, Nottingham Forest and Sheffield United but appeared to keep failing his exams. By this time he was Manager of Hereford United and master minded their never to be forgotten FA Cup victory over Newcastle United. When they drew West Ham United in the next round Colin invited us over to watch another great performance in holding them to a 0 – 0 draw. We ended up drinking with the West Ham players and when the hotel porter asked us to leave, as non-residents, at closing time Geoff Hurst came over and said to leave us as we were with him. In reality it probably had more to do with the girls we had with us than Terry's and my scintillating conversation!

Colin might have taken a couple of years to pass his exams but he certainly knew how to manage football teams. Among the many clubs that he managed were Athletico Madrid and Derby County. One night at the Club he said he had a guest with him that he would like me to meet and who should he have with him but none other than Jimmy Fryatt (obviously the footballer, not the cat!) This was too much for me, meeting George Best I could handle but Jimmy Fryatt was altogether different. I told him how wonderful I thought he was and not sure how to respond, he said that I was a great DJ. I may have made a complete prat of myself but I had met the great man!

Chapter 5

PROBLEMS AT THE VINE

I was well aware that I had been living the dream – having a great time as a DJ, in love with a beautiful woman and meeting stars of sport, music and Job Centre.

However, as I was floating along, living my life in Utopia, storm clouds were gathering in the form of police. We were visited by an Inspector, who said by turning out so many people in the early hours we were making life difficult for his officers. Two of us got the feeling that a cash payment may alleviate this problem and one did not. We will never know as this is a route that we would not have taken.

From that moment on we continually had plain clothes policemen in the Club. We nearly always recognised them because they would usually have more to drink than anybody else! On one occasion a guy wearing a suit (unusual) demanded a meal. Knowing the problems we had had and suspecting that he was a policeman we made a great mockery of clearing people off a table for him, laying a table cloth on, putting ropes round the table to keep him undisturbed. We were all laughing at the ridiculousness of it when we discovered that he was not a policeman but rather an Estate Agent, who had just moved to the area. We all felt very guilty and I think that Dennis gave him free admission from then on.

Then one Saturday night around midnight as I was taking people "so high you are in the sky" all hell broke loose. Police and dogs entered from every exit. Initially I assumed that there must be an escaped murderer in the building but no, it was a police raid on The Vine Club led by the Inspector, who had visited us. They wanted me to tell the punters to stay still to enable the police to take their details and count them. There was no chance as people were as uncooperative as possible. They eventually left to the boos of all the people still there.

What was the point of all this? They had brought a coach of 50 policemen from outside the area plus a van full of dogs at great expense, to achieve what? The net result of this raid plus all the hours so called undercover police had spent in the Club was that we were prosecuted for allowing one act of violence, two cases of drunkenness and serving two underage girls. The reality was that they could have spent a few nights in any of the local pubs and achieved the same result.

We decided that in fairness to Dennis as licensee, we would vigorously defend the case. We hired a top licensing lawyer from Birmingham and he was different class from the police solicitor. The case of allowing violence resulted from two policemen stating that they had seen a fight break out in front of the stage when they had been doing undercover work in The Club. The first policeman gave evidence that he had seen the fight whilst standing with his colleague by the downstairs bar. Our lawyer asked him how he could possibly have seen the incident at the other end of the room when he had already described the venue as jammed full. He replied unconvincingly that he could just see between all the bodies on the dance floor. His colleague then gave evidence that the two of them had had a perfect view of the fight because they were looking down from the balcony! When asked what he would say if told that his colleague had stated that they had seen it from downstairs, he replied that he would say that our lawyer was trying to trick him. So that was that case thrown out!

With the two underage girls that we were accused of serving alcohol to, it transpired that the girls had been bought the drinks by two boys. Whilst we could have been prosecuted for allowing underage drinking on the premises we were actually accused of serving them so that was also thrown out. The two cases of drunkenness were even less substantiated apart from somebody falling off their chair, we were found guilty of one of those and fined £50. Afterwards even our lawyer did not know which one we had lost but explained the guilty verdict was just a consolation prize to the police. We thanked our lawyer, who from the start had maintained that the police over-reaction to The Club was absurd and retired to the pub to celebrate.

As we sat in the pub with our double brandies it seemed like a great time to discuss how we saw our future progressing. I stated that we needed to get another Club to help share some of the expenses and there was one in Nantwich which would suit us. Terry said he had had enough of the Club and that Launderettes were the future and Dennis said that he wanted to go and live in Australia!

We had been aware for some time that Astra would like to buy us out and we agreed that we should open conversations with them. Our value was much reduced when the police applied to have our licence revoked. It was time to move on to our different futures so we sold The Vine Club for a pittance two days before the case to revoke our licence. When we attended court our friend the Inspector was there with files of evidence and witnesses to ensure that he really nailed us this time. There was a lovely moment when the Magistrate announced the case of the Police application to revoke the licence of The Vine Club Newport, and Dennis walked over to the Inspector and handed the licence over to him explaining that he could have it with pleasure as we no longer owned the premises!

It was a very sad way to end but in reality The Vine Club had run its course and it was time for us to lead different lives. It had certainly been one of the happiest times of my life and I could only be grateful to Dennis and Terry for making that call to me in Aberdeen. The Vine Club had gone from nothing to being an institution and so many people were responsible for that. Some are mentioned in this book and others not. But I raise my proverbial hat off to them all because we really did have the time of our lives.

Dennis had held it together and nothing would have been achieved without him. He also became a great friend and I look back with sadness that once he went to Australia I never saw or heard from him again. Terry and Sue stayed in the area, where Sue owned a Hairdressing Salon and Terry took over as Landlord of a local pub. It was really the end of The Vine Club as when it reopened it was as Main Street. I will ever be thrilled to have been a part of that incredible five year journey. I was a lucky boy.

Previously, before we sold the Vine Club, I had the wonderful experience of going with Linda to the little Island of St Helena to get married. Once she accepted my proposal there was only one place that she would get married and that was home.

This was some adventure for me as my only experience of international travel was a day trip to Rhyl! St Helena is billed as the remotest place on earth. It is a volcanic Island 10 miles by 6 miles and is in the South Atlantic with the nearest land being Namibia. It has around 5000 inhabitants. It is most famous for being Napoleon's last place of abode. The only way to get there was a fourteen day trip on a Royal Mail Ship, which took twelve passengers. This somewhat concerned me as I used to suffer travel sickness sitting on a coach. However when we arrived at Southampton I was fortified by having taken my quells and having been given important advice like do not have an alcoholic drink for the first 48 hours.

Once on board I started to feel quite queasy, which seemed to amuse the steward and my travelling companions as we were still in dock. In conversation with the steward I explained my concerns should we have a storm in the notorious Bay of Biscay. He helpfully informed me that the Channel could be just as bad and that they were anticipating a gale!

The Gale Force 9 duly arrived and I felt so bad that I immediately broke the no-alcohol rule and downed a double brandy. Linda of course was a natural sailor and indeed in later life was to spend much of her life working aboard ships as a Croupier in Casinos. By the time that we were called for our seven-course dinner, nine of our travelling companions had taken to their bunks. The other one left mid meal as did the person serving us but we managed the full meal and to then return to the bar to the admiration of the crew. We hit another big storm in the Bay of Biscay and using the same formula survived that although our luggage did go flying across our cabin a few times.

The result of this was that for years to come I would boringly tell an extended version of the voyage, explaining that I was a born sailor. This was to be proved totally incorrect when many years later my then 10-year-old son Ben and I went on a boat to see the seals in Capetown. Being handed a sick bag when we boarded should have given us a clue!

So, after fourteen days at sea on our way to St. Helena this incredible Island came into view. It was night time and the Jamestown harbour was all lit up making a sensational vision. The Chief of Police boarded the ship to clear us for immigration. He spent five minutes clearing eleven of the passengers and half an hour clearing me (long hair has a lot to answer for!) We then had to climb down the gangway on the side of the ship and board a small launch to take us ashore.

It was a warm night and despite the lateness of our arrival there was a throng of happy people on the waterfront most of whom seemed to know Linda. We were met by her Mum and Dad, Rowie and Wilson and her sister Deborah and after many conversations we set off to Sandy Bay on the other side of the Island. I was to learn that a ship's arrival was one of the happiest times on the Island as it meant people were reunited. Conversely the ship leaving was one of the saddest as people never knew when or if they would meet again. Tragically this was to desperately affect us as when we left the Island Linda was never to see her Dad again.

Linda's family lives in 20 or so acres including a banana plantation, cattle, goats, sheep and hens, hence the name Coffee Grove! Their hospitality was fantastic and Linda's Mum, Rowie, was a delight and really made me feel welcome. Evenings spent at home consisted of the generator going on because there was no electricity, followed by a meal, listening to Country School (local radio), a family sing song with them all playing musical instruments and a few cans of Harp larger. The ladies would then retire and Wilson would get the whisky bottle out and we would put the world to right whilst getting to know each other better.

In hindsight these were precious times, although they often resulted in me being sick in the bushes! The music on the Island was mainly American Country, no doubt influenced by the people who went to the American base on Ascension Island to work. At weekends we would go dancing normally to the Silver Strings Band, with whom Wilson would join in with his guitar. There was no television on the Island and it seemed a better place for everybody making their own entertainment.

Wilson was a strong personality, typified when he drove me to the St Helena Radio Station and told the Radio Controller Tony Leo that I was a DJ and he must put me on the radio. When Tony said he would sort a slot out for me in the next few days Wilson explained that he meant now! So in no time I was broadcasting to the Island! Tony was a great guy and an outstanding radio performer. We got on very well and I was to go on and present a family request programme from the UK for a few years. There was also a cricket match between an island team and the rest of the Island, which Wilson insisted that I played in. Fortunately I scored runs and took a few wickets to ensure that I did not let him down. I regarded that appearance as my International debut!

The wedding arrangements were going apace and I was introduced to Gilbert Legg, who I was told was to be my best man! I think that he was chosen because he had the next longest hair on the island after me. But he turned out to be an inspired choice. The remoteness of the Island obviously meant that I would have no family or friends from the UK at the wedding so Gilbert arranged in the morning for me to ring everybody. In the lead up to it Wilson asked me to go with him to help slaughter the sheep and goats and was probably less than impressed when I opted to go with the ladies to help with the flower arranging! We got married at St Pauls Cathedral (not many people can claim that!) and had the most wonderful day. Although 'Help me make it through the night" was probably not an inspired choice for our first dance!

The whole visit to St Helena was the most fabulous of experiences with the family and the general friendliness of the Island making me unbelievably welcome.

Despite this I was happy to return to the UK and behind the turntable at The Vine Club. On my first night back I blew my mind leapt off the stage, fell over a chair and broke both my elbows. So Linda had to take on rather more wifely duties than she might have expected! The show of course, went on with somebody else helping out by putting the records on. Little was I to know at this happy time that within a year of this The Vine Club would be sold and I would be out of work.

Chapter 6

UNEMPLOYED – AGAIN!

Unemployed, I started to apply for jobs for which I thought I was a perfect match. Sadly those doing the employing did not necessarily agree with me and it was a little disappointing to realise how many people could be wrong in their assessments.

After a couple of months of failure I decided to apply the Frank Sinatra tactic! This needs explaining and is obviously nonsense but somebody once told me that the reason that Frank Sinatra had had more women than anybody else was because he asked more. This is flawed in many areas including the question of whether or not he did actually have more women than anybody else. I think that was unlikely – the bit that he asked more – and I honestly believe that perhaps being a massive star of screen and stage and being incredibly rich may also have played a part!

As a very happily married man I did not need to apply this tactic in the female area but rather with regard to jobs. So each week I bought The Stage and applied for every job that wasn't technical and did not involve dancing! It was astonishing how often I did not even get a reply. I fully understand that I may not have been the perfect applicant for the job of General Manager of the Halle Orchestra but they might at least have replied to point out the area where they considered me deficient or at the very least, booked me to do their Christmas Disco!

Then at last the tactic worked and I got not one but two interviews. The first was as Assistant Manager at the Windmill Theatre at Littlehampton and the second was for the Deputy Manager's job at the Queensway Hall at Dunstable. The interviews were on consecutive days and we were going to have to put our faith in Linda's new to her, but very old car. With great imagination we called her Guj (her registration was GUJ!) and we had become so used to her breaking down that on any long journey we would pack for that eventuality. Many a time we would be happily sat on a rug with a picnic and transistor radio blaring out on the side of some road, so much so that many of the AA team came to know us well.

Linda was the driver as I had been a bit unlucky in my attempts to learn. Both Jimmy Davenport and Terry offered to teach me but for no apparent reason withdrew their offers after my first attempt with them. Even Linda, a lady of great patience, gave up after asking me to park the car, which as a result of a slight mistake on my part had shot across a flower bed and ended up against a wall!

So with not a lot of confidence in Guj we set off to Littlehampton with an overnight stay in Arundel planned before Dunstable the next day. The car did its job of getting us to Littlehampton but I did not do mine. I thought that I did a brilliant interview explaining how I could book lots of up-and-coming bands, do some discos and make them lots of money. I was therefore rather deflated when after the interview the guy who showed me out explained that I had got the whole thing badly wrong and that they did not want to make any money as that would result in them losing their subsidy and their council budget. He also explained, more brutally than he needed to, that I certainly would not be getting the job.

Next stop was the Queensway Hall, Dunstable, where I was due to be interviewed by the General Director of Recreation, Bryan Gee M.I.R.M., and the Queensway Hall Manager John Garforth A.I.E.M. The initials impressed me until I realised that one was Member of Institute of Recreation Management and the other was Associate of Institute of Entertainment Management, both of which anybody could be if they worked in that industry! Bryan Gee was ex-Mecca and a very different animal from the people at Littlehampton. John Garfarth was to go on and have a major influence in my career. Bryan Gee was delighted to hear about Discos and Bands being brought to the Venue, particularly as part of his remit was to provide more entertainment for young people. He was also a very busy man as he was responsible for a new Recreation Centre that was due to open next to the Queensway Hall, so he was wasting no time. He offered me the job, which must have been a disappointment to those waiting to be interviewed, and said he would test my keenness by asking me to start on Monday.

This was obviously good news but also a bit of a shock and I quickly had to come to terms with moving to Bedfordshire and to starting work in a very different environment from being co-owner of The Vine Club. We decided that Linda would bring me down on the Sunday, for which we had booked an hotel room and then once I had gone to work I could move into the accommodation that they had said would be provided. Linda returned to Newport to sort things out there and to work her week's notice with Woolworths.

I arrived at the wonderful Queensway Hall, described by Hawkwind as the venue that most resembled a space ship (I could not see that myself) and reported to John Garforth. John was many things, but an arranger of accommodation he was not and he took a very little interest in the fact that as of now I was homeless. In desperation and not having the funds to book into a hotel or guest house I ended up sharing a room in a pub with an Irish labourer, which was an experience I would not recommend. The next day I recounted this situation to Ann Norcross, who managed the box office and she was absolutely brilliant. She immediately rang Personnel and told them that this was outrageous and that they needed to sort it out immediately. She was so impressive that within an hour the Head of Personnel came to see me. He promised me a Council flat and that until it was available I must come and live with him and his family! It was incredibly kind of him and after a couple of days of putting up with me he pursued the search for a flat with a certain amount of vigour! By the following Monday we had a one bedroom Council flat in Eddywick Drive in Houghton Regis and Terry had hired a van and brought all our possessions down (a van did not need to be a very big to achieve that!), whilst Linda drove down with Jimmy Fryatt the cat.

Initially life at The Queensway Hall was quite difficult. Bryan Gee was a man of standards and I was to discover this in my first week when he descended on the venue with a ruler, when I was the manager on duty, and started measuring the overhang of the tablecloths. I was summoned with a "Mr Shrouder over here quickly" to be told that on the tables there was a difference of as much as two inches between the two sides of the tablecloth. This was a serious matter and not to be repeated!

A couple of weeks later the police were called when somebody had their purse stolen at a flea market. I allowed the police lady to interview the victim in the Manager's office and when Bryan Gee arrived on the scene he went mad, explaining in a raised voice (that means shouting!) that nobody must ever sit in the Manager's chair other than Mr Garforth. When I asked if it was alright for me to sit in it when I was the Manager on duty, I got very short shrift. "What does it say on the door – it says Manager – Are you the Manager? – No you are not, so you are therefore not allowed to sit in that chair!" All a bit bizarre but suffice to say that nine months later when I was leaving he asked me if I would go with him to Jersey to be the Entertainments Officer of Tourism. So it would be fair to say that our relationship did improve.

John Garforth was to prove to be one of the most inspirational people I ever worked with. He was a very interesting man and had spent six months in Pentonville Prison as a conscientious objector, who refused to do National Service. He was also a prolific author having had 15 books published as well as writing books from the scripts of The Saint TV series. Whilst I was there he had a book "The day in the life of a Victorian Policeman" published. Not sure how you can write a book about one day when I am feebly attempting to write a book about a lifetime!

We hit it off immediately and we agreed that I would do a disco every Monday night for the 11–17's and a Saturday morning show for the 5–10 year olds. He called me Laughing Sam and insisted that would be my title as a DJ – so goodbye St Sam and hello Laughing Sam. He also instructed that no bands playing the venue would get paid unless they allowed me to introduce them. I think that John had a few drinks when he decided this but he stuck rigidly to it. When Procol Harum insisted that they had a long intro tape to introduce them he stood his ground and the compromise was that I introduced the intro tape!

I was fascinated by the shows John had booked into the venue. For him the highlight was the BBC's Friday Night is Music Night introduced by Robin Boyle. It was a sell-out of course and John was in his element dealing with the BBC and being very much the front man. This was followed by Peggy Seeger and Ewan MacColl, and then came the great American harmonica virtuoso, Larry Adler.

I popped round to see him and check if he wanted to be introduced. He duly, but politely. declined and since in no way shape or form could he be described as a band that was fine by me. Larry Adler was a charming man and I will continue to remember his opening words until I lose my faculties. It went along the lines that "I am truly thrilled to be playing Dunstable. When I first arrived in this country I gave my agent copies of rave reviews that I received when I played two sell-out shows at Carnegie Hall and asked him if I could play Dunstable. My agent said Larry you cannot just play Dunstable like that. So I worked hard and after selling out the London Palladium I returned to my agent and said now can I play Dunstable. He said Larry you just don't get to play Dunstable that easy – Frank Sinatra he never gets to play Dunstable. Six months later I was appearing on "Give us a Clue" on the radio and I made a real mistake and said sorry I am really useless! The phone went and it was my agent "Larry you are ready for Dunstable"!

We also had the "Arthur Askey Show" which consisted of a singer and spec act doing the first half and Arthur the second half. He was my Dad's favourite and had been around a million years so I was delighted when he asked me to spend the first half having a cup of tea with him and chatting. What I came to realise was that despite his incredible career, talent and experience and the fact that he was playing Dunstable, Arthur was still very nervous about the show and that he did not want to be on his own before going on. I was to come to realise that this was quite common with comics. Of course Arthur went on and was loved by everyone – a privilege to have worked with him.

The Discos were a great success with Monday night a sell out with 1000 11–17 year olds. I would like to say that Laughing Sam was a major factor in this but we did it as a Double Discomania and the other DJ was Bruce Benson, who was excellent and a great showman when getting people up on stage. I learnt a lot from Bruce, who at the time was on a local radio station.

The Saturday morning show was also doing well with cartoons, competitions and me hosting it. As a result of these two events my popularity rose with both Brian Gee and with Cllr Jones, who was Chairman of Recreation and always came in on a Saturday morning to help out. Afterwards John and I would have a drink with him and he would give us Chairman's approval for anything that we wanted to do including booking bands.

By now John was on a Disco role so he decided to do a Classical music disco!! Poor Ann Norcross was press ganged into being the DJ and she performed valiantly every Friday lunch time in front of 6 or 7 blokes eating their sandwiches and reading the papers! Every now and again John insisted that we rang Whipsnade Zoo and asked if we could borrow a live bear to chain up outside the Queensway Hall with a placard advertising our Classical Disco! The calls were never made and we duly reported back that all the bears were busy!

I was now booking quite a lot of groups and I had great fun doing the Disco and introducing bands such as Kenny and Mud. These were the days of mass hysteria and we had to create a pit to put security in to help lift fainting girls out of the audience. Once they reached the stage they would immediately recover and make a rush for one of the band. Sadly of the many girls that had used this ploy not one of them ever made a rush for Laughing Sam! At the Mud concert I made the mistake of playing a Bay City Rollers record and the whole audience booed and shouted some quite unpleasant things at me! It was at the Mud show that I first met Derek Block, who was a top promoter and he really fitted the bill with camel hair coat, very large cigar and security. Our paths were to cross many times.

Other bookings included the Rubettes, who on the same night were on the recorded programme Top of the Pops. It was quite an experience watching them singing Sugar Baby Love on a supposedly live show, whilst they sat next to me. I also managed to book Ken BoothE on the day his recording of "Everything I Own" went to number 1 and the day after the Sun had done a full two page spread about him mentioning that he was playing Dunstable. I did not feel quite as clever when less than 100 people turned up!

We also had to hire the hall out to the public to put on their own events. On one occasion we rented it out to an Irish promoter who was putting on Big Tom and the Mainliners and on the booking form he estimated an audience of 150–200. The bars were privately run by a guy called Peter Aitken, who never let us anywhere near them, and he arranged for two bar staff. On the night I would estimate about 3000 people turned up and despite our intervention the promoter kept selling tickets. The Bar was in chaos and John and I both agreed that the event was totally out of control and that there was nothing we could do so we went to the pub! I am ashamed even writing that but at least I wasn't the licensee!

Most boring of all were the Dinner Dances which went on until 2.00am and the Manager on Duty's only job was to count the cloakroom money. It was as a result of these that I got to know Ken Price, who as General Manager had opened the new Recreation Centre.

Ken suggested that when I worked these nights I should come over to his venue when it closed at 10pm and have a game of squash with him. Excellent idea! Ken and his assistant, Brian Strange, were Olympic weight lifters and as such had received much publicity locally. The first event from which I could escape was the Masonic Lodge's Ladies Night and I duly slipped over to the Leisure Centre and lost a sweaty game of squash after which Ken suggested that we had a swim and then a beer. In principle a good plan but somewhat let down by the admission that I could not swim. I explained that nobody had been able to teach me starting with Miss Rushworth at Southport Baths, who used to put a ring round me and then forget to pull it leaving me spluttering underwater. He was not fazed by this and over the coming weeks he achieved the impossible and I have mentally thanked him on every holiday in the sun ever since.

Ken's story of how he became an Olympic sportsman was fascinating. He lived in Yorkshire and was a good all round sportsman playing good level cricket and football. One night he was watching the Olympic Games and decided that he was going to compete in the next one. When he explained this to his incredulous wife he answered her query about what on earth was he going to do by saying weight lifting because it was all about technique. Ken then dedicated the next four years of his life to getting into the Great Britain team. Unbelievably he achieved this. When I asked if he enjoyed it the answer was 'no' as he had put so much pressure on himself but once he achieved his aim he carried on and travelled the world with the Great Britain team eventually becoming captain of it. Inspiring stuff from such a lovely man.

During the times we met up Ken often mentioned that one of his life guards used to be in a band. I would yawn and explain that everybody I know used to play in a band but he would always mention the fact and said that he thought they might have been half decent. Eventually the guy in question came over to help with security for one of our pop concerts and I got the chance to chat. I was embarrassed to find that the musician that I had showed no interest in was Mick Abrahams, founder member of Jethro Tull and later front man for Blodwyn Pig! He was having time out from music and wasn't interested in forming a new band just for the pleasure of playing the Queensway Hall!

Dunstable was a very happy period in my life and as well as the fun at the Queensway Hall we really enjoyed the rest of the experience. Needless to say I joined Dunstable Cricket Club, which proved to be a particularly friendly and social club. My first match was away at Barnet and I suggested to Linda that I would be back by 10pm and she should come up to the Dunstable

Club House for then. I got that wrong by 5 hours as they dropped me off at the flat at 3.00am!

We had a good few days when Terry and Sue and Jim and Kath came down to coincide with a Bedfordshire game at Dunstable (Well not the ladies!). The game was highlighted by a Dunstable non-playing member saying that he could recognise any gin. We bought them and if he got it wrong he paid for the round. Annoyingly he kept being right until we got so fed up that we gave him a Barcardi, which after one sip he immediately said that we couldn't fool him and he knew it was Cornelius Gin! Our day with him got better when he was asked to sort out the squashes for the drinks interval. It was with great hilarity from Jim, Terry and me and bewilderment from the players that he took a tray of 15 scotches onto the field!

Back at the Queensway Hall Bryan Gee was now a jovial fellow and he suggested that we have a competition to see if John and I could get more stuff in the media than he and Ken could do for the Recreation Centre. Luckily I had got friendly with Mike Rowbottom from the Dunstable Gazette and we often went to the local folk club together. Once I told him of the bet he ensured that any bit of nonsense we came up with was printed whist serious stuff from them was ignored. As I explained to Bryan Gee it is not what you know but who you know – he was not amused! Mike and my paths were to cross again 25 years later when he was with Central Television and came to the Oxford Apollo to record me presenting Harry Secombe with a glass vase to commemorate his last ever performance of Pickwick.

In one of our after the Saturday Morning Club drinks with Cllr Jones, I casually mentioned that I had been offered Little Richard for £2000. Normally we booked our acts on a percentage basis, so paying a guarantee of this magnitude went against policy and was not covered in the budget. However after a few pints we all convinced each other that we couldn't go wrong with a star as big as Little Richard so after yet another pint Cllr Jones said, "Go for it – you have the Chairman's approval!"

I got very excited and managed to get lots of media coverage that we were opening the box office on the Sunday at 10am with tickets being sold on a first come basis. Come the day there I was opening the box office slightly surprised that people were not queuing round the building indeed even more surprised that there was no one there! That is the way it stayed and at midday I bought two tickets myself for Linda and a friend and they were the only tickets that we sold that day. Things did not improve and come the day we had only sold a third of the tickets and Bedfordshire Borough Council were heading for a massive loss.

It became worse than that. I was informed that Little Richard had caused problems everywhere and had never done more than 40 mins of his contracted hour set. On the night The Wild Angels were the support act and by the finish of their spot there was no sign of Little Richard or his band. Needless to say John and I took to the bar to discuss it and decided that when – or if – he turned up I would not pay him the £1000 cash he was due in advance of the show having been paid the other £1000 already. Also I would tell him he would be paid after the show pro rata for how long he performed. Suddenly there was an air of excitement as a fleet of four black Merecdes arrived. I met each one and whoever got out first I would say "Excuse me are you Mr Richard?", only to be told he was in another car.

In the end a white Rolls Royce arrived and the main man got out. Relief! I took him to his dressing room. His manager then approached me for the cash and when I explained our plan he went ballistic and shouting for Richard to come here right now. I feared the worse but Mr Richard just said "That's cool man, Little Richard will do the show". He then went out and delivered the greatest 65 minute of Rock `N' Roll that it has been my pleasure to witness.

'Mr Richard' played the gig as though it was crammed full and Long Tall Sally with him standing on the piano playing with his feet will stay with me for ever. Straight after the show I paid his manager who suggested that as I had said pro rata Richard had played five minutes over the contracted time I owed them more money – I think that he was smiling as he said it! When I went to see Little Richard in his dressing room he was doing an interview for Melody Maker which he immediately halted to greet me. His manager was desperately trying to get him out as he had another show to do in a London Club but he was having none of it. I gingerly asked him to sign a photo for a member of staff who had asked for it. With a big smile he signed the photo to the lady with "love and peace from the King of Rock `n' Roll, Little Richard". He then decided that there was no one more important than the Queensway Hall staff and he kept saying "God Bless the Staff" as he insisted signing a photo for every member. His Manager was by now apoplectic and the net result was he arrived two hours late for his London Club gig and then refused to go on anyway!

Despite the euphoria of the night in the cold light of day the facts were that I had lost South Bedfordshire Council a lot of money so it was probably a good time to move on. That was exactly what I did. John had encouraged me to apply for better jobs (I hope because he liked me rather than wanting to get rid of me!) and I had just been offered the Deputy Entertainments Officers job for Rochdale Borough Council and I accepted it very swiftly before anybody told them about Little Richard!

Chapter 7

GOODBYE DUNSTABLE, HELLO ROCHDALE!

So it was goodbye to Dunstable and hello Rochdale. Linda gave up her job at Aircall without a murmur of protest although she had made lots of friends there, Terry and Sue came down with a van to help us move and all seemed well. On this occasion the Council were on the ball with regard to accommodation and we moved directly to 41, Town Mill Brow without even passing 'Go'. It was a high rise apartment in one of seven blocks known as the Seven Sisters. It suited us perfectly and we felt that as well as going up in the world literally we had also done so with the flat as we now had a spare bedroom!

In my excitement of being offered a job that was two grades higher (a local government thing that I will not waste your time trying to explain!) I hadn't really discussed what the job entailed! What it did entail was sitting in an office in Rochdale's Art Gallery taking responsibility for exciting shows like Manchester Camerata. Perhaps the word "shows" should read in the singular because everything was being focused on a new Middleton Civic Hall (that title took some imagination!) which was due to open in four months' time. It was being programmed by the Entertainments Officer to whom I was deputy, a wonderful personality called Francis Lee.

There was nothing not to like about Francis who drove around in a car adorned with "Francis Lee" – Britain's No 1 Super showman". He was a lovely guy who would be able to gain publicity for the opening of an envelope! He had just recently promoted a Tramps Ball at Heywood Civic Hall, another venue controlled by Rochdale Borough Council, and he had dressed up as a tramp with a bill board advertising it and had walked the streets. He was accosted by a lady councillor who told him that he was demeaning his position with the council to which Francis replied "With respect Madame, I am an Entertainments Officer not a public Health Officer"!

Francis was ex Mecca and we hit it off immediately. This did not help the fact that I was stuck in the Art Gallery planning a series of lectures with a budget of Zilch. I had just booked Peter Lever, the England fast bowler, which is as good as it got when I got a call to go to the Director of Leisure's office, who was another good guy, named David John. He explained that they had budget problems and would I help out by doing two jobs and whilst remaining as Deputy Entertainments Officer would I also be the new manager and the person responsible for opening Middleton Civic Hall. Would I ever!

This was a daunting task but a great opportunity and in no time I was housed in a porta cabin next to the building site that was to become my dream venue. Initially there was just me to deal with all queries and to plan staffing the venue. I got lucky because my first appointment was Pat Schofield who was supposedly to be my secretary but in reality got involved in all aspects of getting the place ready to open.

I must admit that I had great fun employing people to work there for when we opened. I worked on two rules – one that I didn't employ anybody that I didn't like and secondly they needed to be interested in entertainment. This was crucial because to make the venue work people had to be flexible and help out in all areas, which was to be proved when our team of cleaners all volunteered to work backstage for the panto.

Francis was well under way programming the opening but it now became mine as well to work on. He generously agreed that anything that I promoted I could put my name to as he would do with his shows. So I could tag an advert with Sam Shrouder for ROCLAS (If you need help with this – it stands for Rochdale Library and Arts Services – pretty obvious) presents. He also agreed we would take charge of all arrangements for respective shows but would work jointly on the marketing. This was to work perfectly but when agreeing to me repeating the Dunstable disco he insisted that Smiling Sam was an improvement on Laughing Sam and he would not entertain a return to St Sam!

The opening programme that he had already arranged included four performances of the Good Old Days, The Band of the Grenadier Guards, a mini circus and the Joe Loss Orchestra.

For the opening day Francis had arranged a grand opening in the morning for anybody who would like to turn up, an afternoon concert by the Middleton Operatic Society and a dance at night featuring the 15 piece Big City Sound with the music of Glen Miller. This was to prove to be a rather ambitious programme for the first day of a brand new and untried venue.

The great day arrived and the good and the great and the not so great arrived for the grand opening. This went off moderately well with important people saying important things. Unfortunately it went on longer than anticipated, which meant we had a bit of a panic preparing for the afternoon concert. To install the major part of the seating we pressed a button and the bleacher seating descended on us. Not this day it didn't! We had to manhandle it, no doubt causing untold damage to get it in place as the audience was literally coming in. Once the concert was over we had the even greater problem of preparing the venue for the evening's dance.

By now we had the engineer who had installed the bleacher seating and his expert advice was that it was broken and unusable and we would have to cancel the evening and wait for it to be repaired sometime next week. Not an option and luckily Tommy, our head cleaner and a great character of the "show must go on" variety said that if we all joined in we might be able to manhandle it back into the wall. Also by now we had the floor expert, who said that if we did that we would do thousands of pounds of damage to our very special, all-purpose sprung floor. We had no choice and Tommy took charge.

We all shoved and pushed, took pieces of wood out of the floor but got it back vaguely where it should be. The next panic was to set up for dancing with tables and chairs for as many people as possible which took us to our next problem. The venue was licensed for 600 but that was far too many for a dance where everybody wanted to have a table. Francis, of course, had sold 600 tickets.

In they came carrying bags with their dancing shoes in and the mayhem commenced with people seeking out Francis and myself to demand we get them a table. As always he handled it with great charm whilst I just about survived with considerably less charm. As the alcohol flowed and our patrons got in the spirit they all crammed onto the dance floor where there was not enough room because we had too many tables and chairs! As 1.00am approached my team and I had been on site for 17 hours and we had a drink in the knowledge that the end was near and nothing else could go wrong.

This was not to prove the case. As licensee I had to get a special hours license for every event at which we wanted to serve alcohol after 10.30pm and they were not easily obtained. I had been given a long lecture by the magistrate about the dire consequences of serving after the 1.00 am extension and not having all drinks finished by 1.10am. We had a brilliant bar manager in George Gorman and I had emphasised to him that we must strictly adhere to the licencing regulations. George dutifully made sure every member of staff was aware of this. At 1.00am I collected all the tills in to do my next job, which was to do the cashing up – I soon learnt the art of delegation! At 1.15am George buzzed me to inform ME that the Chairman of Recreation and The Mayor were demanding a drink and would not take no for an answer. This resulted in a rather unpleasant scene starring Cllr Sanderson, the Chairman of Recreation.

When I arrived to sort it out he instructed me to get them both a drink. When I refused he told me that as Chairman he was instructing me to get the drinks and I told him that as licensee there would be no drinks served. This got more and more out of control and after 10 minutes the Mayor, who I liked, said "Sam can I have a drink or not" and having been told not he departed. The Chairman then lost the plot banging me in the chest and saying I was to report to the Chief Executive on Monday to be sacked! I suggested that if he wanted to continue his diatribe it would be better in my office rather than with an audience. He did this, sat down and we had a power cut! So my first day at Middleton Civic Hall I worked 19 hours and was to be sacked on Monday!

On the Sunday we had the Middleton Band with Irene Stevens of Opportunity Knocks fame (No, me neither). I then received a call from the Sunday People saying that they had been informed that I had been assaulted by a Councillor the previous night I was then contacted by the Council Chief Executive, Mr Towey, a pleasant enough chap, who was trying to sort out the mess. The deal was that I would say nothing to the press and he would ensure that the Chairman was reprimanded and apologised. That seemed fair to me and I got on with the show.

On the Monday I hosted the first Double Discomania as Smiling Sam along with Gordon Collins as the other DJ. I was strutting my stuff, when I was told somebody needed to see me. In the space of a record I saw Cllr Sanderson, who apologised like he wanted to kill me, and returned before the record was finished.

My fellow DJ Gordon Collins was a top guy and a very good DJ. He was fantastic with playing the right music allowing me to do competitions and other Tomfoolery! As I was writing this book he contacted me right out of the blue, 40 years after we had last been in contact. He had gone on to be a very successful business man, retiring at the age of 52. He was also almost as statistically anal as me and had kept a record which he still had of the attendances for Double Discomania. He used to ring our great box office manager Tricia every Tuesday to get the figures. Apparently in nearly four years it only failed to sell out in 16 occasions. Sometime after I left, the Council in their wisdom, decided not to renew his contract and the following Monday the attendance dropped from 1000 to 100! And I thought that it was me who was the star!

Life settled down after that and was great fun. The Monday Night 12–17 year old disco was a great hit with a 1000 kids queuing to get in every week. In the unlikely event that anybody from Middleton Licensing Department is reading this that figure should read 600! We were also getting 500 youngsters a week for our 5–11 year olds Saturday Morning Club. This generated the money to promote other concerts and I did a series of soul bands including Edwin Starr, Chairman of the Board, The Crystals, The Tymes, which all did fine. We also had lots of other shows and Middleton Civic Hall was flourishing. One of the special nights was Ken Dodd's first appearance at the venue in front of two sell out audiences and as is the legend he finished the following day! As we sat in his dressing room in the early hours he was in great form, called me Young Sam, which he has done ever since, and unbelievably gave me his phone number in case I wanted any help or advice. What a Star! Our paths have crossed many times and he has continued to be one of the artistes that I really look forward to seeing both on and off stage.

Two days after Ken's show we had our first televised event when the BBC recorded Andre Previn conducting Besses o' th' Barn Brass Band. Things were really on the up.

Then came another great experience when we had our first pantomime, Aladdin. The "star" was Roy Lance, who was magnificent in an old style panto way. Roy directed the show and was very much the main man both on stage and off in the Nelson Firth production. He knew that I was wet behind the ears and helped and supported me in every way. He was fantastic at doing all the PR and publicity although secretly he couldn't get enough of it! He was a great upholder of Theatre protocol and when the guys from

The Fourmost waltzed past the box office and went backstage to see him he was furious and insisted that they apologise to Mr Shrouder and that in future they would ring in advance and he would arrange tickets for them.

Aladdin also had Bill Waddington, old style comic as Abanazar and a great double act The Twain Brothers. Bill Waddington was to go on and have a major, long running part in Coronation Street. I loved the show although the only other Panto that I had seen had been 26 years earlier at the Garrick Theatre, Southport. Pop singer Vince Eager had been the star and I had never understood why in the middle of the show he had suddenly found a guitar and a band and started singing.

Whilst Aladdin was on, a group of Travellers had moved on to the car park and seemed quite friendly although the milk started disappearing and some of the younger ones started displaying their bare bums to the audience as they arrived. All pretty harmless but a couple of the staff decided to apprehend two of them and having done so brought them to me as though I would have the slightest clue what to do.

At a loss I asked them if they wanted to see the show that everyone was queuing for. "Yes please Mister" came the reply and so I sat with them throughout the show. It was a wonder to behold as they sat fixated by what was unfolding in front of them. As I gave them an ice cream in the interval they were full of questions – Why was the boy Aladdin a girl and why Widow Twankie was a man – there was no fooling them. At the end they both thanked me and one said, "Mister that is the best thing ever in my life". As well as giving a special experience to two lovely boys we also never lost another bottle of milk nor had a bare bum displayed!

Chapter 8

CRICKET, WRESTLING, PUNK AND GELDOF!

Although I spent most of my life working, needless to say, I did find time to play cricket. When we first arrived it was a joy to find that we could look down upon Rochdale Cricket Club's Dane Street ground. Terry and Sue had come visiting for Easter, which was late that year, and it coincided with Rochdale's net practice.

Terry always had his cricket gear in the car, as one does, so we went down and asked to join in. Terry cut an impressive sight in his Shropshire County sweater and causing all batsmen numerous problems. My leg breaks did not seem to have quite the same effect. As Terry and I were chatting he said I will bowl you into their first team. When I queried this he said that he would pitch the ball up a little further and just to play him off the front foot and when he bowled a short one it would be wide of the off stump. This ploy worked and meant that I dealt with him better than the other batsmen.

Afterwards we retired to the bar which was being run by one of the players, a genial chap called Alistair Bollingbroke. By the time there was only the three of us left drinking we had all become great friends and have remained so to this day. Come selection and there I was in the heady position of being in Rochdale's first team to play Crompton in the Central Lancs League.

The great day came and their Pro was Parvez Mir the Pakistani Test Player and ours was David Ash ex-Yorkshire and Middlesex. David opened the batting and bowled left arm spin. The day was a disaster and we were heavily defeated. On the Monday the 14 man selection panel decided that this was not good enough and made six changes to the side. To my surprise the way I walked to the wicket and took guard obviously impressed them enough for me to retain my place.

The season was a great adventure with lots of drinking and visits to Indian Restaurants plus some great characters which included John Raby, Tony Kearns, Roger Sanders and Gerald Shooter. Indeed if I hadn't had to go on the cricket field it would have been an unqualified success. I just managed to keep my place by scoring 20 or 30,or taking the odd wicket just as I was about to be dropped. In its heyday this great ground used to get around 7000 people to watch the likes of Learie Constantine. But those days were long since gone and the main stand was dilapidated and the crowd in the main consisted of a few hundred coming for the afternoon once the pubs closed. It would be fair to say that I was not their favourite player. After one batting failure one guy in the pavilion seats announced to all and sundry that if he had his way Rochdale would not pick any bloody Germans. In fairness his mate put him right by explaining that I was from Poland and what did they know about cricket!

Things went from bad to worse when we played Littleborough, whose professional was Joel Garner, the West Indian fast bowler. In the first over their opening batsman hit a magnificent off-drive off Tony Kearns, our mickey-taking medium slow bowler. It was four all the way until Shrouder flung himself to his right to take one of the finest catches ever seen at full stretch and inches from the ground. The problem was that nobody did see it as the ground was more or less empty. What the crowd did see two hours later was the sight of Joel Garner going to sweep David Ash and getting a gentle top edge and the ball looping to extra cover. The celebrations started, the dangerous Garner gone and David Ash one wicket away from a collection (5 wickets or 50 and a collection was taken and was an important part of the Pro's earning capacity).

The celebrations had to be halted when somebody pointed out that inexplicably I had dropped the catch! The crowd started booing, Garner hit Ash's next two balls for 6 and I had become the crowd's enemy No 1 with somebody trying to present me with a bucket when we came off!

Things went from bad to even worse when we played Radcliffe away. We had not won a match but this was going to be our moment. With nine wickets down they were miles behind us and our inspirational skipper Bernard Burke turned to me to break the last wicket stand to ensure we got full points. One of our supporters was so thrilled with our impending victory that he had bought pints of beer for all of us and taken them to the dressing room. This proved slightly premature as by the time I finished bowling the match was lost! Folklore has it that this was entirely my fault, although to this day I blame Gerald Shooter who was keeping wicket and in my opinion missed a stumping chance. His opinion was that it was two feet outside the leg stump and went for 4 byes and that was my fault as well.

There were better moments but not very many. I did get the Stockport Pro John Holder out, stumped by Dai Lodwig who was obviously a much better wicket keeper than Gerald Shooter. John Holder has, of course, appeared at many Test Matches but not as a batsman but rather as an umpire. On his return to Royton he apparently claimed to all and sundry that a bloody Disc Jockey got him out!

I also batted for a while against Joel Garner as a result of a cunning plan. He had recently hit someone who had displeased him on the head with a bouncer so Alistair and I decided to go to the Ladybarn Pub in Milnrow where he normally drank on the Friday before the game. He was at the bar so we joined him with a jovial "Hiya Big Bird how are you doing man?". Once he had established he was playing us the next day he asked how we were doing. I explained that I was having a dreadful time with the bat because I was having trouble with my glasses and I couldn't see the ball.

The next day as he was bowling Rochdale out, I stuck around as he consistently pitched it up to me. After a while his captain got annoyed and said along the lines of, Bird give him some chin music (By now we were all talking like West Indians!). But Joel was not for moving as he patiently explained that I had trouble with my glasses and couldn't see! Alistair needed no such tactics as he got fifties against Garner and the two other big name fast bowling pros Colin Croft and Geoff Lawson. Alistair's natural modesty ensures that he only mentions this once in each conversation he has! Rochdale was a great club to be part of and Linda was made very welcome – probably because she volunteered to help with the teas.

One of the many shows presented at Middleton Civic Hall was wrestling. This was provided by a great guy named Brian Dixon whose wife was the lovely Mitzi Mueller, the British and European Ladies Champion. She would enter the ring to 'She's a back breaker!" which was penned by the Scaffold. Her bouts with Hellcat Haggerty were a joy to behold and restoring one's faith that good eventually always triumphs over evil!

My relationship with Brian did not get off to a great start as during my Dunstable days I had booked a wrestling show for the Bossard Hall in Leighton Buzzard from a rival promoter called Terry Goodrum. Part of the show's attraction was that it featured the masked avenger Kendo Nagasaki.

For those not aficionados of wrestling I should explain that a masked wrestler could only retain his mask until he was defeated. The fact that he was masked naturally meant that nobody knew what he looked like, which obviously opened the way for imposters. Unfortunately on this occasion there were two Kendo Nagasaki's wrestling in the area at the same time. Brian was promoting a show with the genuine one the main attraction and they were somewhat miffed that we were advertising another one.

Their response was to arrive mob-handed with a number of wrestlers, including the very likeable Neil Sands, and they climbed into the ring and ripped off our Kendo's mask. Once they had gone I obviously had to maintain that our Kendo was genuine and that their behaviour was a disgrace and that I personally would be reporting them to British Board of Wrestling Council!

Our relationship survived that and with Mitzi and Linda becoming good friends we had some great nights out together particularly at Fagins Night Club in Manchester.

We also saw a lot of Terry Gennoe (of Telford Sunday League fame) and his wife Angela. Terry had been sold by Bury to Halifax Town but they still lived in Bury. We had an interesting few days together in a caravan in Clarach Bay. Having decided to walk along a cliff edge to Aberystwyth for a couple of drinks we got way-layed in a pub which had no people but a singer called Memphis Short. We kept drinking on the basis that we could not desert him until there was no chance of us moving. We were joined by some Germans, who, due to language difficulties, kept saying Bobby Charlton to us and we would say Uwe Seeler to them and then buy another round. At closing time one of the German guys went and bought a round of a pint of bitter for everybody including the girls with the result that Terry and I had to drink most of them. We were marching along the promenade singing "We'll keep a welcome in the hillside" when a kind lady adopted us. Explaining that we could not possibly go back along the cliff in our state, she insisted that we all stayed with her. After some protest we did this although we did lose Angela's brother Al, who we found in a hedge the next day.

You will get the picture from this that Terry was indeed a dedicated footballer! Despite this incident Southampton paid £50,000 for him. To celebrate his transfer into the big time Linda and I decided that expense was no object and we should book the best restaurant in the area The Moorcock.

We had never been there but had heard great things about it so when Linda booked she was a bit surprised to be told that we did not need to make a booking. When we arrived all was revealed as we had the wrong Moorcock! It was dirty, had a cracked window and served ham, egg and chips. It was so bad that we had the best night ever.

After a very successful period at Southampton, Terry moved on to Blackburn Rovers, where he went on to make a record number of appearances as a goalkeeper. So all in all a fine advert for beer! Like so many of our friends Terry got divorced. He then met and married Susan and had a great time as goalkeeping coach with Blackburn Rovers, Celtic, Newcastle and Aston Villa. They are a lovely couple who have just started enjoying their retirement.

To add to the social whirl that was Rochdale, my childhood friend Nick Hall lived in a farmhouse on the moors near Todmorden with his girlfriend Alison. They certainly knew how to throw a party. They were that good that I cannot remember them! What I do remember, but wish I didn't, was Nick persuading me to join him in playing tennis for Milnrow. I think the general consensus from the other players was that I should stick to cricket, whereas the members of Rochdale Cricket Club, if canvassed would undoubtedly have suggested that I stuck to tennis!

Back at Middleton Civic Hall things continued to go well. One of the bonuses was having Mike Harding living in Middleton. He regularly popped in and as well as using the venue when touring he also did his end-of-tour show there. This seemed to involve half of Coronation Street as well as other artistes and was highly entertaining. I recently went to see Mike after a show at Tewkesbury and we both recalled the same story. It was when he came to our Saturday Morning Club and a friend of his was performing Old MacDonald's Farm. He arrived as a cherubic 5 year old blond boy who responded with and on this farm he had a shit!" I remembered at the time that Mike's laughter drowned out everything else.

Life at Middleton was about to change with the introduction of Punk Rock. I received a call from Nick Leigh, who was working for Derek Block, suggesting that I got in at the start and put on some punk bands as they were going to change the music scene. I was not totally convinced but agreed to take a three-band package for £100. The advance sales were not great with a couple of hundred tickets sold. It was on a Saturday so I disappeared to play cricket leaving George Gormon, now Hall Manager, to open up if I was not back in time.

I rushed off the field at Milnrow with Linda waiting in the car to get me to the venue. I arrived to astonishing scenes with hundreds of punk rockers and lots of police all milling around. I let myself in the stage door and the first person I saw was George. When I queried why he had not opened the doors he replied that he had and we were sold out – wow! The first band was not really punk and did alright but then came the next one and everybody starting pogoing and it was incredible to behold as there was just so much energy both on and off stage – I was hooked.

The band were The Adverts and I remember having my photo taken backstage with Gaye Advert (obviously very reluctantly!) It occurred to me that the next band would not be able to top The Adverts. How wrong can you be as The Damned absolutely took the place apart, with the audience going crazy. The only slight downside of the audience reaction was that as they were at the height of their pogoing they would gob (spitting to you and me!), but I was just overwhelmed by the whole show.

Unfortunately the evening was not to pass without incident as Rat Scabies, The Damned's explosive drummer, was drunk and annoyed as he had been trying to count people as they came in and reckoned that as the band was only getting £30 I had ripped them off. I explained that if they were being taken advantage of it was not by me as I had just booked the package. He was not convinced. I was also doing my Smiling Sam's Disco in between the bands, which with no punk records was probably not wise. At the end of The Damned's performance I went on stage to collect my records only to be confronted by Rat, who then went on to launch each record individually into the audience. My "Excuse me Mr Scabies there is no need for that" fell on deaf ears and I had to scramble around the hall picking up my platters or what I could salvage of them.

So soul was out and punk was in! I next booked the Boomtown Rats for £100. We sold out well in advance and all was going smoothly as the equipment arrived and was set up, the support band turned up as did the Rats apart from Bob Geldof. As I chatted with the rest of the band they said that he had a problem with his voice and was seeing a specialist but was definitely travelling up to Middleton. He was not overly concerned on the basis that if Geldof was travelling he would play.

By the time Bob arrived the support band were playing, the place was heaving and he could hardly speak! So my job was to go on stage to tell

1000 punk rockers that the Boomtown Rats would not be appearing. Bob was great as he insisted that the whole of the band would come on stage with me and promised that they would do a replacement gig at the same fee.

So I went on stage with the good news and the bad news. The good news was that the gear was here, the band was here but the bad news was that Bob had been told he would be endangering his voice if he attempted to sing. I added that there was even more good news as the band had agreed to schedule a replacement gig for which your tickets are valid and tonight is free with Smiling Sam's Disco to follow.

You might have expected problems but the audience were superb and many actually applauded the announcement (Probably not at the thought of even more of Smiling Sam's Disco!) Their agent said that they would not do a replacement gig for the same fee as they were now getting a minimum of £1000, but Bob Geldof said they would and we had a sensational night when they returned.

We were now regarded as one of the major Manchester punk venues, with The Buzzcocks and then The Clash quickly following. We were then selected by the legendary Tony Wilson to house Granada TV's show featuring Tom Robinson, XTC and Mink DeVille. Next up came The Jam managed by Paul Weller's dad John. He always had a thing about not wanting to pay 10% commission on the merchandising.

This was to prove the case through the many gigs Paul did at Apollo theatres both with The Jam and Style Council. We used to have a bit of banter with John calling me a thieving bastard. Many years later when Wychwood Festival started I thought that I would call on our old friendship to see if John would do us a favour and get Paul to play the gig. The conversation went along these lines "Hi John it is Sam here."

"Who?"

"Sam Shrouder – Middleton, Blackburn and Apollo Theatres."

"Oh I remember you, you were a thieving twat!"

"That's me, we did have a few laughs."

"What do you want?"

"I wondered if Paul would like to play this new festival, Wychwood."

"Fuck Off!"

Over the years, I had obviously created a special relationship!

Chapter 9

FROM SID LAWRENCE TO THE SEX PISTOLS AND TIME TO GO

With money coming in from the Discos and Bands we were able to be more adventurous with our bookings and Jasper Carrott supported by Victoria Wood was our next sell-out show. We also added Radio 1 DJ Peter Powell to one of our sell-out Double Discomanias. He was thrilled to see a sell-out for his appearance until it was explained to him that Monday night always sold out. In fairness to him when I paid him his £300 he insisted that he took Linda and I into Manchester for a meal.

Not all artistes were happy playing Middleton Civic Hall. Sid Lawrence really lost the plot when I played Joe Loss "In the Mood" before his band came on. He said it was his signature tune, which I must know, and to take it off. I told him I didn't know that and when he exploded at my ignorance I asked him if he knew what mine was. Astonishingly he did not know! For those even slightly interested it was and is "Red River Rock". He went away slightly bemused.

We also had lots of functions, which included a Darts and Dominoes presentation. This consisted mainly of lots of guys with their local pub landlords, drinking and having a good time. Julie Goodyear did the presentation and was excellent with lots of witty comments aimed at the prize winners. At midnight for some bizarre reason they had booked a comic and a young lad came on and did his best to entertain a room that was very rowdy and was making their own fun. He got little or no reaction and was obviously a bit upset when I went to his dressing room after his spot. It obviously did not affect his career as Lenny Henry went on to be a great star.

Francis Lee proved an absolute joy to work with and fully justified his Britain No 1 Supershowman tag. He saw a potential stunt in everything we did. For the Jubilee he insisted that we would be the only venue in the UK to have a breakfast cabaret dance. I had to get a licence to enable us to sell alcohol from 8.00am and the punters had four hours of fun. Francis aimed to dress up entirely in Union Jack clothes but was horrified to find that you could only buy Union Jack clothes from Japan!

Turning a negative into a positive he went on to Granada TV to protest and within a few days he had received every possible clothing item in Union Jack style including shoes and umbrella. That was typical of Francis. When he forgot to get a piper to play the New Year in at our dance it was no problem. He borrowed some bagpipes, kitted himself out in the full regalia and mimed to a record that I put on. Due to the marvellous effects of alcohol I am not sure that anybody noticed! He also put on a nappy and was the New Year's baby, this was definitely not a pretty sight.

One day Francis rang me up and told me he had excelled himself by offering £1,250,000 for the Loch Ness Monster dead or alive so he could put it in Hollingworth Lake. We were falling about laughing when the BBC TV and Granada contacted him to do a piece with him by the lake. Some people might have thought Rochdale as a dour northern town but not when Francis was around.

Unfortunately this latest stunt did not amuse the council hierarchy and absurdly he got a written warning for offering council money without permission! It also resulted in some bizarre letters to the Rochdale Observer on the line of – 'I have been waiting four years to get my Council house guttering repaired and the Council are wasting their money on this' – yours disgusted of Rochdale. Even Greenpeace suffered a humour bypass and wrote to complain about the dead part of the offer, which obviously was inciting people to kill monsters!

Like all good Theatre Managers I had invented a ghost, with the story being that on the original market place which had been on the site of the Hall, a hundred years ago a 17 year old girl had hung herself because she was being evicted from her pottery stall. Unfortunately this got out of hand with there being numerous sightings and staff being afraid of being in the premises on their own! Things took a further turn for the worse when The

News of the World contacted me to say they wanted to bring a priest to exorcise the ghost! I had to explain to people that I had just done it for a publicity stunt but by now nobody believed me. No doubt forty years on people are still talking about the ghost.

Francis and I started going to the Institute of Arts and Entertainment Management meetings where it was good to mix with others in our line of business. At one of these meetings they decided that if you wanted to be an Associate of the Institute you would have to pass an exam and that they would recommend to all Authorities that they should not employ people without this qualification.

We were both horrified and argued strongly against it but to no avail with Francis pointing out that you could not learn to be a Supershowman from a book. I had already taken the decision after my academic failure at school that in no circumstances would I ever take another exam, so that condemned me to only ever being able to be an Affiliate member, which did not totally devastate me! However this was to prove not to be the case as many years later I was asked if I would be the Vice President of the Institute with a view to being President the following year. This was too good to miss and I did a year and a half overseeing life time achievement awards lunches for Ronnie Barker and Harry Secombe. At the end of my stint I was made a Fellow of the Institute and entitled to use the initials FIAEM behind my name. All this without passing the exam – there has to be a moral there!

In my own mind I had done a pretty good job running Middleton Civic Hall both in the Acts that I booked and as a DJ and compere but of course others see you with different eyes! With no comment whatsoever I include a passage written in the autobiography of Mark Burgess, the lead singer of Chameleons Vox.

"Until this time, though, the only places you could see and hear these new bands around Manchester were in the city centre. Middleton, however, was about to play host to the best of them. Middleton Civic Hall first opened its doors in the mid-1970s but it had struggled to attract the patronage of the town's youth and thereby justify the enormous amount of ratepayers' money that it had cost to erect. Initially it had housed the annual Christmas Pantomime, the occasional hearing aid exhibition and a twice-weekly ballroom

dancing session for the town's old-age pensioners. I'm tempted to say that demand for the hearing aids rose dramatically amongst the older generation over the space of the following six months but that would be pure speculation. In any event, Middleton Hall's only concession to teenage angst up to that point had been a Monday night disco hosted by a curious chap called Sam Shrouder.

Sam, the resident DJ, with his long blond hair, huge spectacles, white frilly shirt and stars and stripes trousers, was a seriously gruesome spectacle as he danced back and forth across the stage to the rebellious sounds of The Stylistics and vintage soul music. His disco nights were always packed the for simple reason that there was absolutely nothing else in the town for a teenager to do. Too young to drink in bars, a Middleton teenager would normally have a tantalising choice between the local community centre, with its table tennis – usually with only a single remaining bat – street corners or burglary.

Due no doubt to Sam's apparent ability to pack them in at the Civic Hall, he was appointed chief booker, given a substantial budget, and sent off to find fresh material to feed to Middleton's culurally-starved youngsters. Surprisingly, old Sam, to the delight of many – but to the horror of the local council – came up trumps. Late in 1976 he set off on a talent-spotting mssion to London and began dishing out Civic Hall contracts to a whole host of new bands eager to find gigs up north. These bands included The Damned, The Jam, The Slits, X-Ray Spex and the Adverts months before punk rock became a household name. By the time the gigs came up the following year, the punk scene had exploded out of London and these obscure, strange-looking bands were all the rage. Sam's contracts had to be honoured, and Middleton Civic Hall consequently became a Mecca for all those hungry for the new scene, finally making some money into the bargain. Of course for those more used to the wholesome, soothing sounds of The Stylistics, the sight of Dave Vanian of The Dammed dressed as some kind of vampire gravedigger was a bit of a shock to the system, but once they realised that these colourful characters weren't actually going to vomit on them they began to get the hang of it and started enjoying themselves and for those of us already familiar with the scene, it provided a considerable saving on bus and train fares.

I remember the excitement that I felt when I read in the local paper that The Damned were due to play at the Civic Hall. I'd been exalting the merits of this band, amongst others, to my mates over the previous six months, but they were seemingly unimpressed. That said, hardly anything of note ever happened in Middleton, so I was able to persuade quite a few people to check them out; all of them subsequently spiked their hair within a year. Sadly, the local authority's response to Sam's shrewd entertainment coup was to sack him in order to appease the multitudes of outraged parents who had come after them with gnashing teeth."

This had been sent to me by my friend and nephew Quin Marshman who had gone to see the band after being to Wychwood and had bought the book. I find it somewhat reassuring.

Despite the views of Mark I stayed in the job and was then challenged to provide entertainment in Rochdale Champness Hall with the people of Rochdale complaining that Middleton got the good shows and that all they got was the Manchester Camerata (Yes they were still doing the Town Hall but the audience had dropped from 60 to 40!) Champness Hall with 1300 capacity was the biggest venue in the Borough but was owned by the Methodist Church and this was to come back to haunt me!

Our attempts to entertain the good people of Rochdale went well initially with sell-out shows with Mike Harding and wrestling and a large audience for Irish entertainer Brendan Grace. I then upped the stakes and booked The Bunch of Stiffs tour, which featured Elvis Castello, Ian Drury and the Blockheads, Wreckless Eric – Nick Lowe and Larry Wallis – all of whom were contracted to Stiff Records. The Rochdale Observer kindly pointed out that this was not what they had in mind when they campaigned for more entertainment in Rochdale.

The show sold out well in advance and was a fabulous night as everybody strutted about in their tour T Shirts with "If it ain't stiff it ain't worth a fuck"!

I was a little concerned when the Methodist Minister, Reverend John R Jennings, popped in to see what it was all about, but I need not have worried as the following letter praises our efforts.

CHAMPNESS HALL

ROCHDALE METHODIST MISSION

DRAKE STREET

ROCHDALE

OL16 1PB

Telephone 45731

THE REV. JOHN R. JENNINGS, Minister
Mr BOB BLOUNT, Warden
Mrs. K. M. HIRST, Secretary
Mr. GEORGE H. HEAP, Trust Treasurer
Mr. JIM DONEGAN, Mission Treasurer

Mr. S. Shrouder,
41 Town Mill Brow,
College Bank,
Rochdale.

27th October, 1977

Dear Sam,

<u>Stiffs Concert 24th October, 1977</u>

Our congratulations on the excellent way in which you organised and conducted the concert on 24th October. As you were aware we were apprehensive - with reason, having experienced various pop concerts here during the past 2 years, booked through, but not organised by ROCLAS.

This concert was entirely different, to date we have discovered no seat breakages or vandalism as has happened previously. And Bob says "as far as he's concerned you can come back tomorrow" That, coming from a caretaker is praise indeed.

Every best wish,

Yours sincerely,

John R. Jennings (Rev.)

Rochdale Champness Hall letter

72

With this ringing endorsement I decided to go for the biggest punk attraction and booked The Sex Pistols for £1200 against 70%. With no concerns I placed the following advert in the Rochdale Observer Saturday edition.

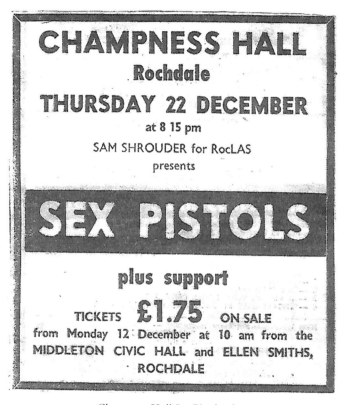

Champness Hall Sex Pistols advert

This innocent action resulted in mayhem. I was rung on the Sunday and instructed to stop the ticket sales and to report to the Chief Executive on Monday morning. I was also informed that The Methodist Church was taking out a High Court injunction to ban the show. The nice Reverend John R Jennings was quoted as saying, "We regard this booking as an insult to Methodists and an insult to the decent folk of the Borough"!

At the meeting on the Monday was John Towey (Chief Executive), Cllr Aspinall (Chairman of Recreation), his deputy, Francis Lee, David John and little old me. John Towey attempted to guide the meeting to cancel the show whilst ensuring there was no blood on the carpet. The Vice Chairman was an odd man who was outraged by the very thought of The Sex Pistols appearing and that the person responsible should be dismissed.

Francis and David were very supportive and both said that they took full responsibility for the show being booked. (People in local authority did not usually make these sorts of gestures, so it was much appreciated). John Towey, in an attempt to calm things down, pointed out that we book more than 400 shows and perhaps booking The Sex Pistols to appear at The Methodist Champness Hall in Christmas week was possibly an understandable error of judgement. His desire to bring peace to the proceedings failed as the Vice Chairman did a complete turnabout saying we are not having any churches dictating to us what we do, we pay to hire the venue and the show must go on!

The Chairman agreed, the Chief Executive looked unhappy and I put the tickets back on sale for the Tuesday morning, when they sold out with lots of kids bunking off school for a second day. On the Wednesday at the full Council meeting the show was brought up under any other business and was banned!

A number of Councillors stated that the officer who had booked them should be censured and Cllr Mrs Pamela Hawton said that many young people also enjoyed hitting old ladies over the head but that did not mean they should be allowed to! I had agreed with The Sex Pistols management that we did not need to pay them the contracted £1200 and made sure we got maximum publicity for the band's generosity.

The pages of letters in the Rochdale Observer were a joy to behold with me either labelled as a hero or the devil incarnate. Nice one Rochdale said: "The Sex Pistols provide very unhealthy and sick entertainment and it is right to ban them in every town in Britain. I don't mind the kids having fun but have kids nothing better to do but watch this evil rubbish? Pop music over that last 10 years has been very poor. We need more people like Johnny Cash and Jim Reeves in the top ten. I wonder what the kids in the USSR do for fun. In Russia children are reared in a different way, which is why they are healthy and the best at Sport"!

The whole Sex Pistols saga had been fascinating but not really a great help to my Rochdale career. Not that I cared as I had just been appointed Senior Entertainments Officer for Blackburn! I had adored my time at Middleton Civic Hall, where the team to a person had been a joy to work with and it had been a great privilege to open the venue.

By the end of my time working for Rochdale Borough Council, I was running Middleton Civic Hall, putting on shows or not putting on shows at Champness Hall, putting on Discos at Rochdale College and Heywood Civic Hall, with not much time for anything else.

It reminded me of a double page spread on Francis and I that journalist Stan Westall did for the local paper. Francis described us as the two finest showmen in the UK (he normally said the world!) and followed it up by saying entertainment is our world and that we eat it, sleep it, talk it and think it and as such we work up to 80 hours a week. He was asked what our wives thought of us working such long hours and particularly at holidays and weekends, when other people are enjoying themselves and he replied that they accepted it as part of the job. He might have got that slightly wrong as we both ended up divorced!

So goodbye Rochdale and thanks for the memories and hello Blackburn.

Sadly, 40 years later, Linda and I were at the wedding of cricketing friend Alistair Bollingbroke's daughter Joanne to Martin Culshaw in Rochdale. Before the great event we decided to drive to Middleton to see what shows the venue now put on. We got lost and could not find it. Eventually we ended up in Tesco's car park. When I asked a passer-by where it was, he told me I was standing on it. It had been demolished a year earlier – how sad.

Chapter 10

LAUGHTER AND TEARS AT BLACKBURN

I jumped at the opportunity to be Senior Entertainments Officer for Blackburn particularly as it had the mighty King George's Hall with 1800 seats and a 2000 standing capacity. It was also another two grades up the Local Government ladder (this is still too boring *to* bother *to* describe).

Needless to say I did not take into account that we had recently moved to a lovely but impractical house on the moors outside Littleborough nor how it would fit into Linda's life. Throughout my time at Middleton she had uncomplainingly driven over there for the end of the show to bring me home as I still couldn't drive. Blackburn was too far for this arrangement so in the end I got a council flat (again!) where I would stay after shows. Needless to say this was not an ideal arrangement but in my excitement generated by my new challenge this fact rather passed me by.

On arriving at Blackburn, who should I find starting as well as the newly appointed Assistant Director but dear old John Garforth. We were delighted to be working together again and John generously told me that I could do all the programming and take the credit or otherwise for what I put on stage whilst he would be responsible for all Classical Music and would create the first ever Blackburn Festival. This was to prove to be a massively ambitious project for which the £4,000 budget was also to prove to be somewhat inadequate.

As well as King George's Hall I had Windsor Theatre (it really was just a hall but we renamed it) Regency Hall, various outposts and the responsibility for children's entertainment in the Parks. This I knew about but what I was not aware of was the great team of characters that awaited me. It was good enough to be back working with John Garforth who was still trying to get a live bear to advertise shows, although this time from Belle Vue! However for good value there was Geoff Peake nominally my assistant, who as well as being part of everything we did also ran a progressive rock night on the Fridays. We also had Peter Brennan, who kept us out of trouble (some of the time!) on the administration side, and Val Sweet who, as the secretary did many things including trying to find John his live bear!

Quentin Seed ran the technical side extremely well but was undoubtedly bewildered by some of the strange requests that came his way, particularly once John was in Festival mode. But I ended up sharing a very small office with the greatest character of them all – John Jardine, Promotions Officer. We were to laugh our way through two and a half years together, starting with when I got all the staff together in Windsor Hall, and as I stood behind the bar and explained that things were going to be different and in future we would do everything with style and panache. I then tripped over and fell flat on my face which resulted in John saying to all and sundry that this was a good example of style and panache resulting in extensive laughter as I picked myself up and joined in!

I immediately started planning the Double Discomania for Monday night and the Saturday morning club. John and Geoff found me my Disco partner John West. John West's publicity said that he was very popular in Denmark which was not a lot of good in Blackburn! However he turned out to be a great music man allowing me to do all the competitions and promotions. The two shows were a good start and both proved very popular with Double Discomania attracting more than 75,000 customers in its two years.

It was also the plan to start bringing in top groups, particularly using my punk connections. This was to prove to be a problem as I was told that it had been agreed to let one company put on all the groups. I said not anymore and thus headed for a showdown with the two promoters. One had just left being social secretary at Preston Polytechnic and the other was Andy Grimshaw, whose mother was a great Blackburn character. She owned a number of pubs, opened the Lodestar night club and was reputedly the first ever topless barmaid in Blackburn. So when I arranged a meeting with the two guys and Margo turned up as well I knew that this was not going to be easy. Their view was that they should be allowed to carry on and that it was not acceptable for an outsider (Me!) to come in and stop people from Blackburn from providing the music.

It was a good time for me to remember that I too was from Blackburn, having lived there for the first 6 months of my life and I also explained that they could promote as much as they wanted on my terms but I also would be booking bands because that was part of my job. Andy Grimshaw got a bit excited, the other guy could see the way it was going, and Margo threw the towel in and got out a big bag of sweets and offered me one! She also wished me luck and we parted friends.

The other guy was Phil McIntyre who went on to be one of the top promoters in the world and we went on to be good friends. Many years later he was responsible for bringing 'We Will Rock You' into the Dominion Theatre, of which Apollo then owned a third and had the management contract.

The first band that I got to play King George's Hall was The Jam, obviously as a result of my very close friendship with John Weller! They were followed by The Rezillos, The Clash, Judas Priest (costing slightly more than the £35 we paid them at The Vine Club) and of course The Be Stiff Tour with Wreckless Eric. Mickey Jupp, Jona Lewie, Lena Lovich and Rachel Sweet.

Sat in the very small office I shared with John Jardine he asked me to ring Stiff Records to get posters etc to promote the show. So I rang their number and was somewhat surprised to be answered by Harrow Police Station this sent John and I into uncontrollable giggles, which must have bewildered the police constable who had taken the call. Sharing an office with him was an hilarious experience. He was a great one for graphs and at this time was using a graph to try and stop smoking. He had to grade the pleasure he got from each cigarette from 1 – 10. The idea was that bit by bit he would reduce his smoking by eliminating the ones that gave him least pleasure. However he continued to smoke to the same level for three months to make sure his graph truly reflected the varying merits of each cigarette. By the time the three months was up he got bored with this campaign and took his graph down and carried on smoking as normal!

To those with the slightest bit of interest the most pleasurable cigarette was the one after sex! (I am sure his wife Sandra was pleased that he shared this with me!) and the second most was the first cigarette you had with a pint in your hand!

When Terry, the Head Steward, popped into our office to bemoan his luck generally and particularly the fact that someone had stolen his bike, John was at his most consoling with a "Don't worry Terry these things go in cycles"! Terry himself was a bit of a character and is fondly remembered for when at a large Asian wedding where everybody had taken their shoes off and left them in the foyer he tidied them all up and put them into bin liners! The chaos that followed was a joy to behold as Terry tried to explain that he thought he was being helpful!

Our next project was to sort out what we were going to do for Parks entertainment for children in the summer. Previously a juggler or a man on stilts would appear unannounced and entertain any child who happened to be there. But things were about to change, as everybody enthusiastically threw in ideas. The result was a Roadshow to do a tour of the parks and playgrounds with Willie the Wizard, Punch and Judy, John West's Disco and me to compere and run all the competitions. John Garforth got involved and insisted that I had photos done so that I could sign them for the youngsters!

John Jardine worked his magic on branding and publicity. It was to be the BOB (come on follow the plot – Borough of Blackburn!) Roadshow 1978 Tour for Fun in the Sun. This proved to be tempting fate on our 16 date tour as it rained just about every day! Quentin and his team went out every morning to build a stage and put the sound system in and we artistes arrived at 1.30pm just in time to go on stage for the 2.00pm show! Unbelievably despite the weather it was a great success with large crowds turning up. By the end of the tour we were able to announce that more than 15,000 had turned up during the run, making it the most successful show of its kind in the country. Obviously 15,000 did not turn up but it sounded like a good number.

The shows were coming in quick and fast although for the first time we were having problems with some of the punk shows. The Council were concerned with the amount of gobbing going on and at The Buzzcocks show Pete Shelley stopped mid number and said that he would go home and have a cup of tea, if people kept spitting and throwing things. Sounded reasonable to me! But at the end of their encore they spat at the audience threw beer all over them, smashed their equipment up and left the stage! They were followed by American punk band The Dickies which resulted in quite a lot of fights breaking out.

The following week we had The Skids. The Blackpool punks had come to fight the Blackburn punks and we had a near riot on our hands. It really erupted midway through The Skids set; I had to stop the police and dogs coming in by promising to control it. I went on stage spoke to lead singer Stuart Adamson and took over the mike. Everybody stopped fighting to listen as I explained that the Council did not want these shows but I was still putting them on but if we had trouble they would get banned – so do me a favour and enjoy the band. I got a fantastic round of applause and for a moment I thought I had saved the world. However immediately after the applause the fighting restarted, the police joined in, the dogs attacked anybody and everybody and we had a full scale riot. The world was very definitely not saved!

By now the balance of the shows had definitely improved as we had George Melly, Jasper Carrot, The Dooleys (remember them?) Ian Gillan, Michel Legrand, Showaddywaddy, Lindisfarne and Lancashire favourites Fivepenny Piece and The Houghton Weavers. But the result of all these shows was that I spent most of my nights in my Blackburn flat.

Linda had been very homesick, particularly after her Dad Wilson, at the age of 46, had died during my last year at Middleton. I received the telegram on Christmas Eve and she was naturally devastated. We agreed that Linda should get three months leave from her job working for an Examination Board in Walkden and have a trip home to St Helena Island. When she returned, she decided to change jobs and became a croupier with Ladbrokes. Our lives had become incompatible whilst I was obsessed with the joys of the job and with many tears we decided to separate. It was a heart-breaking situation and as a result I moved full time into my somewhat grotty flat in Blackburn. This parting was to prove to be the end of a chapter but not the book.

Back in the important world of show business I had a pantomime to arrange. We again tied up with Nelson Firth to produce it and Mother Goose was to star Nicky Martin of New Faces fame and Mitzi Mueller, who, having refused all previous offers of Panto, fell for my charm and agreed to do Blackburn or maybe she was just doing an old friend a favour. It also had a fabulous dame in Ian Moore, who turned out to be a Southport supporter – so obviously a fine chap – well in this case lady!

John Jardine took charge of the publicity and insisted that he and I dressed up as brokers men and visited every neighbouring town with poster and leaflets. It worked a treat with him organising the press for every visit. There was no doubt that we got rid of far more print and got lots of interest due to our costumes. We travelled in John's campervan and were able to stop and have a cup of tea between towns. Such glamour. The Panto was great fun and we were able to boast record crowds. Not sure that we actually had record crowds but we were certainly able to boast about them!

The Director of Recreation was a gentleman named Mr Sykes (he probably had a first name but I was not privy to it). We had crossed swords a few times and I was irked that he never came to any of our shows, particularly the pantomime. This was a very busy period for us as we were also running events in King George's Hall as well as the Panto in the Windsor Theatre (As you already know it was only a hall). Come the New Year's Eve Dance we had a sell-out crowd to dance to The Bob Watmough Orchestra and Smiling Sam Shrouder (that guy gets everywhere). The problem was that we had no bar staff because the council would only pay normal time whilst the pubs paid triple time. So poor Dennis, who was in charge of the bars, stood forlornly looking at a queue the length of the venue. So I rang Mr Sykes at home to get his decision reversed and he got very agitated as he, like the rest of the council employees, was on a ten-day holiday. Voices got raised (we shouted!) and he said he didn't care how many staff we had and it was nothing to do with him and don't ever ring him up again at home. During my rant I also added that it was a disgrace that he hadn't even bothered to see Mother Goose.

The team at King George's Hall were magnificent and rang family and friends to get them to come and work behind the bar and we got a full complement and I told Dennis to pay them double time.

During the panto run we used to get a bus load for just about every matinee from Brockhall Hospital. The hospital had 1600 patients with various mental problems. They also had a saint of a man called Frank who was in charge of all their social activities. We used to welcome them with open arms and put them in the balcony which only had four rows and they had it for their exclusive use. I got on really well with Frank and always ensured that the Panto cast visited the hospital to meet patients and staff alike. At this particular performance they were there in all their glory when Mr Sykes, obviously stung by my criticism, came to see the show and without speaking to anybody went to sit in the balcony. This conjured up the wonderful possibility of, at the end of the show, Mr Sykes being put on the bus back to Brockhall! He would be explaining that he was Director of Recreation and they would be saying that of course he was and just hold hands with Napoleon and get on the bus!

By now more and more of the top promoters were using King George's. MCP brought heavy metal heavy weights, Iron Maiden, Def Leppard and

AC/DC. Maurice Jones had started the company but had brought in Tim Parsons as a partner. Tim was a bright spark and we hit it off immediately. We went on to do thousands of shows together during my time with Apollo and in later years we met up on golf courses (He won on every occasion but he did take it quite seriously! He obviously got bored by this so went to live in Cape Town!).

We got lucky with another major promoter in Mel Bush, who was trying to fill the last date on his David Essex tour. It was early evening and he had rung quite a few venues only to find that they were closed, but we never closed so when he rang us as a last resort, we found him his date by moving a few things and got our David Essex date. At the time he was massive so this was a major feather in our cap and another sell out show.

Other major promoters such as Danny Betesh from Kennedy Street Enterprises, John Curd from Straight Music and Stuart Littlewood started using us but the one major promoter we could not get was Harvey Goldsmith. This was until they were struggling for a date for Manhattan Transfer and we obliged. It was always my policy to meet every act that played the venue at the stage door and take them to their dressing room, letting them know that they could have anything they wanted as long as it was tea, coffee and sandwiches! This was often declined as their rider would include copious alcohol including rare brandies plus an exotic buffet made up totally of things that you could not buy in a supermarket.

Billy Connolly was a delightful exception with his only requirement being a pot of tea. After I had looked after the act I would then chat to the tour manager, establishing opening times, set times and merchandising deals, all of which could cause some debate. Once done we would have a good old gossip. On the Manhattan Transfer show, I was desperate that we should make a good impression to enable us to get more of Harvey's shows. The tour manager was Kenny Stephens and I told all of our team that he was to be treated like royalty and that we must let him have whatever he wanted to ensure Harvey got good feedback. When they arrived I asked some scruffy guy which of the touring group was Kenny Stephens and once he was pointed out I was there making a big fuss of him. The scruffy fellow tried to have a chat with me but I had no time for him when I had got Kenny Stephens in my radar. I was even stood next to him to watch Manhattan Transfer come on stage. I was somewhat surprised to find that the scruffy fellow, who had been a bit of a nuisance, was introducing the band.

When I asked Kenny who the guy was he looked at me oddly and said that he thought that I knew him as he was Harvey Goldsmith! A quick allegiance change and goodbye Kenny and hello Harvey! I should point out that I went on to do many shows with Harvey and that on all occasions I was in his company he was always immaculately dressed. (That is not true but I would not want to upset him!) I should also point out that my wife sat next to him at some function and described him as the nicest guy she had sat next to as he didn't just talk about himself (in this industry we have a habit of doing that) but shared genuine interest in what she did. He also did me a big favour by giving us a Rolling Stones warm up gig for Glasgow Apollo. The story of that is later on in this riveting book, just in case you were thinking of not bothering reading anymore!

One of the bonuses of the job was to see acts that you might not have bought a ticket for, but then discovered how talented they were. One such act was Roy Castle who turned out to be a brilliantly versatile performer. He held the audience in the palm of his hand proving to be a fine trumpeter and a very funny man. For some reason we had dressed the stage with a number of pot plants that then became part of his act including them as though they were members of the audience. In the circumstances it seemed only right to present Roy with one of the plants in memory of a great show. He was obviously so moved by the generosity of Blackburn Borough Council that he left the cheque for the gig in the dressing room! When I forwarded it on to him I got a lovely reply which included, "incidentally the pot plant I was given in fond memory is alive and well and taking over my greenhouse. Telling my tomatoes how it used to be on the stage and that it is the only Azalea in Equity!" Roy was a great guy and a special talent.

Another show that fitted in to the same category was Mary O'Hara. She was a delight both on stage and off stage. She had given up her career following the death of her young husband and became a member of the enclosed order of Benedictines. She was there for 12 years and then had left and resumed to give her gift of harp playing and wonderful soprano voice to the world. She had enormous success and had had three hit albums – the latest having been recorded at The Royal Festival Hall – which had gone silver. The Mayoress of Blackburn had obviously not been aware of this because when I took her backstage to meet Mary she said "Eh love you have a lovely voice – have you ever thought of making a record!" I normally did not let councillors backstage but she and her husband were the exception as they did a great job for the community and they even let me compere their Charity Gala.

When everybody had gone Mary and I had a coffee and sandwiches and she asked if I could explain the finances for the show. She was getting less than a third of what I was paying and she had to cover the costs of the other musicians and the hotel bills! After our chat she was able to negotiate a far better deal.

Life was not all glamour in Blackburn as John Jardine and I had to do auditions and then run a heat to find a winner of the Senior Citizens Talent Contest. We were both dreadful gigglers and at the most inappropriate times we would collapse as some old dear would be doing a Gracie Fields number. We were even worse when John's wife Sandra's Uncle Jim turned up with the worse jokes you have ever heard, not even remotely funny but the more we laughed, the worse they got. It back fired because we put him in the final and nobody laughed. Two weeks later John came in and said that Uncle Jim had died and before I could stop myself I said "Yes and he did two weeks ago as well". This is an inappropriate and not very funny show business joke! The winner was 78-year-old Alf Young who was very funny. Unfortunately when he did his spot in the final at Preston Guild Hall he exceeded the time limit and was disqualified. He had practiced long and hard to ensure that he was in the time limit but had not taken into account that the audience would take time laughing. The audience fell about and he overran by three minutes. It just added to my belief that comics are a tortured breed.

The following year we played safe and selected a singing duo. I had just passed my driving test in bizarre circumstances when I forgot to signal for the first half of the test, stalled during the three-point-turn and when asked what the outside lane on the Motorway was for had answered overtaking and turning right! I certainly had not learnt to drive but John thought it would be amusing if I took our double act to the final at the Southport Theatre in my Ford Escort which had a slow puncture and the gear stick which would come away in my hand! My passengers, apart from John who just giggled were terrified and after one emergency stop the gentleman's toupee fell off. They were in such a state by the time they got there that they did a dreadful show, avoided me and caught the bus home!

John Garforth meanwhile was running his classical concerts and plotting the Blackburn Festival. It would be fair to say that by now John was an alcoholic of the, 'I like a drink so I will have a drink' breed. He would come to work with a gin bottle and glasses clinking in his briefcase. But despite this he had more flair and imagination than anybody I ever worked with.

John's classical series featured the Liverpool Philharmonic Orchestra, who for me epitomised everything that was wrong with the subsidised arts. The first time I saw them they went down brilliantly, getting a great response from an audience that demanded an encore. I could not believe that they did not oblige and when I asked why it appeared that they had to leave by 10.00 pm or the musicians would claim overnight payments. They were soulless and their behaviour was in marked contrast to The Prague Symphony Orchestra. They came back and did three encores and then when we applauded the violin soloist when he entered the post show reception he disappeared and returned with his violin and gave us 15 minutes of sheer musical magnificence. He had the music in his soul.

John's Blackburn Festival was to be no mundane event either as his artistic side took over adding more and more adventurous events. It was a sign of things to come when the media, who were always very kind to me, turned on him at the first opportunity. There was to be lots of Festival merchandise including an avalanche of T Shirts. John had got the best price available to buy them and ordered them. Sensible enough to most people but the fact they were from Portugal made front page news in the Blackburn Evening Telegraph. With "outraged of Blackburn" saying what a disgrace it was that here in the heart of the cotton belt this man was ordering T shirts from Portugal. John had followed Council directives by getting three quotes and taking the cheapest but needless to say nobody from the Council stood up for him. It was an ominous start and a sign of things to come.

An added bonus to the Festival was the arrival of John Garforth's two Festival Assistants Freda Lawther and Helen Lovell, and they immediately bonded into the frivolity of the office. They became the focus of all John's ideas and plans and obtaining all that was required to make them happen. One of the events that John was planning was a cycle of Mystery Plays to be performed every Saturday for 6 weeks at such venues as outside British Home Stores. For those of you not entirely sure what a mystery play is let John Garforth explain:

"In the middle ages every town of the stature had its own cycle of Mystery Plays. These were performed around the time of the Feast of Corpus Christi, by the various trade guilds.

The mystery cycles clearly had their origins in church ritual, but they were secular events and the church authorities came to disapprove of them so strongly that they were eventually banned (Think Sex Pistols!) and the texts of the plays destroyed. But as with most things concerning centralised authority the tradition lingered longer the further away from London and the manuscripts of four different northern mystery cycles have been preserved. It was not surprising that the church authorities looked askance at these festivities as for these people of the Middle Ages there was no such thing as form. With them drunkenness is found with the most mystic adoration, debauchery with the most lofty moral idealism, cynical ridicule with passionate worship, laughter with the solemnity of sacred thoughts. It is natural that this grotesquery should be reproduced in what is in some ways the most typical of medieval creations the mystery play".

So now you know!

The plan was for the Players and Entertainers to arrive on a cart with many festivities taking place before the performance of The Mystery Cycle, which will not have taken place on the streets of Blackburn for over 500 years. The question was that on the basis that nobody was around 500 years ago, was Blackburn ready for this innovative dose of culture?

John had now lost interest in live bears and was instead demanding a fire eater from Freda and Helen. When they came out of his office to enlist everybody's help we were all somewhat amazed when David Green, with us on work experience, said that he was a fire eater! We all agreed that we needed to audition him, so he said that he would go home and get his stuff. He duly returned with his equipment which looked suspiciously like it had just been bought! John Jardine named him The Great Flambeau and had also rung the Blackburn Evening Telegraph to send a photographer to record the audition. So there we all were and The Great Flambeau went for it big style with flames shooting skyward. The weak link in this was that the audition took place in King George's offices with the result that the fire alarms went off, two fire engines arrived in such a short time that it did credit to their service and to Blackburn Evening Telegraph for a superb photo and a lovely story. It is my belief that David had never done fire eating in his life but had grasped his chance for stardom and nipped out and bought the equipment. This belief was rather supported by the fact that David's six weeks spent on a cart every Saturday doing his act resulted in him returning with various burns, no eyebrows and hair reductions! The Great Flambeau also signed up for the BOB Roadshow's "Stay Fine in '79" tour. He was a real trooper and regardless of wind, rain or sun (not often) The Great Flambeau performed to the pleasure of many, regardless of his own safety. A blessing that the days of Health and Safety were not upon us yet!

The opening of Blackburn Festival duly arrived and John Garforth had been as good as his word, in organising well over a hundred events with Freda and Helen, whilst my own involvement was to be as a compere. The grand opening was to be conducted from the roof of King George's, where The Mayor and other dignitaries were to witness a cascade of rockets, a searchlight beamed into the sky with responding bonfires blazing simultaneously from the surrounding hills. It was all meticulously planned with the boy scouts building fires around the Borough. Nothing was left to chance apart from the weather. On the night in question the heavens opened, the dignitaries got drenched, the fires went out and the rockets did not function. John deserved better but the fates were against him and just about everything that could go wrong, chose to do so.

One of the biggest attendances was for the Napoleonic Skirmish which was over two days and included two Mock Battles and the re-enactment of one of the many riots of the Lancashire cotton workers in which the troops were called in. It was very expensive to stage but thousands of people enjoyed a fabulous spectacle. The only weak link was that the arena was surrounded by a small wall so that the audience instead of going in via the box office and paying, just stepped over the wall!

We also had a Jousting Tournament, advertised under John Jardine's slogan of "Joust about fun for all the Family"! But probably the most popular event was It's a Knockout to be contested between the four Authorities in the Red Rose Festival. All went well as we built up to the final, where I looked out, as the compere, at many thousands of punters all having a great day. I adopted my best Stuart Hall skills (obviously not in all things!) and all was going well until the teams had to push a massive beach ball with a young lady trying to stay on top. There was lots of falling off and clambering back on, to the obvious mirth of the crowd and compere, until a girl fell off and did not try to clamber back on. She was injured with a possible broken neck and not to be moved until an ambulance arrived. Even the ebullient compere found it hard to find many laughs in this scenario! The crowd drifted away and another event was spoilt, John and his team did not deserve this.

There were many other outside events including a Rock Festival with local bands, and The Lurkers, Grand Water Spectacular on Queens Park Lake, an

Army Tattoo and The Blackburn Spectacular with Parachute teams, clowns, blindfolded driver with X-ray eyes, escapologists and a Mini Circus. The weather was unkind but lots of pleasure was given to many people and it was fair to say that Blackburn had never seen it's like before.

Lots of indoor activities were also part of the Festival including my favourite, The Pub Entertainer of the Year. This entailed Freda and myself going round local pubs judging different heats. Visiting pubs with a very attractive woman, what was there not to like! The final was held at Romeo and Juliet Night Club and was a great success until the comic provided by the club, came on. By this time nobody was going to pay any attention as the pub landlord treated their clientele. His act had won some TV talent show and was based on holding a rope with an elephant constantly pulling on it. I should explain that it was an imaginary elephant! Nobody took any notice and he walked off after five minutes and nobody noticed. It once again made me reflect on the life of a comic.

John Garforth had also decided to hold a beauty contest for Miss Red Rose, which included the three other Authorities in the area with the final at Colne Municipal Hall with the compere being – of course! I would not want to miss this! The rules were very strict and contestants had to live in each Authorities' area, but John was not going to let this bother him. We had applications from all over to be a contestant for Miss Blackburn to then compete for Miss Red Rose. The mail he received was a joy with some of the applicants sending in nude photos.

In the end we had a contestant called Suzanne Hughes, who came from Morecambe and went on to win Miss England. John explained to her that she had an imaginary granny who lived in Blackburn and that she lived with her. John warmed to the task of getting her as much publicity as possible. This included pictures of me dressed as Napoleon and Suzanne as Josephine lying on a bed in some historic house. I should point out that I was getting paid to do this!

Once she won Miss Red Rose, John's friends in the press got onto the story that she did not live in Blackburn and therefore should be disqualified! John and his team had also arranged a fashion show at Romeo and Julie's to be hosted by David Hamilton. Of the many items of merchandise were Festival Plates designed by Brenda McDonagh from the Councils Art Department. They were excellent but not selling so when David Hamilton was heard discussing plates with Pete Murray on their Radio 2 handover it seemed too good an opportunity to miss. So it was arranged to present him with a Blackburn Festival plate and get the required photos. Unfortunately he was late so Freda had to pick him up from Preston Station. It was agreed she would tell him about the plate and we would get the photo as soon as he arrived. However all was not as it seemed as he explained that meant something completely different and pointed out a young lady in the audience and said he had had a really good plate with her! I had never heard the expression before or since but apparently him telling Pete Murray that he had had a really good plate in Blackburn was enough to get the word banned on the BBC! John compered the final event which was a Festival Finale Dance with a cabaret spot for Charlie Williams and the six weeks of fun, mayhem, disasters and triumphs was over.

Unfortunately the finances for it were not great and the merchandising had not done as well as hoped although in fairness there is not much demand for boaters in Blackburn. We even found a photographer sneaking round trying to get a picture of unsold T Shirts etc. The excess T Shirts were duly shipped to a charity in Africa and in every disaster appeal I used to look in the hope of our T Shirts being worn!

Once we were aware of the losses it made we all met up to put together a Festival for the following year with lessons learnt and some more commercial activities added. The six weeks had given a massive lift to the area and people had definitely never seen the like before. However once Mr Sykes was aware of the losses it was immediately decided that there would be no more Festivals.

The Festivals certainly changed my life as I had fallen in love with Freda, which was somewhat complicated by the fact that she was married and had two lovely daughters. Despite that we were to go on and get married.

Once I had ended up living in Blackburn I had left Rochdale Cricket Club for the delights of Cherry Tree in the Ribblesdale League. Until I started playing they probably thought that they had made a useful signing with the local paper heralding that Cherry Tree had signed leg spinning all-rounder Sam Shrouder from Rochdale in the Central Lancashire League. Sadly that was as good as it got! I got the bowling yips for the first and only time and on my debut against Barnoldswick I bowled one of their batsman with a ball that bounced three times and the crowd laughed! As at Rochdale I just about did enough to stay in the first team but it was not much more than that. On one occasion one of the Umpires was David Hargreaves, who worked at King George's Hall, and when asked to bowl I chose David's end.

I had been born to appeal, which I did loudly and theatrically, every time the ball hit the pads with a radius of a foot either side of the stumps. On this occasion it might have been even wider and the batsman looked astounded that I had the temerity to appeal, no matter David's finger went up with a, that's out Mr Shrouder!

At the time Cherry Tree had an outstanding 17-year-old in Kevin Hayes who went on to play for Lancashire having captained Oxford University. Kevin's path and mine were to cross again. Cherry Tree was a very social club and I made good friends with Peter Benson who was the most social of them all. I also enjoyed the company of Eric Kinder who I was to come across many years later when he was managing Blackburn Rovers under-21 in a friendly with Southport.

There were shock waves at King George's Hall when the Council allowed the British National Party to hold a meeting in our Regency Hall. There were massive demonstrations against it but in fairness to the Council they had no choice as Blackburn was the first Council to have a British National Party candidate voted in. By law if a party had a Councillor they were entitled to use the same venues as any other party. We were told we could only have two staff in the premises so John Jardine and I volunteered and then duly hid in the hall balcony so we could observe Kingsley Reed, the BNP's Councillor. It was so bizarre as to be funny. Their doorman had a spider's web tattooed over his face and was a skin head, with short trousers and Doc Martins. Some seven people turned up and they were all as nutty as Kingsley Reed apart from one old lady, who I genuinely thought had turned up for something completely different, perhaps a tea dance! It was a pity the demonstrators stopped more people turning up as anybody who witnessed his racist rant could not possibly have voted for him. Needless to say John and I got the giggles!

Our "Stay Fine,79" Roadshow was a great improvement on our first one, which now apparently had played to a record breaking 22,000 children (well it sounds better than the previously exaggerated 15,000!). We had the perfect act in Hanleo and Katrina who worked with snakes, did fire eating, the bed of nails and washing with broken glass. If there was ever a, do not try at home act, this was it. I was particularly fond of Katrina who performed in all weathers in a very low cut ball gown; although when it was muddy she wore wellies as well. The kids and parents loved it, Crazy Tramp made them laugh, John West did the Disco and I compered and ran lots of zany competitions and a talent contest. The crowds were great everywhere and we played to a record breaking – Think of any number you like over 22,000 — I went for 30,000!

King George's continued to attract the big names including The Ramones, Sham 69 and Ralph McTell. I particularly enjoyed Ralph McTell and I seem to remember taking him across the road to The Jubilee for a pint or more and not only was he great company he also got his round in. He was followed by the legendary Chuck Berry, who was so legendary that when he wandered into a full bar before the show nobody thought that it could possibly he him. I loved his show, duck walk and all, but he was not in the class of Little Richard.

When we had The Three Degrees I was delighted to do my usual and take them to their dressing room and ensure that they were provided with the usual sandwiches and coffee. All three were delightful and very polite but then their manager came up, slammed the dressing room door and followed it with a lot of shouting and a few slaps. It later transpired that he thought that they had ordered the sandwiches and the cost would go against their fee! Peter Brightman, who was later to bring the Bolshoi Ballet production of Spartacus to Dublin for us, did the honourable thing and drove the manager back to London mid show after he threatened one of the bar staff. We had sold out the second house but had a few back seats left in the first so good old Frank from Brockhall had come to the rescue and brought a bus load. They had a ball and at the end of the show when everybody rushed to the front they joined in and as everybody chanted for The Three Degrees to come back on stage they focused on the bald musical director with chants of Kojak!

We also had a sell-out show with Suzi Quatro and when I went back to see her after the show she was giving some terrible stick to one of the boys in the band. When I mentioned to one of the other band members that it seemed a bit off, they said it was OK because it was her husband!

Not all shows were sell out and glamorous successes and the saddest one that I did was Hylda Baker. It was to be one of her last ever shows, we sold 81 tickets and I couldn't move her to the Windsor Theatre (alright Hall!) as we had the amateurs in. When I met her she had a dreadful problem getting up the stairs to her dressing room, and rightly bemoaned the lack of a lift. The show was a shadow of the great star she had been and not long after she went into a home. I always regretted putting her through the ordeal and wished that the Promoter would have cancelled the show.

Top groups kept coming though with Generation X, The Police, The Ramones, and the Clash.

While all this was going on we were also planning our next Panto, Jack and the Beanstalk and how to improve on Mother Goose, which had broken all known records (I think that you get the idea!) On one of Linda and my visits to Fagins Night Club with Brian and Mitzi, I had been massively impressed by a double act Burk and Jerk. To anybody who would listen I said that they would be the next Cannon and Ball and they even had a record on sale. I pressurised the Panto producer Nelson Firth to go and book them and I was delighted when he succeeded and added them to the bill, which included Mr Blackpool Duggie Clarke (of course you remember him!) and our own favourite Panto Dame Ian Moore. I was so excited by the booking of Burk and Jerk that when they came to play Blackburn's Romeo and Juliet I arranged for the King George's team to go, in the knowledge that their fantastic comedy would inspire everybody to sell tickets. They had by now changed their name to Brian and Michael and had a massive hit with Matchstalk Men and Matchstalk Cats and Dogs which greatly added to the package.

The show started and my heart sunk as they sang a load of songs with no humour or jokes at all. My King George's colleagues were looking at me as though I had lost the plot. As soon as the show finished I was in their dressing room saying I had booked a comedy double act and whatever else they were, they were not that.

"Brian" explained that with the success of Matchstalk Men they had dropped the comedy to concentrate on their musical success. As I explained that may be the case but I needed them to bring back the comedy for the Panto. Michael was all apologetic and said they would work on it but "Brian" who did not look like Brian was not so keen. It transpired that the original Brian had declined the opportunity to go full time due to his milk round, and the current Brian had produced the record and then filled in the vacant spot!

Michael, who had written the hit, was great and managed to bring lots of comedy to the Panto whilst "Brian" was a bit wooden and obviously saw himself as a musician. Needless to say the Panto was a massive success and broke all the records of the previous year! (In reality we had a few less punters as we lost some coach loads due to snow!)

Michael and I became good mates, although he did have the habit of setting fire to the paper every time he found me reading one! I was delighted when he agreed to do our BOB Roadshow – 80 miles of smiles tour and it was certainly a massive boost to have someone with a Number One hit record. He was brilliant with all the kids and played a major part in the BOB Roadshow, breaking all known records for any BOB Roadshow anywhere in the world!

Old favourites continues to play King George's with the great Ken Dodd selling out two houses, Mike Harding doing yet another sold out show, and northern favourites The Houghton Weavers continuing to pack them in. They had two great front men in Tony Berry, who had a fabulous voice and Norman Prince who added the humour. Norman went on to write the song for Southport's trip to Wembley in 1998 and I bet you cannot wait for the story!

However, my time was running out and I was looking for other opportunities. Nelson Firth wanted me to join him and take a version of the BOB Roadshow to play on the front at Blackpool. It is a sign of my incredible vanity that I even considered it! But I was due my Sex Pistols moment and it came in the unlikely package of Andy Williams and his 30 piece Orchestra. I was offered one of only eight shows he was doing in this country for £18,000, an astronomical sum for 1980.

Part of the deal was that we had to completely redo the dressing room including adding a shower and toilet. This was the moment I had been waiting for to take King George's to the next level. I grabbed the chance, agreed to all the dressing room requirements and signed the contract for £18,000. This caused uproar with Mr Sykes demanding to see me and insisting that I immediately cancel it. He did point out that he had sent me and everybody in his division a memo instruction that nobody must commit to spend £50 or more without his personal permission! I had taken over my green book in which I kept the accounts for every event I had been responsible for and that I was in profit by £32,000 and actually had a budget of £20,000 to spend so in real terms I had £52,000 to spend and therefore I did not need his permission.

This was not a view that he agreed with and he was very angry and outraged that I had not consulted him in advance of signing the contract. I explained that if Frank Sinatra had rung me and said that he was only going to do one more show in his life and he had chosen Blackburn I could hardly say hang on Frank I will have to go and check with Mr Sykes! This argument did not impress him either! After a lot of shouting I explained that the contract was signed, the show would happen and it would be the greatest moment of King George's life. He explained that I had broken every rule in the book (I obviously had not!) and that I had not heard the last of this (I obviously had not!)

The media were massively supportive and took my line that this was the biggest ever entertainment event Blackburn had experienced. The Radio Blackburn phone ins were full of it going from does this young lad not know that Gracie Fields once played King George's Hall to it's an absolute disgrace that the Council should be paying this money to some foreign singer when all the services were being subjected to cut backs!

On the Saturday that the tickets were due to go on sale a reporter from The Evening Telegraph rung me to say that they were running a front page story on Monday quoting the Chairman of Recreation saying he was outraged by the decision to book Andy Williams at such a cost, that at no time had he been consulted and that the Officer involved had broken numerous Council rules. He wanted it to be understood that at a time of severe cut backs he totally objected to the decision and the behaviour of the Officer. At the time of the call people were queuing right round the building so I asked the guy to send a photographer and to ask him to run the picture alongside the article.

We had two box office girls in Raz and Anthea and bless them they worked nonstop all day, by the end of which we knew we were on the way to a sell-out show and more profit to the ratepayers of Blackburn. The paper duly ran the photo on Monday's paper along with quotes form the Chairman saying he was absolutely delighted with the success of the ticket sales and that he had always been very supportive of his team and their ability to bring an American Superstar to our town. The people of Blackburn should be very proud of him and his team! That's politics I suppose!

Having sold the tickets our next problem was to provide the required standard of dressing room. Everybody, apart from me, got involved with this project probably breaking every council regulation along the way! Geoff Peake used a contact in the Works Department to get a shower and loo redirected to King George's Hall from its proposed destination of a council house. So in the unlikely event that somebody from Blackburn, who is still waiting for the said items that they were promised in 1980 is reading this – apologies but your sacrifices enabled the show to happen!

Freda with the help of members of our crew took charge of furnishings and decorations with a beg, steal or borrow mentality. People worked through the night, carpets were laid, shower etc. were installed and the final result was stunning. We had a dressing room fit for a star at no cost to the rate payer. But Andy Williams was not the first to use it because that honour belonged to 12 year old Robert Jenkins. Robert had written to me asking how much it would cost to rent King George's for his magic show. It was too good to miss so I rang Robert, who came in to entertain the office with an array of tricks and illusions and we all agreed that we must put his show on. So it was that one lunch time Robert left the Andy Williams Dressing room with a star and Roberts name on the door to perform for a hastily arranged audience of 32 and nearly as many again from the nation's media including TV. It was a fabulous occasion and The Daily Mail headlined their review with 'A Star is Born....Just Like That!"

The staging of the Andy Williams show was another area that we needed to demonstrate we could compete with the best and this is where Ron Lewis came into his own. When Quentin had left as our Technical and Stage Director we had just three applications for the job. One didn't turn up for the interview, one ran discos in Colne and the other had regularly worked on The Royal Variety Show. Not a difficult decision to choose Ron, who it has to be said, had a somewhat unorthodox approach to the job, a lot of which entailed being in the pub, however he was an artistic genius – obviously not when he was in the pub!

On one occasion we had Motorhead appearing and their road crew were going crazy because our crew had disappeared. Just as I was uttering dark threats re Ron and his gang I got a message that he wanted to see me in the pub, so I stormed over ready to be slightly unpleasant. However there were the entire crew with a pint for me and a speech from Ron who presented me with a silver goblet from them inscribed "To Sam. Thank you for saving Blackburn's entertainment"! What could you say other than order another round of drinks and think sod Motorhead!

Ron would sometimes work through the night to create his staging masterpieces and he saved the best for the Andy Williams Show. He was an unsung hero but he played a major part in ensuring that our shows were presented with style and panache, which I think is where I came in!

The great day arrived with our two sell-out shows and I duly greeted Andy Williams at the stage door to take him to his dressing room. As we climbed the many stairs I explained how the whole staff had worked together to create his dressing room. When he had looked round the en-suite dressing room and the tastefully decorated and furnished lounge area he asked me to let the staff know that he had played all over the world and, including Vegas, he had never had a finer dressing room. This was obviously not true but didn't I love the guy for saying it! In fact I loved him so much that I presented him with a Blackburn Festival plate – well we did have rather a lot left!

American comedy duo Stiles and Henderson did the first half and I was stood at the back to await the moment he came on stage as his 30-piece orchestra waited and the lights went down. I felt a gentle tap on my shoulder and there he was dressed totally in white with his arms full of roses, he gave me a big smile as the spotlight turned to the back of the theatre as he entered. The audience stood as one and went crazy. It was one of the best moments of my life as I just stood there watching him approach the stage with tears flowing down my face. Against all the odds Andy Williams really had come to Blackburn! His show was magnificent, oozing class as he sang hit after hit. He obviously broke all box office records known to man and on this occasion I can truthfully say, that he more than doubled the existing record! After the show he was incredibly gracious in posing for photos and signing autographs and telling people that along with Paris and Las Vegas, Blackburn was now his favourite place! We bid each other a fond farewell and he promised that next time he toured the UK we would be top of his list. All the team who had worked the show were exhilarated and a few of us not wanting the night to end went to a nearby Italian Restaurant and when we entered, who should be there but Andy Williams, clutching his Blackburn Festival Plate, and his entourage. To end a very special night he came over to our table to meet the rest of our team and to thank them.

It was now time for me to move on and I had been very fortunate that a number of promoters including Tim Parsons, John Curd and Phil McIntrye had recommended me to Paul Gregg who had just started the Apollo Leisure theatre chain which had amassed Glasgow Apollo, Oxford New Theatre, Manchester Apollo and Coventry Apollo in an eighteen month period. I had never met him but was very aware and impressed by what he was doing. I had mentioned this a few times to both Johns so when I was told that Paul Gregg was on the phone I assumed it was John Jardine and another merry jape! It wasn't! Paul said he had been asking amongst the promoters if they could recommend any Managers and quite a few, who I had obviously bought drinks for, had kindly recommended me. He went on to invite me to meet him and David Rogers, the financial brain behind the company, at Coventry Apollo. I readily agreed, never thinking that those two people were going to have a massive effect on my life both as colleagues and as friends.

Unfortunately I had chosen to have an Afro-Asian hairstyle, which not only was a complete failure but had also turned my hair orange! It was not the look that I wanted to present at my interview but I put on my best (only!) suit which was green and headed for Coventry. I hoped that I cut a dashing figure with my orange hair and green suit but I later learned that after I left the room David, not prone to witticisms, turned to Paul and said that it was the first time he had ever interviewed an inverted carrot! Despite that they offered me the Managers job at Oxford New Theatre plus being in charge of Downtown Manhattan Night Club.

Paul was an inspirational figure and explained that they were tilting at windmills and were very much the outsiders in the theatre world, but we were going to have lots of fun and work very hard. We would be in the office at 9.00am, an hour before all show business offices opened, and that we would be in our theatres at night meeting the promoters and producers as well as the artistes. I was completely sold on the Company, the two of them, but not on the job, which I turned down because the Managers of the theatres had no say in which shows were booked and that was part of the job I loved doing. After a number of promoters asked me why I had not taken the job and I explained they obviously told Paul, who again rang me to meet up as he had the job that I really would want He offered me the job of being responsible for all the Theatres and for booking them. Wow! He gave me the best job I could ever want and I was excited to join what turned out to be one of the greatest theatre stories of all time.

Apollo were based in Oxford, as that was the first theatre in the group and as I prepared to move I reflected on what a fabulous opportunity Blackburn had been. I had been part of a great team led by John Garforth and we really had lots of fun. The press were very kind to me on my departure and I got a lovely letter from Mr Sykes, who it turned out was called Paul. So if on previous pages I might have seemed to be critical of Paul Sykes, please ignore me as he was obviously a fine fellow!

Leaving Blackburn resulted in me being apart from Freda, although it was to be only temporarily, and also her many friends that also became mine particularly Colin and Clare Brindle, who I had become very close to. My final sold out show at King George's Hall was Don McLean who finished his performance with "Crying" and so did I! But goodbye Blackburn and hello Oxford!

Chapter 11

APOLLO TAKE OFF

This book does not, nor was it ever intended to chronicle the incredible rise of Apollo Leisure to the very top of the theatrical tree. It is merely my personal journey and memories of an incredible period.

Myth has it that the company's success was based on the chemistry between Paul Gregg, David Rogers and myself. Like all myths there is an element of truth in this but it also does a massive disservice to the many incredibly talented people without whom the story would have been very different.

I was incredibly fortunate to get the opportunity to work with the greatest visionary, in Paul Gregg, that I ever met and with the greatest financial operator in David Rogers. I arrived at the right time to make the duo a trio. For the two of them to achieve their ambitions for the company they needed a third member to balance two very strong characters and for me it was a case of the right place at the right time. It helped that they both quickly became great friends to me.

There is no doubt that without Paul's plans and ideas there would have been no success story just as there is no doubt that without David's control of the finances and sometimes sheer bloody-mindedness the company would not have survived. They were both especially talented people but they did need that third person particularly as they often could not agree. That third person could have been anybody but it just happened to be lucky old me.

My first take of life with Apollo was whilst I was working my notice at Blackburn but was invited to the opening of The Apollo Victoria, where the first show was a week of Shirley Bassey. This was a great adventure and I arrived mid-afternoon to see what I could help with. The answer was that if I could paint or lay carpets I was in demand but otherwise I was not needed. The Theatre looked as though it had no chance of being open on time but there calmly masterminding it, was Keith Wells on behalf of the Wigan Company that was responsible. Keith was to join Apollo as the Development Director, and as he always did, got the venue open on time as the last bit of carpet was laid.

The drama was added to when Shirley Bassey said she could not possibly use the glamorous recently-decorated dressing room as the smell of paint would get on her chest and she would not be able to sing, which obviously would have been a bit of a disadvantage! A dehumidifier was bought, but the lovely Shirley moved and used an undecorated, unglamorous dressing room.

Little was I to know that Miss Bassey and dressing rooms was going to be an important part of my life. Whenever she played our theatres where she would play multiple dates, it was my responsibility to be there on the first night and not to leave until she was happy. There were always changes required and I would make sure that they were achieved. The biggest challenge came at Manchester Apollo, when after the show I was in her dressing room with her manager, her dresser and the promoter Tony McCarthur for MAM. She had done another great show and was in good form as everybody constantly asked her if everything was OK. She would say that everything was fine and I was thinking that I could get away and not have to be there for the second night, when somebody else asked her if she needed anything. She was obviously bored by now with this question so she answered that she was not happy with the loo as it smelt of men and that the carpet must be ripped out and it should be completely retiled by tomorrow night!

As she was leaving she gave me a kiss and a carnation, which meant that I would happily have built her a new dressing room! Obviously I could not have done that personally due to my building deficiencies but I would have searched the earth to find somebody who could! The job was done and on the next evening I popped in to see her before the show to check that she was happy with the re-tiled loo, she was apart from the minor fact that the smell of the glue might get on her chest and stop her signing. This was important as she did not tell jokes and could not juggle. You will possibly also have picked upon an on running theme to this! On this occasion the dehumidifier did the job, Shirley was happy, did her usual sensational show and I was able to escape.

I have obviously digressed beyond the moment in September 1980, when I reported for work for my first day with Apollo Leisure in an office attached to Paul's house in Boars Hill, Oxford. I felt immediately at home both with

Paul and Hilary, Gill, Georgina and Nicky who were the rest of the team working there. We were very privileged as the rest of the Apollo staff worked in Park End Street in the centre of Oxford. An added bonus was that Paul's wife Nita would wander in with food and would often blow a whistle for us all to stop work for a glass of wine! It was my sort of office!

On my first day Paul took great pride in showing me a very sporty Ford Capri which was my company car (A big mistake!) He wanted me to have a test drive but on the basis I would not have a clue how it worked I declined saying I would rather start working with Hilary on what was booked in the theatres, which at the time were Glasgow Apollo, Manchester Apollo, Coventry Apollo, Oxford New Theatre and the newly purchased Apollo Victoria. I was dreading having to drive the car to the Cotswold Lodge Hotel where I was staying at on the other side of Oxford.

I had not learnt to drive despite passing my test and in Blackburn had avoided going into the centre as I wasn't very good in traffic! I waited till Paul was on the phone, waved goodbye, and managed to hop the car down the drive and then out of sight got the handbook out to try and find out how it worked. More by luck than judgement I managed to get the car to the hotel while sweating profusely and wondering if I could catch a bus into work the next day!

That evening I wandered into Oxford (on foot!) to check on the Downtown Manhattan Night Club, (DTM) under the Oxford Theatre as this was also one of my responsibilities. The first person I encountered was Mike Adamson who went on to be not only the most important person in the whole of Apollo for making our theatres a success but also a close friend. However I am not sure that we got off to the best of starts. In the words of Mike, who at the time was the Theatre Assistant Manager but also had been coerced into running DTM. I burst in with a "Hi! My name is Sam Shrouder and I'm the new Operations Director (I was exaggerating because at the start I was General Manager!) and I am told that you are the Night Club expert in this company. Well Mike I have great experience in this business, I was a DJ you know. This is great, Mike we can do plenty of promotions together and look here I have a range of sample promotional vouchers to hand out at the door. What do they get for a voucher on a Thursday, I asked? Blasts from the Past and Plastics Fantastic, he replied! Well, I thought, this guy's either a genius or a lunatic. I didn't have the heart to tell him that I wasn't the Night Club Manager."

Later that evening I was in the Theatre meeting Jo Weston, who was the Manager, and she introduced me to her Assistant Manager, Mike Adamson! I had to explain to her that she was a bit confused because Mike is the Manager of DTM!

The next day I managed to drive back to the office, park with a sigh of relief, ready to commence ringing all the promoters and to start filling the gaps in the diary. To my horror Paul immediately asked me to drive to the Apollo Victoria. This was obviously way beyond my capabilities so I suggested that I caught the train as I was not sure how to get to Victoria. This was not possible as I was to deliver a load of boxes of leaflets.

So started the journey from hell! I nearly hit a few vehicles and also got lost, ending up on the wrong side of the river (I will never criticise sat navs again!) I was trying to read the map and when I came to a fork in the road I stopped to try and work out which way to go. This enraged the taxi driver who had come to a quick stop behind me and he kept his hand on the horn. By now I was near to having a breakdown so I got out of the car and explained he could do that for as long as he wanted but it would be more constructive if he gave me some directions, which he did. Miraculously I arrived at the front of the Theatre. Problem solved it seemed but not so as there was nowhere to park and I ended up a mile way in a multi storey car park. I would like to point out here and now that if you are the owner of a 4x4 that was scratched in a multi storey car park that day it was entirely your fault because if you had had a smaller car I would not have touched you and scratched my car on its first full day of use. So no apologies from me!

My lack of driving skills were to be a major feature of my life with Apollo. In my first nine months I had six accidents. Freda and Ian had separated not long after I moved to Oxford and she had rented a house in Blackburn with Andrea and Stephanie. My usual plan was to drive up to Blackburn, hopefully to arrive in time for us to have a drink in The Red Lion. I failed spectacularly to do this on a number of occasions including closing the M6 during a Friday rush hour. This was as a result of hitting the barrier in the centre and then catapulting back to hit a barrier on the inside. There were bits of car all over the road but mostly I was fine. The police who dealt with it were very understanding as an officer explained to me that this could have been caused by excessive speed or ice on the road. It was July!

As I was already on nine points I was grateful that they took no further action. I (my insurance) did have to pay £1000 to replace the barrier and for some time I toyed with decorating it or putting posters on it, which seemed reasonable as I had paid for it. I also managed to split the turn off to Preston and the M6 resulting in me careering off the road into a field between the two. This did shock me slightly but I managed to limp to the Trickled Trout who initially would not let me use their pay phone.

On one of my less impressive driving performances I managed to have two accidents on the same day! On joining the A34 on the way to the office I did not notice a lorry on the inside and collided with it doing no harm to me but considerable damage to the car. I had to be in Birmingham that evening for a show at The Alexandra Theatre so I borrowed a pool car, which was a bit complicated to drive resulting in me running into the back of the car in front as I joined the M6 (again!).l also managed to get done for speeding twice in the same day!

The response to my driving mishaps probably summed up the culture of the Company with everybody finding it very funny and Paul lending me his spare Jaguar. He did point out on one occasion that I was becoming uninsurable and had been withdrawn from the pool insurance and that the cost of mine at over £2000 was more than 50 per cent of the whole of Apollo's car insurance! He also said that he would appreciate it if I took a little more care as he did not want his life disrupted by having to visit me in hospital in Carlisle. Not sure why he came up with Carlisle as I have never been there in my life but the sentiments were understood if not acted on! I was also designated to drive Paul to hospital when Nita decided that he was having a heart attack (probably indigestion) and the general consensus was that if he was not having a heart attack at the start of the journey he certainly would have by the end!

At the start Apollo was an Isle of Man based company with Lionel Becker an accountant, who started it with Paul, as its Chairman. I knew that he was important from the start because he always had his name on the posters! Julian Harper was also an Isle of Man based director and was always good fun to be with, and a particularly good influence when times were tough, which they certainly were when I joined.

Within the first fortnight I had visited the five theatres and had to pinch myself that I was in charge of them all. My biggest concern was Coventry Apollo, which was managed by Andy Simpson (Fallus to family and friends), who had in his ABC days been Paul's boss. He was the one person who might have queried my appointment but he could not have been kinder and as I was leaving the theatre after a show he shook my hand and said he thought that I would be perfect for Apollo and just what was needed. That was a magnificent confidence booster and I really enjoyed working with him and we became good mates as well.

The manager in Glasgow was a law unto himself and I was uncomfortable how the theatre was run. In Manchester Lionel Becker's nephew John Becker was the manager and we got on well although I am not sure that he was particularly impressed to have some new guy turning up and wanting an input to how it was run. Oxford was managed by Jo Weston, who was excellent and with whom I had a great relationship. Oxford received lots of Arts Council product including Welsh National Opera and it was a major boost that Jo had an Arts background.

The guy who managed Apollo Victoria seemed to dress as a cowboy and it was obvious that we were not going to be able to work well together. In financial terms the Apollo Victoria was our biggest problem. Whilst we attracted some of the biggest stars including Dean Martin, Sammy Davis Junior, Liza Minnelli, Cliff Richard, John Denver and Shirley MacLaine the deals were such that if we did not do near capacity business we were running at a loss. For me it was living a dream meeting them all including going out for a Paul hosted dinner with John Denver. But all was about to change as Paul had done a deal with the producer Ross Taylor to bring in The Sound of Music. The show was to star Petula Clark, Michael Jayston, Honor Blackman, June Bronhill and John Bennett. We were entering a new world and a show with eight performances a week with great potential for front of house sales was obviously the way forward.

Any normal person would have watched how it did before getting involved in other shows, but not Paul Gregg. He had been to New York and had seen the black musical "One Mo Time" at the Village Gate, starring Vernal Bagneris. By the time he left America he had done a deal to bring it into the West End and for it to open before The Sound of Music. There was a slight problem with this as we did not have a theatre to put it in. Not daunted by this he took me along to a meeting with the old pop impresario (think Billy Fury) Larry Parnes who owned The Cambridge Theatre. By the time we had left I had another theatre to run. Paul had done the deal to lease the theatre in the knowledge that at Christmas John Pertwee and Una Stubbs in Worzel Gummidge were already contracted. We had little time to sell it so we took out a TV package. To everybody's surprise this lovely show was a minor hit.

In the meantime The Sound of Music had opened to good but not great business I got on well with Ross Taylor most of the time but there would be the odd bust up particularly over the placing of the programme sellers and the brochure sellers. The theatre maxim is that the house has the programmes and the brochures belong to the producer with the theatre taking 25% commission for selling them. We therefore gained most from selling the programmes so with David Roger's encouragement the public were always greeted with staff selling the programmes. However, contractually we apparently were meant to have the brochures first in line (I trust that you are following this – the world of Rock and Roll was never this complicated!) This resulted in threats of legal action and a quick reversal in policy. Luckily for me the General Manager of the production was Max Howard and he was a fabulous guy, who ensured that any problems were ironed out without blood on the carpet. We became the best of friends and in no time I was playing cricket for the Sound of Music team in a game Max had organised. I seem to remember that Michal Jayston, as well as being a very pleasant person to have in the theatre, was also a very good leg spinner.

Max was outstanding at his job, doing it with real style and ensuring that there was a great relationship between the cast and the staff. Petula Clark was a real star and always very friendly although sometimes seeming a little sad.

I remember Max and his partner Caroline coming to our house for New Year's Eve, when there was no show and saying that he had thought of inviting Petula because she was on her own, but did not like to as he was not able to contact us. What a shame as my stock at the local pub would have improved dramatically if I had walked nonchalantly in with Petula Clark!

Meanwhile One Mo Time was in need of recasting as Equity had only agreed for the mainly American cast to do it for a limited period, as well as about to become homeless. It might have been a good time to bring it to an end and make the most of Worzel Gummidge but this was not Paul's style. So he took me along to meet Veronica Flint Shipman to do a deal to take over The Phoenix Theatre. For some bizarre reason Jo Weston, who had taken over the management of the Apollo Victoria whilst overseeing our growing London empire, and I were sat in the office of the Cambridge Theatre interviewing potential cast replacements. This really was a case of the blind leading the blind!

One of the big bonuses of One Mo Time was their American Company Manager Peter Schneider. We dined regularly together and I liked him a lot. After One Mo Time he became our head of productions, overseeing, amongst other shows, Camelot. He left in 1984 to head up the Arts programme for the Los Angeles Olympic Games. He was a talented man and it was no surprise that he went on to have an incredible career with Disney including being head of Animation and also Theatre Productions. In what goes around comes around sort of way the great relationship Peter had with Apollo resulted in him placing the massive hit show The Lion King many years later at our Lyceum Theatre.

Life was about to become very difficult in London as One Mo Time closed at The Phoenix to go on a not very successful tour and then Sound of Music closed meaning that we had three West End Theatres to find products for. To the theatrical establishment we were very much outsiders. To a certain extent we had to return to our roots and programme concerts. One of our successes at the Apollo Victoria was a season of Freddie Starr and Hot Gossip. As a result of this we decided to put Freddie into The Cambridge Theatre for a limited run. Freddie, who I liked, was not at his best and a night at The Cambridge Theatre with 17 people in the audience and Freddie heckling Mike Newman, the opening act will rank alongside some of my worst memories.

We had a few shows that really worked at the Apollo Victoria including Dash with Wayne Sleep and Fiddler on the Roof with Topol but in general it was a financial struggle that was getting worse. In trying to find a show for The Cambridge I was sent to Plymouth Theatre Royal to see their production of The Mikado. I loved it so we, along with Bill Kenwright, put it into the theatre.

The problem with this decision-making was that I loved just about every show I ever saw. I would come out of shows and people would be saying that it was a disaster and I would be saying that I really enjoyed it. They would look at me in astonishment and say the lead kept forgetting his lines and the scenery fell down! I was just so in love with it all I just would not see these slight imperfections! So I was not a man to decide that a show should come into the West End. I was desperate for it to work and Andy Phipps, who was managing The Cambridge would ring me every night with the figures but it was to be a flop. Bill Kenwright never once mentioned my lack of judgement and as he was in all my dealings with him he was an absolute joy to work with, indeed one of the truly great men of theatre.

So whilst all was not well in London we were also having mixed fortunes in the provinces. Glasgow Apollo was an iconic venue and regarded by many bands as the greatest Rock gig in Europe. It had been, as Greens Playhouse, the largest cinema in Europe. With its 4000 seats it had stood alone as the biggest concert venue outside London but Arenas were now popping up all over and Glasgow Council were planning to build the Scottish Exhibition Centre with over twice the capacity. It was also in such a dreadful state with a couple of managers who had not mastered "Give unto Caesar that which is Caesars"! But despite all that, what memories! It had an atmosphere unlike any venue. When the place was rocking, the balcony went up and down as well! It had to be measured every year and if it moved by 6 inches we would have to close. The Council always chose Status Quo's annual visit to measure it. I wonder why! It was recorded as moving 5'/2 inches which was sufficient to ensure that I never stood under it!

You would never go and see an act before the show as they would complain about how shabby everything was but after the show they would be buzzing as the Glasgow audience was like no other. When Dionne Warwick was touring we had a real panic. The show before Glasgow was in Bridlington she protested that the venue was so run down that she told the Orchestra not to change and do the gig in their jeans whilst she wore a track suit. We all reacted the same – if she thought Bridlington was bad, wait until she got to Glasgow Apollo.

I was told by Paul to cancel what I was doing and get up there and Tony McCarthur from the promoter MAM was told the same. We obviously had to see her before the show and Tony, who was a bit of a charmer managed to distract her sufficiently to ensure that she and the band were dressed appropriately. As always the sell-out Glasgow audience were magnificent and after the show she was really bubbling. If you sold out Glasgow you got a trophy with Apollo written down the side. They cost about £1 and we had a job lot of them but no matter how big the star they were always thrilled to get one. Dionne Warwick was no different and as she left the theatre she held it up like the FA Cup. Tony had arranged to have dinner with her after the show and he invited me to join them. When she came into the restaurant she was still holding the Apollo Trophy, which then sat in front of her for the entire meal. It did occur to me that Bridlington must have been really bad!

One of the worst nights there was when David and I had to go as it had been reported to us that there was a fiddle on the door and there was. The manager had gone to London to see Paul and was dismissed and I had to suspend the head of security to enable us to properly check what was happening. To make matters worse the promoter of the show had previously complained about what was going on and had brought up a team of people to watch the exits. I called the security together explained what had happened and suggested that with the promoter watching all doors they should be whiter than white. The fiddle was pretty basic with compliment slips with seat numbers on being sold. Just as I thought I would go and watch the show, which was UB40, the promoter came rushing in to say he had caught one of our security offering to let one of his guys through an exit door for a fiver. When he pointed the guy out he was one of my favourites, he was also massive. I had to sit him in the office and very gently explain that he could not continue. I should add that David was nowhere to be seen at this stage! After what was a horrible night David and I popped into Lauders Bar across from the venue for a well-earned pint. When I went to pay, the girl behind the bar said that a gentleman had already paid for them. When I looked over it was the guy who had just left our employment and he smiled and raised his glass – only in Glasgow!

One of our most remarkable shows was when Harvey Goldsmith agreed to do a warm up gig for The Rolling Stones stadium tour. I was told that I could only announce it one week before at midday and that if anybody found out before that, the show would not happen. So I had to get the tickets printed with no name on them and fly up to Glasgow to be ready to put them on sale at midday. I rang the local radio station at 11.55 and asked them to announce the show on their 12 o'clock news. At about 12.10 people started running up the street, taxis started arriving and lots of cars stopped to drop people off to join the queue. The effect was remarkable with the queue stretching down the street and by 4.00pm with tickets limited to 4 per person the show was sold out The show of course was sensational and I watched a large part of it from the side of the stage – what a privilege to see Mick Jagger strut his stuff from such close proximity and this was work! Our contact at the Radio Station was at the show and when I went to thank him for putting it out on the news he just as quickly apologised because they had not been able to mention it on the news. At many a marketing meeting or conference I would always mention (must have got a bit boring!) that it is possible to sell a show out by telling just one person.

Many years later I was again telling this story, Gerry Tait, an outstanding Divisional Director, and obviously tired of the repetition of this tale asked me if I knew what really happened. I told him that it was obvious the guy told the people he worked with; who then rang people that they knew and it just went round like wild fire that The Stones were playing Glasgow Apollo hence this stampede to buy tickets. Gerry said, "No, what really happened was that he did not get it on the news as requested but he mentioned on his show straight after the news!" I prefer my version!

The worst experience I had at the theatre was when I booked The Wolfe Tones, an ageing Irish Folk Group. The promoter was Peggy Jones, who I liked and she had done many Irish shows around the theatres, so it all seemed very harmless and indeed what could go wrong? The answer was everything!

It appeared that they were banned from every Glasgow venue as a result of the sort of audience they attracted as a result of their pro IRA rhetoric. Despite this I was reassured by the many coach bookings made by Catholic priests. The police were not at all happy and said that we were inviting trouble. I thought that had I better be there for the show, which had sold out. I was not overly worried on the basis it could not be any worse than the Skids at Blackburn. I certainly got that wrong as it was one of the most terrifying nights of my life. The audience was dominated by the lunatic fringe of Celtic supporters with their shirts off and carrying the Irish flag and sinister looking people wearing balaclavas (I realise that there is a contradiction here as if they were wearing balaclavas how could I know that they looked sinister – but trust me they did!). It soon became obvious that the event was completely out of control, the security were a target so I withdrew them, pipes were being ripped from the walls so we had some flooding and The Wolfe Tones were making highly inflammatory statements that were whipping up the audience even more.

I felt it was my responsibility to be in the theatre to check what mayhem was taking place but after a guy in a balaclava grabbed my hand to join in singing 'One Ireland, United We Shall Be', I beat a hasty retreat! At the interval the head of Police asked to see me and told me that the place was completely out of control and what was I going to do about it. That was a bit of a coincidence as I was going to ask him the same question! He instructed me to make sure that in the second half The Wolfe Tones would tone down the political content. As I went back stage I realised there was no chance of this as they were having a whale of a time and getting a better audience reaction than even the Rolling Stones did. I went into their dressing room on the basis that I was the only guy who would let them play in Glasgow and as such they needed to return the favour. They were on a high and insisted that this was their act and they would continue. In the corner was a guy in a long black leather coat (I have one myself and I think that they look great!) and shades and he looked even more sinister than the other people who looked sinister. He asked me to leave the dressing room and wait outside. After a few minutes he came out, shook my hand, thanking me for letting the band play The Apollo and guaranteed that they would tone down the second half. I was later told that he was one of the top IRA men in Scotland. I'm not sure whether that was true but he is now my friend and had saved my bacon.

I went back to the Police Chief to inform him that I had sorted the problem out. Neither he nor I will ever know if that was the case as he left the building and I never left the office!

If the building was looking ramshackle before The Wolfe Tones it looked like a building site after it. Our contract stated that the promoter was responsible for all damage done during the show so as Peggy Jones was taken round the empty theatre she saw just about all the revenue disappear as it was withheld to pay for all the required repairs. We did approach Glasgow City Council's Chief Executive to say that The Apollo was becoming non-viable and we were thinking of closing it. As becomes a guy who had "Glasgow Smiles Better" emblazoned on the front of the Town Hall, he was fantastic. He said it would be a tragedy for the young people of Glasgow if we closed before the new Scottish Exhibition Centre opened and agreed to give us a grant to keep the venue open. So Glasgow Apollo continued to entertain the young and gradually fall down.

Our other prestigious concert venue was Manchester Apollo, which continued to be very successful with major acts playing multiple dates there. One of the best shows I ever saw was Rod Stewart there. I went to see him before the show to tell him his hero Dennis Law was in the audience and it was like talking to a boxer as he bounced up and down in front of me. From the moment he came on stage, the audience were on their feet and singing every word of every song. I have seen him a few times but this was Rod Stewart at his best. I also enjoyed seeing Engelbert Humperdinck there and after the show the promoter Jeff Hanlon, one of the real nice guys in the business, said come back and say hello to him. We got in the dressing room and Jeff was deep in conversation with one of the band so when I saw Englebert standing on his own I went over said hello and how much I enjoyed the show, had a pleasant chat about the tour and said my goodbyes. As I was leaving Jeff followed me and asked what I thought of Englebert and I explained that he seemed a good guy Jeff started falling about laughing. He told me that I could not know what he is like as I had never met him, because the guy I had introduced myself to was his brother!

I was delighted when Kennedy Street's Danny Betesh, one of the legendary promoters, put in four nights of Barry Manilow and quickly put the first show in my diary. A sell out show and the very pleasant company of Danny, what could be easier?

Driving up the M6 and managing to avoid all other cars I was in fine form as I turned on the radio to catch the national news. My mood changed quickly as the last item said that Manchester City Council would take an injunction out to stop the remaining three Barry Manilow concerts if members of the audience lit a candle or held a lit cigarette lighter in the air. This was nigh impossible to stop as when he sang "One Voice" it was the highlight of the show with the lights going down and everybody holding a candle. It was a fabulously theatrical moment and I couldn't see Barry Manilow wanting to lose it.

The Manager of Manchester Apollo, Ian Coburn, had done everything possible to take charge of the situation, including selling the punters torches to create the same effect. A bright ideal (Sorry about that – couldn't resist it!).

Danny had told Barry about the matter but he suggested that I also talked to him to stress the seriousness of the situation. It was with some trepidation that I broached the subject but Barry could not have been more understanding. When the show started there were 30 Council Staff, who were obviously delighted at the opportunity of seeing Barry Manilow for free, whilst doing their best to spot somebody with a naked light to ensure that nobody else would be able to see him. When the moment came for him to sing "One Voice" he was brilliant. He asked his fans as a special favour to him not to light candies as he felt it was dangerous. To the best of my knowledge nobody did, those with torches provided the scene and Barry Manilow had saved the day! Phew!

Apart from Glasgow the other provincial theatre that was in serious trouble was Coventry Apollo. I loved going there partly because it was a historic theatre and partly for the joy of being in the company of its manager Fallus Simpson (We have already established that he was Andy to the world and Fallus to his friends – and we were friends). He did everything to try and make the theatre viable including when David complained about his petty cash bill of around £7 (By a long way the smallest of all the Theatres) he responded by putting in zero bills for the next two months! He was an old style manager, who insisted on calling me Mr Shrouder in public.

He had a very complicated love life and his many admirers would come to the shows and it would be a regular occurrence that he would say "Mr Shrouder do you mind if we hide behind the pillar as I do not want that lady to see me!" I came in one evening and he had a list of complaints letters to deal with. Everyone else used to send written replies but he would let them accumulate and then spend an evening ringing them up. Most of the complaints come from women and I am certainly not going to comment on that! On this day I asked him how it was going and he said very well Sam (We were in the office!) I have so far got three dates!

It is interesting what people complain about and following a Dexy's Midnight Runners concert we got a complaint from a school teacher who had been sat in the back row and because people had stood up he couldn't see the show from his seat. It was so obvious that it was what a Dexy's audience would do that I refused to give him a refund so he took us to a small claims court. I was so incensed by this that I foolishly tried to fight it. I made a very eloquent submission explaining that at certain style of music concerts people stand. It cannot have been that eloquent as I lost the case and had to give him a refund plus costs. It was also explained to me that we should have asked everybody to sit down so that the bloke at the back who did not want to stand could see the show!

When I joined Apollo, Paul was in habit of paying guarantees to get shows to Coventry in particular. I was really against this as I have always maintained a percentage split is the only fair way to do it. On this occasion he had guaranteed a production of My Fair Lady for which the producer was Cameron Mackintosh. On the opening night I was chatting with Cameron and he asked how the business for the show was and I said that we were going to make a considerable loss on the production. Now this was not the incredibly successful and rich producer Cameron Mackintosh this was the, it's early in my career needing every penny I can get. Cameron Mackintosh. Despite this he immediately said that he would re-do the deal and give us the show at cost. Not only did he say it, he actually did it, coming back with a revised deal. I have never forgotten this gesture (well obviously not, because if

I had done, I would not be recalling it now!) and he was always a joy to deal with and his team lead by Nick Allott always reflected this style. All the success that they have achieved has been totally deserved for his incredible creative talent along with his desire to make the theatre industry as a whole, thrive.

One of the highlights of our programming Coventry Apollo was when Paul persuaded the legendary producer Harold Fielding to bring his 2 Ronnie's show. Business was brilliant but could have been better and Harold used to keep ringing the box office and then justifiably complain about how long it took for his calls to be answered. In the end this resulted in some quite heavy exchanges of correspondence.

It was agreed that Paul and I would go to Harold's office to sort out the problem. When we arrived he said that knowing that Paul and I were northern he had arranged for some scones! Needless to say all differences were quickly sorted as we tucked into the scones! The show itself was special as were both the stars, although very different. I would go and see Ronnie Barker to check he was OK and he would stand at his door saying thank you for everything and that he was fine and that was it. In later years as President of the Institute of Entertainments Management (I may have mentioned this!) I looked after him for a lunch time before presenting him with a life time achievement award. He was fabulous company and later sent me a letter that the actor J.L. Toole had sent the manager of The Lyceum, a theatre we had gone on to own, which read "Dear Miss Terry, I don't think I was quite up to the mark in 'Trying a Magistrate' today – so I shall fine myself five guineas – will you kindly hand the fine to The Royal Eye Hospital – Yours Sincerely J.L. Toole.

Ronnie Corbett was very different with a massive welcome and invitationinto his dressing room and a drink to go with it. He would also insist that if I had any family or friends in during the run that I ensure that they went back to see him. He was just always great company. On one occasion I passed him in the street and he immediately remembered my name (people have a habit of not doing this!) and insisted that we went in the pub outside The Cambridge Theatre. He chatted away and as always was fabulous company.

The success of the 2 Ronnie's was a beacon of light in a theatre that was struggling. Just about our last throw of the dice was to put on a panto starring the up-and-coming star, Michael Barrymore.

Michael was fantastic and the business was not! I remember that he did a portion of the panto standing on his head in case there were any Australians in the audience! Michael was a comic genius and a lovely guy to work with. He would do any publicity request and chat away with anybody who was our guests. After one of the performances Freda and I went out for dinner with Michael and his then wife Cheryl. They were both great company but what stayed with me was when Michael said that he had never seen a pantomime before appearing in this one. He went on to be a real star and regardless of what happened later in his life he was always a great pleasure to work with.

The loss on the panto was a serious blow to the future of Coventry Apollo but in a last desperate attempt to keep it open we approached the Council for some financial support. When I went to make the case the Senior Council Officer was David John. If you are following this meandering story you will remember that he was my boss at Rochdale Metropolitan Borough Council. David, bless him, came up trumps and we received a small grant to enable us to continue to run this fabulous theatre. So Coventry like Glasgow was now reliant on council support.

Whilst Coventry struggled, Oxford New Theatre (to later become Oxford Apollo, and then under American Ownerships to become Oxford New Theatre!) continued to be a strong theatre with Downtown Manhattan underneath it continuing to make a major contribution to the dwindling funds of Apollo Leisure. I enjoyed being responsible for Downtown Manhattan, which, with various midweek University Clubs was strong all week apart from Tuesday.

Whatever promotion we did for the Tuesday failed until I came up with a cracker of an idea to make the night a comedy night with entrance by joke only. This gained lots of publicity including a feature in the Daily Mirror. BBC Radio Oxford picked up on it in the shape of a certain Timmy Mallett, who arranged for myself and the cashier to come on his programme and then listeners to ring in with jokes to see what would make the cashier laugh.

The first DTM comedy night arrived and I proudly stood at the top of the steps ready to listen to all the jokes and to take the plaudits for another successful promotion. So you will understand that I was slightly disappointed when only three people turned up all night. We also had to abandon the entrance by joke only as they were Iranian and did not have a clue what we were talking about!

Timmy Mallett went on to do panto for us at the Swindon Wyvern and I got on really well with him. Timmy is a big Oxford United supporter, so we agreed that he would take me as his guest to one of their games and he would come as my guest to a Southport game. It is fair to say that he is quite a vocal supporter! The Southport game he came to was at Stevenage, where having picked him up at his house we sat and watched another Southport defeat. It was a weekend when there was an International break and for some reason The Sun featured our game as the game of the day and in the middle of the paper was a report and a photo of Tommy and I watching the game. The paper reported that Timmy was a celebrity Stevenage supporter. Not like The Sun to get it wrong!

Oxford New Theatre was a fabulous Theatre, well attended with a wide variety of product. I started the job just in advance of the panto, which starred The Krankies and Stu Francis and they were great fun, I knew Stu from Middleton days so I spent quite a bit of time in their company. Ian and Jeanette were very funny and slightly suggestive on the stage and were very funny and extremely rude off the stage! It was a real bonus to be able to leave the office and go and spend some time laughing away in their dressing rooms.

Oxford was very important to the Arts Council with it housing regular weeks of Welsh National Opera, Glyndebourne, English National Ballet and Ballet Rambert plus visits from other major Arts Council-funded companies. Opera was new to me and not an art form that I initially took to and was, of course, totally ignorant of all its subtleties. However I overcame this by going to The Grapes Pub opposite the Theatre with Sheila Nelson, who was part of their touring management. Over a gin and tonic or two she would tell me a few things to mention at the interval. She never let me down and I would get the experts to believe that I actually knew what I was talking about! I had lots of battles over the years with WNO but I had a lot of respect for some of their management. Brian McMasters, who was head of WNO at that time, was a great personality and when he moved to become Director in charge of The Edinburgh Festival we would often meet for lunch and I always enjoyed his company. In later years I dealt with Geoffrey Rowe, who I liked and years later he became Chief Executive of Cheltenham Everyman Theatre where I was on the Board. He was "old school" and very amusing.

There was a great team at the Oxford Theatre, firstly under Jo Weston who then went on to manage Apollo Victoria and then under Mike Adamson. Mike was the start of the policy of promoting from within and giving young Assistant Managers their chance rather than bringing in managers from outside the company. This was an important part of Apollo's success and many people who went on to have top careers in the Theatre industry can thank this policy for giving them the opportunity.

Mike was a prime example of this and as the company grew we were destined to work very closely together and he was a massive part of The Apollo story. The Theatre team included a very talented technical director, Adrian Leggett, who was to go on to be Head of Apollo Productions, but in those days could create the most wonderful staging of even the most low budget show. There was also Maureen Scriven who was in charge of party bookings and was incredibly creative in selling lots of tickets. She also ran a fun office and I would always nip in for a cup of tea if I was in the theatre.

In the box office was Peggy Parson who went on to be awarded the MBE, having spent 61 years working there. I was delighted to be able to get her up on the stage, courtesy of Gary Wilmot who was the star of the show, to do a presentation to her to celebrate this award. I was less delighted when she finally retired, long after I had left, to go to her farewell party to find that nobody from ATG, the current owners of the Theatres, could be bothered to turn up. I ended up making the speech (well there's a change!) and enjoying an orange juice (the management had said there was to be no alcohol) with Debbie Garrick and Roz Thomas, who had made the effort to return to the Theatre to be part of Peggy's day. It was a shabby way to treat someone who had given 61 years of their life to the Theatre.

I was loving every minute of the job and was brilliantly looked after by Paul and David in their different ways. After a few months there I realised that a couple of managers were earning more than me which was fine, indeed I would have done the job for nothing. One day Paul came into my office with an envelope and said that they had decided to readjust my salary. From the way he said it I thought that they had reduced it but when I opened the letter I found I had been given a 50% rise!

It was gestures like this that made you even more dedicated to the job – if that was possible. The next letter I got was to inform me that I had been made The Operations Director and had been appointed to the Board. Also included in this enlarged board was Keith Wells as Development Director,

Blackburn Sam and Jasper Carrott

Blackburn Smiling Sam DJ

Blackburn Panto Promo with John Jardine

Blackburn with Andy Williams

Bowling (ABC) Hanley Face Cream Bango promotion

Ken Dodd signed 10 x 8 inch

Top of the bill at Hammersmith Apollo

Linda and Ben in Maldives

Sam meets Princess Margaret

Sam meets The Queen Mother

Waterford Crystal Awards with Ronnie Barker

Sam in action

Middleton with Bob Geldof and Boomtown Rats

Sam at Old Traffford with coach Tom Reddich and Jackie Bond

Vine Club Noel Edmonds and Sam

Vine Club showing Noel Edmonds the ropes

Vine Club with Linda recording requests show later broadcast on Radio St-Helena

he was a fun guy and we would often meet up for a pint.

My first board meeting was notable for an opportunity for further advancement in my career. During the meeting Paul and Lionel Becker confirmed that a deal had been done with Stuart Littlewood to do some dates with Cannon and Ball, who were massive at the time. That was really good news. What was not good news was that they had agreed to do a 20% commission on brochure sales as opposed to our normal 25%. David had always rightly insisted that this was one thing that was non-negotiable and I had always stuck rigidly to it. When promoters and producers argued about it I had always been able to honestly say that we had never reduced the percentage for anyone. So I was miffed by this part of the deal and kept on arguing about it, with some support from David. The longer it went on the more irritated Lionel was becoming until he asked me if I wanted to be Chairman! I considered this kind offer briefly but decided that it was possibly a step too far at this stage! I declined politely and he stated that in that case perhaps we could move onto the next item on the agenda!

The office at Boars Hill continued to be a great place to work and in being responsible, with great help from Hilary Faraglia, for the programming of the theatres I was really enjoying life there. It was a very relaxed environment with lots of laughter but also lots of hard work. Hilary was in charge of the office but concentrated on getting shows for the theatres.

Hilary was also a good friend which resulted in me making the dreadful decision of having a game of squash with her. It turned out that she was an international player and I ended up a sweaty mess not having got a point while she must have wondered why she even bothered to get changed. I felt that I had to explain that cricket was really my game, so she introduced me to her friend Brian Bowden, a stalwart of South Oxfordshire Amateurs, who I joined and played a number of mid-week games with.

Also in the office was Gill Hopcroft who was my P.A. and really looked after me saving me from numerous errors, whilst there was also Georgie who did a cabaret act with paper plates that is probably best not described here!

After living in a flat in Oxford, I moved to a village called Watchfield, when Freda, Andrea and Stephanie moved down. We were renting a lovely thatched cottage and really enjoyed the village life. On one occasion the village got cut off following a blizzard. There were cars and lorries abandoned on the nearby A420 and Watchfield had to accommodate all the stranded drivers. One of our neighbours, Stef Episcopo, knocked on our door to ask if I would help with digging out vehicles. I reluctantly agreed and followed his orders as did the other volunteers. That evening we were all in the pub and I laughingly said to Stef that he should get the MBE for his incredible work in the snow. He quietly let me know that actually he had already got the MBE!

Stef, his wife Diana and daughters Joanne and Katie became great friends and to this day Stef and I still meet at Cirencester Golf Club and catch up with life as we meander round, normally trying to find where I have hit my ball! This is helped by our other golfing partner, Richard Rollett who, as well as being great company, is the only one with decent eyesight!

The nearest village to Watchfield was Shrivenham and the day after we moved I was down at their impressive cricket ground chatting to the guy mowing the square, a certain Bunny Burroughs. It turned out he was Mr Shrivenham Cricket Club doing just about everything including captaining the first team. After regaling him with my cricketing history, no doubt mentioning Joel Garner, I had talked myself into the first team! There were two games left of a fixture list filled with friendly games. Luckily this was about to change as the club had applied to join the Oxfordshire league. We were accepted and for the 15 years I played there we were in either the Premier League 1 or 2. It was my spiritual cricketing home and really enjoyed my time there.

Joining at the same time as me was Ted Senescall, who had been a pro in the Bradford League and had been known as the Queensbury Flier. As well as being a top quality cricketer he was a great character. He was dour and funny and we happily took the micky out of each other for fifteen years. The club was full of characters with Nigel Tucker being the voice of reason and the best drinker, Chris Sugden being the best player and Howard Moore an outstanding left arm spinner, who looked on disapprovingly at our wilder antics, as befitted a school teacher. We also had an opening batsman called Stevie Jack, a prolific scorer and lovely guy. Stevie became a born-again Christian and did fantastic fund raising events for many needy causes including some that I was involved in. The Cricket Club was great socially and a very happy part of my life.

When Freda and I decided to get married the Greggs and Apollo's generosity was again to the fore. Paul, who gave Freda away, said that as Apollo's present to us they would organise and pay for our reception which was held at their house. No expense was spared with all our friends and family welcomed along with many of my Apollo colleagues. Bo, a great DJ from Downtown Manhattan, did the music, Terry Harrison was my best man and my Mum and Dad and Freda's Mum, Ruthie, marvelled at how the other half lived and Nita cut Keith Well's tie off! Not sure why! A couple of characters from our village were so impressed with the occasion that they told Paul that if he ever needed anything knocking off to just let them know!

In the early days I enjoyed meeting up with Kevin Hayes the cricketing prodigy I had played with at Cherry Tree. Kevin started at Oxford University, after a year playing for Lancashire, at the same time as I started at Apollo. He had said previously that he was worried that he might not fit in but nothing could be further from the truth. A few weeks after he started I asked him if he would like a lift to Blackburn at the weekend, but he declined as he was going to a sherry party! A few weeks later I casually asked what he was doing next week to be told that he was playing at Wembley! He had been picked for the Oxford versus Cambridge game without ever mentioning that he was playing football. He went on to captain Oxford and it was a great joy to go to The Parks to see him captain the combined Oxford/Cambridge team against the West Indies, and to watch him go out to toss up with Viv Richards. Some people have all the luck!

Chapter 12

STARLIGHT AND STARS

Back at work the three West End Theatres were proving a drain on our resources and it was decided that we should produce a musical at Apollo Victoria. This was obviously a high risk strategy but we were running out of options. Paul did the deal for us to present Camelot staring Richard Harris and Fiona Fullerton. At one of our board meetings, Peter Schneider came in to run us through the finances of it. In his usual blunt American way he finished by saying that if you guys do this you are crazier than I thought. We did and we were!

The show was fraught with difficulties and Richard Harris was incredible star quality but difficult. Michael Rudman had been brought in to direct the show but Richard Harris was not happy with him and wanted him removed. I was disappointed with this because Michael was a top quality director but more importantly he was married to Felicity Kendall! Paul had previously arranged a small dinner party for Michael and I had won the star prize of sitting next to Felicity. Now in reality if she has, is, or will write her autobiography her sitting next to me is unlikely to feature but for me it was a great joy and she was charming. So no Michael, no Felicity! Frank Dunlop, from Edinburgh Festival took over and had Richard's respect – most of the time!

When we did our preview, and charity performances I was spell bound. I thought that the show was magnificent and Richard Harris had an incredible charisma and aura. The audiences seemed to agree and we were getting standing ovations at every performance. The opening night was sensational with Richard Harris alone taking 13 curtain calls. When we went to the opening night party the theatre industry were gushing in their praise. I was too new to this to know that the theatre industry is always gushing in their praise to your face. People were saying "Darling you must be thrilled – it will run for ever" or "Sweetheart you have a smash hit on your hands".

It was fantastic as I believed every word, particularly as I adored Camelot. This would be the answer to all our problems, and we could now concentrate on getting long running shows for The Cambridge and The Phoenix. So we were all in high spirits indeed when we went down in the early hours to Fleet Street to pick up all the first editions.

We all sobered up very quickly as we found out that this wonderful show was not wonderful at all, indeed it was a turkey. There was hardly a half decent review. It seemed so unfair as the audiences were loving it but on the word of a few hard bitten journalists, who spent their life either loving or hating shows, we were going to struggle to bring in the level of business that we needed. We were not helped by the show taking place during the period when the IRA had launched a campaign by bombing on the mainland. With Richard Harris being an outspoken Irish man we were very much a target. On a regular basis a couple of police would arrive and say they had received a call that there was a bomb on the premises detonated to go off during the performance. Initially we evacuated and then we had 20 police, sniffer dogs, and vehicles with sirens and blue lights arrive with a senior police officer telling us to go into evacuation mode. It seemed a member of the audience had seen a package with smoke coming out of it stuck behind a radiator and they were taking it very seriously.

When the staff were gathered and told about the package a slightly embarrassed usherette explained that it was her Chinese meal, which she had put there to keep it warm before eating it after the show. What it taught us was that when only two policeman turn up to tell you that they have had a call about a bomb on your premises they are not taking it very seriously because if they do you will get the full works as we did. From that moment on it was an unwritten rule that we never evacuated unless instructed to do so by the police.

Camelot ran for a while but incurred heavy losses, which we were not in a position to fund. We were then called to a meeting with our bank manager, who went through our figures and then said "Gentlemen you are fucked"! I was astonished both with the sentiment and his style of portraying it. I very much hope he lived long enough to see how unfucked we became.

Lesser people would have thrown the towel in at this stage but Paul, David, Lionel and Julian were made of sterner stuff. Julian and Lionel with their Isle of Man connections put a deal together that involved Pools and

Horse Racing multi-millionaire Robert Sangster becoming our Chairman, with Lionel stepping down to Vice Chairman and Ken Paul, a representative of Robert Sangster, joining the Board. Whilst at the time I was not privy to the individual shareholdings it was obvious that Paul had relinquished a large amount to the Isle of Man group to make this work. Robert Sangster was obviously not interested in theatre and never attended a single show including Royal Galas. I only met him once which was after a board meeting on the Isle of Man when we were invited to his house, The Nunnery, for lunch.

After the meeting I ended up travelling with Ken Paul who knew the back way so arrived well before the others. On arrival Robert and Ken had disappeared leaving Robert's wife Susan Peacock and me. Susan was Australian and very chatty and I enjoyed her company and continued to do so once the others arrived as I sat next to her at lunch. On our little plane back to Kidlington we were all laughing and I was telling Paul, David and Keith that now that I was friends with the new Chairman's wife I would put a good word in for them. This did not last long as on the following Monday the paper headlined that Robert Sangster had left his wife for Susan Lilley!

Ken Paul was an astute business man and a lovely guy if always a bit flustered. A typical meeting would involve him turning up late followed by some personal chaos. On one occasion he arrived with "I am sorry I am late boys" followed by "Oh, no, I have picked up somebody else's jacket on the plane". This went on for five minutes with him bemoaning how he could possibly have picked up thewrong jacket with everybody coming up with useful suggestions such as ring the airline. Then suddenly he said that it was OK because it was his jacket after all! He then said he must ring his secretary and rung his mother by mistake! He was a good guy and played his part in David, Keith and myself receiving shares in the Company. One phone call changed the whole future of Apollo and indeed the theatre industry. The phone call to Paul Gregg was from Andrew Lloyd Webber asking him to come and see a workshop for his new musical. We were all intrigued and Paul duly went on a Saturday when he had intended going to the FA Cup Final. What he encountered was a number of people on roller skates pretending to be trains.

It was, of course, the early stage of creating the hit musical Starlight Express. Andrew was looking for a theatre and with the ambitious creative designs of John Napier, Apollo Victoria was just about the only theatre that could house the show. With the intention of having trains racing all round the theatre we were in the position of having the space and design of theatre that could accommodate it. Andrew had put together the very best of West End talent to create the show with Richard Stilgoe doing the lyrics, David Hersey the lighting, Arlene Phillips the choreography as well as it being directed by Trevor Nunn. Andrew had written some fabulous music and with Richard's lyrics helped to create a very special theatre experience. Whilst it was going to take in the region of three months to get the show in, we all believed in the project (I think!) and it was with great excitement that I watched the first preview. I was mesmerised and I thought that the show was magnificent, and I know that I always think shows are magnificent but this one was even more magnificent than the others!

The audience was totally entranced by Rusty and we agreed that nobody could do it like a steam train. The show ended with Poppa, the aging steam locomotive leading the company with "Light at the end of the Tunnel" and I could not help but think how it might be just, that for all of us at Apollo.

In our wildest dreams nobody could have anticipated that when Starlight Express finally closed in 2002 having run for over eighteen years it would be at that time the second longest running musical of all time. Audiences adored it and came back to see it again, tourists flocked to see the all-action musical.

To his eternal credit Andrew and his Really Useful team never took its success for granted. The show was regularly freshened up with new music being written. There was also no chance, after everything that had happened, that we would not treat it as a special guest in our theatre.

I had always been convinced that theatres are a place of magic and that it was an insult to that image not to have them in their finest condition. I regularly did inspections of all the theatres to ensure that we retained our sparkle and that the staff were not only smart and presentable but also chirpy and welcoming. But no matter how high my standards were Paul Gregg's were even more so and his visits raised terror in all of us and always resulted in him finding something wrong.

Often he would instruct Keith Wells or Steve Lavelle, his successor, to stop what they were dong and immediately go to the specific theatre to arrange for areas to be redecorated or recarpeted etc. It would drive hell in David and me because the money was not in the budget but Keith and Steve knew the script and would nick the money from someone else's budget.

Paul was, of course, right. I remember many years later giving a talk to a Civic Theatre seminar about the importance of looking after the audience in every way and how we presented the theatre. As is my want I probably went on for a rather long time! I was followed by Philip Hedley, Director of Stratford East who told a story about Joan Littleton, the world famous director. On one occasion on the opening night of a show that had people coming over from the USA for and just before the doors opened she was on her hands and knees scrubbing the steps. When one of the staff queried why she was doing it she looked up imperiously and said "I am expecting guests aren't you?" In a couple of minutes Philip had made the point far better than I had managed in far longer. Needless to say I nicked his story and told it regularly.

I loved Starlight Express and watched it on a regular basis. The good and the great came to see it and for a while we were the hottest show in town. On one occasion I got tickets for some friends and their daughter and the day after the show their thanks seemed somewhat over the top saying that it was the most wonderful thing that had ever happened in their daughter's life and they would never be able to thank me enough for arranging it. It turned out that as the house lights went down a gentleman came to sit in the spare seat next to their daughter, who could not believe that she was now sat next to Michael Jackson! It would have been churlish to explain that I did not even know he was going to be in for that performance!

The theatre manager for most of the run was Peter Hancock, who was a big part of the success of making Apollo Victoria a very special place to visit It was also where Andrew De Rosa, who was to go on and have a very influential career with the company, cut his teeth as Deputy Manager. In later years I went annually with my son Ben and we would thank the show for the fact that we had a house to live in! It really was the light at the end of the tunnel.

The first sign of our change in fortunes was when Paul and David did the deal to buy the iconic Bristol Hippodrome from Stoll Moss. This was particularly significant as it was Stoll Moss' last provincial theatre and they had sold because they could not make it work financially. Along with Birmingham Hippodrome and Manchester Palace, which we later bought, it was regarded as one of the three most important provincial theatres. In deciding to buy it we were not in the days of massive business plans. The fag packet came out and basically the question to me was could we run it and make at least as much profit as we made from Oxford. That was easy as the answer was yes, the fag packet was put away and we got on with the job. One of the joys of buying a theatre is that you give them a cheque for the purchase and they then give you a cheque to cover the advance monies for future shows. On this occasion we received a third of our purchase price. The buying of Bristol Hippodrome was a massive statement by us and indeed within three years we were making more profit annually than it had cost to buy it.

Bristol was the first of many that Mike Adamson and I worked as a double act. Mike had been managing Manchester Apollo very successfully, was particularly highly regarded by David and was crucial to our expansion. We both agreed that we would not bring in Managers from outside the Company and that we would promote the young talented and enthusiastic Assistant Managers that we were bringing in which makes it all the more surprising that we kept Stoll Moss' manager in situ, which was a big mistake.

We had already started the young manager's process with Tony Docherty taking over as Manager at Oxford whilst Fiona Thomas, Mike's deputy at Manchester Apollo, took over as Manager there. Mike and I had talents and styles that complemented each other in that I would do all the talking and he would do all the hard work! The problems with Bristol Hippodrome were that it was badly programmed and very badly run, which means that there was not a lot going for it! As soon as we took over we got all the staff together and I made a speech about how passionate we were about theatres, and how we regarded each one as an individual jewel to be cherished. I also pointed out that without Apollo there was every chance that the theatre would have closed as there was no other company out there buying theatres. We were not there to make cut backs (not quite true!) but rather to boost the income with a better programme, more aggressive selling and better margins on front of house sales I also stated that I fully understood that if anybody there did not want to work for us, now was the time to leave. Nobody did and we were left with some brilliant people and some who were very definitely not going to buy into the Apollo experience.

My main focus was to improve our income from the shows, which in the main was achieved by getting rid of the drama weeks for which there would be a poor return and replacing them with concert weeks. We had already proved in Oxford that just one concert could give us a better rent than a week of a play. We were delighted to continue to bring the big musicals, opera and ballet weeks although we sharpened up the deals. This was an easy process and the local media were very supportive once they were reassured that we were not going to rename the theatre Bristol Apollo. So my part of the job was easy fronting it up with a smile and reassurances whilst changing the programming, which by now was second nature to me.

Life was much more difficult for Mike as he based himself at the Theatre and set about dramatically improving the management of it. One of his main bones of contention was they always employed the same number of stewards and usherettes for every show regardless of whether we had 1700 or 250 in.

When Mike tried to explain that this was not sustainable he was met by total resistance from both the staff and the Manager. In the end he just gave them a fist of how many we would want in for each performance dependant on the number of tickets sold.

This came to a head when they all walked out on a sell-out matinee Panto performance and went to the pub. If I had been in the theatre at the time I would have persuaded them to come back with a promise to look at a compromise on rotas and a nice speech. Mike took the other route and sacked the lot of them! He was of course right and immediately solved our ongoing problem but it left him with a sold out theatre with no front of house staff. This problem was added to by the staff that had walked out ringing the Licencing Officer to make him aware that we were now in breach of our licence. By the time he arrived unbelievably we were not.

Some fantastic members of the staff who had fully understood the stance had come to our rescue by ringing family and friends to rush in and help. The theatre's Technical Director was John Randall, who was a lovely old style theatre guy and he was massively helpful in getting the crew to make calls and to help front of house.

We also had a great Front of House Manager in Ghannam Hussain and he totally supported Mike's action and played his part in ensuring that we were able to comply with our licensed staffing regulations. At a stroke Mike had changed the whole ethos of Bristol Hippodrome with the manager leaving to be replaced by Tony Docherty and a somewhat reduced but incredibly loyal team to the standard Apollo wanted to achieve.

One of our first Bristol pantos was to star Les Dawson, who was to prove to be one of the sanest, down to earth, nicest of all the comics. He was also a great star and a massive coup for the theatre. I first met him when he arrived to do the press call and by the time he had walked up to the office I was concerned that he was not a well man. My medical intuition was obviously spot on because, sadly, he had to pull out of the panto due to ill health.

Les was obviously impossible to replace and I was concerned when I was told that Gary Wilmot would be taking over. I should not have been. Gary was tremendous, massively talented and with great charisma. He was so superb in the show that nobody who had bought their tickets to see Les asked for their money back – now that is superb! We got on really well and were destined to meet up regularly as he starred in Guys and Dolls on tour having done so in the West End.

Freda and I were invited to his wedding and we became good friends. A few years later he was selected to be the guest of honour at The Variety Club of Great Britain Christmas Lunch at The Grosvenor Hotel in front of 700 guests who were mainly stars of stage and screen. Paul, who was to become Chief Barker and would raise over £11,000,000 for needy children during his year, was in charge of organising these lunches.

He was obviously a very busy man and on this occasion forgot to arrange the tribute speakers. Normally there would be three top stars who would stand up and amusingly fete the star guest. None of this was my business as I had not even been invited! The night before Paul asked me what I was doing the next day and after I had told him I had a budget meeting at The Swindon Wyvern Theatre he told me that he might need me to make a speech at Gary's tribute lunch.

I dismissed this on the assumption that he could get someone more suitable and told him that I would go to Swindon and he could ring me if he needed me. The phone call came and off I went on the train to London. You may have gathered that I am not adverse to standing up and gabbling away but this was different. To be one of the speakers in a room where I would be the only person that I had not heard of was rather daunting.

I knocked together a sincere and vaguely amusing ten minutes worth and arrived at The Grosvenor to find I had not been left a ticket for the reception for top table guests. To make matters worse, Frank, the company manager for Copacabana in which Gary was starring, saw me and asked me if I was speaking and on finding that I was, said "Bloody Hell I told Paul that if he could not get somebody famous at least get somebody important!"

This was going from bad to worse, and at the top table I was sat next to John Sachs the BBC presenter who told me he had been asked to speak four days ago but had obviously declined as that was nowhere near long enough to prepare something. I explained that I had had four hours! The toast master came to see me to explain that when it was my turn to speak he would collect me and seat me by the microphone. When I asked who the other speakers were he said that there were none, it was just me! He then spent the next 20 minutes introducing all the many stars in the room. It seemed to me that all 700 guests were better equipped than me for this task.

I decided to have one glass of wine and then keep a second glass to take with me. When the dreaded moment came I picked my glass of wine up to find that the wax from the candles had gone in it! When I arrived to where I was to sit in advance of my talk I found that Jarvis Astaire had given my seat to Miss India, the current Miss World. Now I fully understand that given the choice of Miss World or Sam Shrouder to sit next to there may be those who would choose Miss World!

Luckily Jarvis Astaire went to the loo so I nicked his seat with the result that I was now sitting next to Miss World; however I was unfortunately somewhat preoccupied! The moment came and I gave it my best and they kindly applauded. Julia Morley, who was Chief Barker, was lovely and I think realised that it was a bit of an ordeal and it was sweet of her to write to me saying "It was absolutely wonderful of you to speak at our Christmas lunch yesterday. Your speech was perfect for the occasion".

Previously I had been a bit concerned as I was due to be the guest speaker at the Mayor of Torbay's Ball. But not anymore, every occasion now that I was required to speak at would seem a doddle compared with 700 stars at the Variety Club Christmas lunch!

As well as Bristol we were now running Scarborough's Futurist Theatre on behalf of the Council. This was partly as a result of our relationship with the legendary promoter Barry Clayman who had in place a deal to present the summer season. Barry and his wife Linda were very much part of the Apollo social scene and were fun to be around. I liked Barry a lot and got on very well with him although obviously not all the time as on one occasion when the office had a swear box (obviously suggested by those who do not swear!) I came down and emptied all the money I had into it following a conversation I had with Barry! But I think he liked me most of the time!

The summer seasons, in the early days, were a joy we would all traipse over to Scarborough with our families for the opening weekend and have lots of fun as well as watching the shows. Scarborough was a popular resort and summer seasons with the likes of Cannon and Ball and Ken Dodd were massively successful. For a number of years Cannon and Ball were the biggest selling comedy act and we always looked after them royally to ensure that they continued to play our theatres. Paul even insisted that we created two star dressing rooms in any of our theatres that they played a season in. They were a joy to deal with but like most double acts they liked their own space. The press always tried to make a story out of this when there was actually no story as they got on great.

I ran into Bobby Ball in a hotel in Glasgow when they were playing The Pavilion and we had a show at The Apollo. He was saying that the press had been on to him to try and make a story out of Tommy staying at a spa hotel with a golf course. He asked the reporter "who is sat at the desk next to you and do you live together?" When the puzzled reporter said no and why do you ask Bobby replied that he was just establishing that if you work with someone you do not have to live with them! End of story!

For one summer season Paul and Barry said that they had booked Joe Longthorne to top the bill with Dana second on the bill. I was shocked by this as I had never heard of Joe Longthorne, although I obviously pretended that I had, and also I was very fond of Dana and thought that she should be top of the bill.. When I sat watching the opening night Joe was sensational and I was absolutely mesmerised as his Tom Jones/Shirley Bassey duet brought the house down but his Barnsley Elvis meeting lots of stars was pure comic genius. Dana was great, as always but there was no doubting who the star was. We saw a lot of Rosemary (Dana) and her lovely husband Damian as she played many of our theatres in Snow White including a season at The Phoenix Theatre.

In Scarborough we all went together with children in tow to the funfair where their daughter Grace insisted that I went on the high wheel which I was terrified of but could not refuse. My favourite memory with Rosemary and Damien was going to the Chinese Opium Den at the bottom of George St, where The Oxford Apollo (it had been the New Theatre, became The Apollo and then after 20 years as The Apollo was changed back to The New Theatre by some Americans – I may have mentioned this before!) was. She was starring in Snow White and Freda and I went out for dinner with them after the show.

At about midnight they started some very loud Chinese Karaoke. When Damien asked the waiter if it could be a little quieter as we wanted to chat he was told that everybody wanted his wife to sing a song. Rosemary said she would but only if one of us would join her. Damien and Freda quickly declined so it was left to me to form the double act. I was allowed to choose the song and so it came about that for my first ever experience of karaoke I sang Green Green Grass of Home with a Eurovision Song Contest Winner! I am not sure why but she never asked me to sing with her again!

The Opium Den was also the scene of another interesting celebrity meal. This particular year Oxford Panto was produced by Freddie "Parrot Face" Davies, who got the date on the back of being able to bring Norman Wisdom as its star. I was thrilled that we had got Norman who was undoubtedly one of the finest comic talents of all time. Norman was obviously determined to give value for money with the result that the first dress reversal ran for four hours! Bearing in mind that the ideal panto running time is two and a quarter hours, Freddie obviously needed to instigate some considerable cuts.

The problem was that as Norman completely dominated the show it was him that would have to be cut. He was not impressed by this suggestion on the basis that the audience were coming to see him. Second on the bill was Dino Shafeek (Best known as the Char Wallah in It Ain't Half that Mum) and he had become a friend of mine following a summer season in Scarborough, when we went out for a curry a few times. His role had already been cut to the bone with only two gags, both of which needed Norman to provide the feed and which Norman normally got wrong! So there was no other option for Freddie but to insist that Norman lost some of his beloved act. He did brilliantly to get it down to three hours of pure Norman.

He was, of course, fantastic and it was a privilege to spend time in his company. As always with the stars of the Panto I invited Norman and his girlfriend out to dinner. We sat in his dressing room as he explained that they only both ate curry and drank cider and in those circumstances would it not be a good idea to get a takeaway and have it in the dressing room. When I insisted that I would take him to a restaurant that did curry and sold cider he explained that he was very anxious not to be recognised and would I ensure that the restaurant was aware of this and that they found us a secluded table.

This proved quite difficult as the manager of The Opium Den had never heard of him and had not a clue what I was talking about. Eventually I got him to understand that he was a big star from the theatre and we needed a quiet table. I should have known better! As we entered The Opium Den, Norman's jacket went off his shoulders, his cap went at right angles and he enquired if Mr Grimsdale was the manager! He would of course have been devastated if he had gone to a quiet table with no fuss and not being recognised. The fragile ego of those we worship – Bring back Dana!

As well as adding theatres we were also losing them and in some ways 1985 was a dark year with us closing both Glasgow Apollo and Coventry Apollo within a fortnight in June. Although it was very sad to lose Glasgow, the deal with the Council had always been for them to support us until the Scottish Exhibition Centre opened. This was achieved and the dilapidated Glasgow Apollo was sold and reduced to being a Car Park. Fallus Simpson had gone up there to manage the closure, which was a heart-breaking and impossible job with stuff disappearing all over the place.

Our last show was Style Council so I ended with the pleasure of a bit of "banter" with John Weller re: our brochure and merchandising commission – so nothing changed there. After its closure BBC Scotland did an hour long tribute to the legendary rock gig. Fallus featured heavily with Alvin Stardust narrating. The final shot was of Fallus handing the key to Alvin to lock the building up for the last time. All very emotional.

I also featured in the film having gone to a suite in the London Hilton which BBC Scotland had hired and waited with others for the opportunity to be filmed telling our Glasgow Apollo stories. I was in good company as I sat with Phil Collins, Noddy Holder, John Cooper Clarke and Rick Parfitt and Francis Rossi. Once again I was in a room where I was the only person that I had never heard of!

The Status Quo boys enjoyed recounting how the balcony moved over a foot when they played – if you had been paying attention you will remember that it was five and a half inches of movement and if it had reached six inches the venue would have been closed. Still I reckon that you should never let the facts spoil a great story!

Fallus had been a star leading the Apollo through the desperate time and it was agreed that he should go to the somewhat more relaxing task of managing Scarborough Futurist. Paul also decided, quite rightly, that he should be offered a holiday at anywhere of his choosing as a thank you. Fallus, by this time, was suffering the first stages of Parkinson's but he did not allow this to reduce his enjoyment of Thailand!

On his return all he could focus on was his next visit after which he came back to say that he wanted to go out there to live as soon as possible. We were all delighted for him if slightly envious of the 24 year old lady he had met! Paul and David sorted everything out for him in double quick time, with Paul booking his flights and sorting out the supply of medication he needed, whilst David sorted out his pension. It really was another example of what great people they were to work with. The climate in Thailand helped his Parkinson's and he had a fabulous few years living there with his lady friend before his illness meant that he had to return.

Whilst I was very sad over the inevitable closure of Glasgow, I was completely devastated by the closure of Coventry Apollo. The Council were unable to give us a £40,000 guarantee against loss, although at the same time they had given a £950,000 grant to The Belgrade Theatre. The staff there were fabulous and many had worked for over 25 years at the theatre. We had even taken to laying staff off in the quiet summer months and they understood that it was our attempt to keep it open.

I had been in the theatre a few weeks earlier when Phil McIntyre promoted King with a capacity audience (and 44 seats wrecked!) After the show I was chatting to their vocalist Paul King and he stated that Coventry had been the best gig of the tour, which only made its imminent closure even worse. The last show was Barbara Dickson and I went backstage to say hello and to make sure that she was aware that she would be the last act ever to appear here – which she was.

Needless to say the theatre was full to the rafters and after she had done two encores Barbara came back on stage to say how sad she was that a theatre with the Apollo history was to close. She said that she had been looking at a list of the many great stars that had appeared there and she noted that Gracie Fields had played it so she was going to close with "Sing as you go".

I stood at the top of the stairs going into the balcony and I just sobbed. I felt personally responsible for the great team who worked there, losing their jobs and that this historic theatre that had been entrusted to me, I had failed it. The theatre was sold to Granada for Bingo (well at least better than a car park!) and I was determined that I would do whatever necessary to ensure that no other theatre that I was responsible for would ever again be closed.

I worked on the basis that as long as they were making money Paul would never let them be closed. The target was almost achieved but many years later The Davenport in Stockport was sold despite being profitable when we had a big bid for it from Stockport Grammar School. This provoked quite a fiery boardroom discussion with David insisting that the offer was far too good to turn down, which in business terms was correct, whilst I fought the battle on the basis that it would be dreadful for our reputation of taking on more and more theatres if we were to close it.

Paul managed to reach a compromise between the two of us by doing a deal to sell it to the Grammar School with an agreement that we could run it for two more years. I worked on the basis that whilst there was life there was hope – two years later it closed!

Chapter 13

MORE THEATRES AND MEETING HER MAJESTY

In my role of Operations Director my life changed dramatically with the acquisition of Hutchinson Leisure bringing more than 60 extra venues under my control. The Company had been founded and run by Alan Hutchinson, who, along with his wife Dorothy, had become friends of Paul's via going to Cinema Industry Balls and Events. Alan had sadly died and Dorothy, along with her daughter Gillian and husband Chris, had turned to Paul for help.

So it was that this mass of Cinemas, Bingo Halls, Hotels, Llandudno Astra Theatre and Moorehouses Brewery ended up in our lap. I was obviously particularly delighted to see that the St Helens Hippodrome Bingo Hall was one of them! David was a bit of a spoil sport by quite wisely selling the award-winning brewery as quickly as possible. As I was always very hands-on I set out to tour the new empire.

Keith Wells and David were doing the same and we would normally end up in one of the Company's hotels – The Midland Morecambe, The Sparrow Hawk Burnley, The Clarence, Landudno, Prince of Wales Caernarfon and The Rhos Abbey Hotel. When we ended up together, we worked, drank beer, played pool and discussed all the venues – normally in that order. Alan Hutchinson had amassed this incredible combination of venues, whilst being very penny-pinching in how they were run and it was inevitable that the exercise of which to keep and spend money on and which to sell was in David and Keith's mind from the outset.

On our nights on tour we were often joined by Chris Eddlestone, Gillian's husband, who was a lawyer by trade and extremely humorous company. Julian Harper would also be a very welcome addition from time to time.

Having The Llandudno Astra Theatre was a bonus and it was another of our theatres that housed a Welsh National Opera season. It was also where I saw The Smiths walk off after Morrissey was hit with a coin. Luckily they did return which helped avoid a riot. I also remember going backstage to see Elkie Brookes after a show and she was justifiably not very happy with the state of the theatre. I could have blamed the person that booked her there, but that would not have helped as it was me!

The cinemas were the area that I was most comfortable with and we were able to make dramatic improvements to those we wished to keep. This included a blitz on housekeeping and lots of Keith Wells' paint! We were to go on and build a number of new cinemas and to create a very successful chain, which in later years was overseen by John Merryweather, a nice guy steeped in Cinema experience.

The hotels were somewhat different as we were guilty of the "as we stay in them we know how to run them" mantra. This is always a dangerous concept. We even added another one when we purchased The Lion and Swan in Congleton. Jim Kaye who managed the Clarence in Llandudno was put in charge of all of them and he vaguely knew what he was doing which was an improvement on the rest of us.

I was always receiving complaints about the quality of food at Morecambe Midland Hotel and then suddenly we got a new chef and it all changed with letters now arriving extolling the virtues of the high standard cuisine. I rang Jim to say that whatever else he did he must make sure that we keep the Chef. If he needed more money then give it him but do not even think of ringing me to say that he has left.

The following Monday on our weekly phone call to go through the figures Jim added that he had a bit of bad news to which I responded that as long as it was not about Morecambe's Chef I am sure that we could handle it. When he told me that it was about the Chef and that he had left I went ballistic. Jim kept trying to intercede with a "it's not my fault" but he got very short shrift as I pointed out that of course it was his fault, he was in charge and I had specifically instructed him to make sure that we kept the chef. Obviously I had been wasting my breath. Eventually when he could get a word in edgeways Jim explained that the police had arrived and arrested the chef as he was wanted for murder! Poor Jim was also responsible for the Llandudno Winter Gardens Nite Club and in a similar scenario, we at last had a manager who could control a very rough environment and make it a success. Jim had to ring me that we had lost the manager as he had been caught pushing a wheelbarrow up a hill with the safe in it!

My favourite of the Hutchinson team was Ken Shepperson who seemed to be involved in everything but was specifically in charge of the Bingo Halls. Despite my outstanding career as a bingo caller this was an area in which we were most exposed, particularly with the strictness of the Gaming Board. Indeed Ken had experienced this when he had been arrested for advertising Bingo on the back of a lorry during his days with Star Bingo.

Ken was a lovely guy, and a great character and he humoured me into thinking that I was having some sort of influence whilst he continued to run them all in his own way! He would also point me in the right direction with the other divisions. Ken was a great showman and in his early days he had regularly got stars to make personal appearances and this had included Sonny Liston, the World Heavyweight Champion who he picked up at Manchester Airport and took to the Burnley Bingo Hall to present a cheque for £8000, an enormous amount in those days.

I tried to show enthusiasm for being in the Bingo Halls but one Friday night I was in our Newcastle under Lyne hall with 38 punters, when a customer who noticed my very sartorially elegant red jacket shouted, "Hey you from Butlins, come over here"! Once I had followed her command she berated me that somebody who had only just joined had won the jackpot and would I explain how that was possible.

As I explained that it was possible as she had just bought the right ticket card, but this got me nowhere and I decided there and then that in future I would spend my evenings in our theatres! In many of our halls it was an uphill struggle, no more so that in Leyland. When the National Game with winnings of up to £75,000 was introduced I said to all the punters that this was very exciting and they should all play because one of them might win. This was met with derision with them telling me that nobody from Leyland was every going to win and all the money would go to them down South.

It was obviously with great joy that I returned to Leyland after one of the punters, whilst playing for a full house of £6.50, won the National Game and added over £44,000 to her winnings. I did not really get the response that I had hoped for as they all said they would not play it now because Leyland was never going to win it twice! To make matters worse the lady that did win stopped coming as she was enjoying her winnings. So the only result of winning the National Game was that we had one less customer.

When Ken did retire after 53 years in entertainment, one of his best memories was being invited by Paul Gregg to The Dorchester for Russ Abbott's Tribute Lunch. At one point a massive cake was wheeled into the room and the Rolly Polly's jumped out. I am sure that he was right but I would not know as I wasn't invited! Ken was replaced by Julian Cotterill, who was excellent and with whom I always got on very well. But for me nobody could replace good old Ken.

In my life away from work, the most important event of my life took place on October 11th 1985 when Freda gave birth to my son, Benjamin. If anybody had told me then how much joy he would bring into my life I would never have believed them. When I talk of being lucky this was my biggest stroke of luck of all. Freda had chosen to give birth in Wroughton Military Hospital and when she needed to go in, not surprisingly I was not around as I was, of course, attending important show business meetings in London.

Because of my absence, Freda was taken in by our RAF friend Stef in his uniform; with the result that all the staff were convinced that he was the father and it took me sometime to persuade them otherwise! We were also lucky in that we had willing babysitters in Andrea and Stephanie as long as we were back by 8.30pm for them to go out!

When Ben was five months old Paul decided that I looked a bit weary and the next thing I knew he had booked a ten day holiday in Barbados for the three of us. That in itself was incredibly kind and generous but being Paul there was even more in the planning. He told me that the all-inclusive hotel and the flights were paid for but I would have to buy my own tickets for West Indies v England! This was the quality of Paul that he should do all this for us whilst making sure that it tied in with cricket. Kevin Hayes arranged our tickets with Lancashire's legendary spinner Jack Simmons who came over to The Heywoods Hotel to deliver them. With Ben at five months being quite a handful, it was agreed I would go every other day for the five days. This resulted in me seeing one day of cricket as England had lost by lunch on the third day!

As well as the other things Apollo did we also promoted some touring dates. These were run by a great character called Michael Rouse, who always seemed like a bit of an aristocrat to me. He was also very kind to me and when we had two shows on the same day it was often me who would be the tour manager for the other one.

These included Billy Connolly in Birmingham and he was so easy to get on with that it was a piece of cake and Freddie Starr at the Southport Theatre. The Director of Tourism for Southport was Phil King and he had an excellent system in that once the show went up, he would go to the bar, ask for his bottle of wine and the Promoters bottle of wine and we would go to his office, happily drink our bottles whilst ignoring everything else that was going on.

It was quite clever from his part in that when the settlement arrived I just signed it without checking! If I ended up in one of our theatres when Michael Rouse was tour managing one of our shows, he would be highly entertaining. I remember spending an hour or more having a drink with him and the American star Jack Jones as they told story after story including how they once rented a helicopter to take some girls out – as one does!

He was obviously a real ladies' man as when we had Hot Chocolate, Errol Brown told me that he and Michael were the two greatest at pulling ladies. Michael also liked a drink and could be quite outrageous at the wonderful Managers Christmas Dinners that Paul would meticulously plan. I would find this quite amusing but I think that I was in the minority!

At this stage in Apollo's life David and I used to sit down with every single manager to do their budgets and the manager would be required to sign them off as achievable. These could be quite feisty meetings with David wanting to achieve the highest budget possible whilst I liked a little bit of room to cover unforeseen circumstances. I also worked on the basis that if we budgeted a profit of £70,000 and achieved £60,000 we had failed whilst if the budget was £50,000 we would be a roaring success!

I would prime the managers in advance and I would ensure that they were sat near enough for me to kick them if they got carried away. These sessions were hard work often starting at 8.00 am in one of the hotels and churning our budgets for the next twelve hours. So it was no wonder that both David and I got a bit tetchy or worse. On one occasion we were doing the Bangor Bingo budget and we both completely lost it. The argument was over whether we would get 1000 admissions or 1100 with him stating that both the manager and I must be useless at our job as we were not budgeting for any improvements. The shouting match went along the lines of me saying that if David could get 1100 admissions then he better run the venues and I would do the adding up, whilst he went down the route that he probably should but on these figures he was not sure that I could add up! The poor manager was shell shocked and left without any budget being agreed! If only somebody had suggested 1050 admissions

I also remember an irate David ringing me one evening when I was in a theatre, saying whatever you are doing stop it and turn on the TV. On doing so I watched a hilarious programme with an up-and-coming comedy star as a Bingo Manager in a very badly run Hall. The good news was that it starred Peter Kay, but the bad news was that it was filmed in our Blackpool Apollo Bingo Hall with all the inept staff in the film wearing our Apollo uniform.

I shared David's view that this was not showing us in a very good light, but secretly hoping that we had received a very large facility fee. When I contacted the manager he explained that he had not thought of asking for a fee and just thought that it would be great for the venue and that there is no such thing as bad publicity, which has to be one of the stupidest quotes of all time.

Obviously I have a story for every occasion and I told him about when the multi-talented Marti Caine had done a panto press call at Oxford Apollo (which – you know the rest!) I had gone down to meet her and really liked her, sat her down with the press and left her to tell them what a great panto we had in store. Unfortunately her first question from a Sun journalist was about her being made to sign a form for Equity stating that she would not return to South Africa's Sun City while apartheid existed. She replied along the lines that she could easily rip it up and that animals only lived with their own and it got worse! By the time I realised that there was something wrong there was no stopping her and she had given The Sun its front page headline for the next day.

The result was devastating, parties started cancelling their bookings, the Bishop of Oxford asked the people of the area to boycott the show and the Oxford Anti-Apartheid Group said they would picket the show. I discussed with Barrie Stead who ran our Panto Division whether we should sack her and both agreed that we should. However she was so apologetic, charming and upset by what had happened that she drove down to Oxford, called on the Bishop and had him eating out of her hand and withdrawing his boycott request. Then I joined her in a meeting with the Anti-Apartheid Group. They explained about how life was in South Africa and by the end she was promising to go to one of their meetings to learn more. So we kept her in the show in which she was magnificent, an absolute joy to have in the theatre and the business was down by 25%! Which is a long way of saying that I am not the right person to be quoted "That there is no such thing as bad publicity" to! I think that the Manager of the Blackpool Bingo Hall understood that after we had chatted. On the other side Phil McIntyre and Paul Roberts brought us loads of Peter Kay dates.

David and I had many arguments over the years but they were never personal and never stopped us having a drink together at the end of the evening. I had tremendous admiration for David and learnt a lot from him. He was also a great mate and we even played in the same football team, Shipton under Wychwood, for a few years. As you might guess David was a sweaty, hardworking, tough tackling midfielder and I was a goal scorer!

Because Apollo was such a sociable Company I was also able to get to know David's wife Julie and his two children Katie and Philip. The year 1985 was memorable for a number of reasons but one of the best was when a young lady called Mrs N. Wilson joined our team at The Boars Hill office as a clerk/typist, having been appointed by Hilary on the princely salary of £4,500 per annum. There were a number of dramas in the early days as she went about not being Mrs N Wilson anymore! She was also a very quick learner and very bright and after numerous promotions became Head of Theatre Programming when Hilary left. She went on to marry the lovely Doug and became Nicky Monk.

She was to go on to become the top and finest Theatre Booker in the country. We always had a great relationship as we worked very closely on the diaries to ensure that we got the best product on the best deals. We also became close friends along with Doug and their daughter Lizzie. There is no doubt that much of the success of The Apollo Theatres was down to Nicky and her team who worked in the Theatre Bookings Department.

Many years later when we had bought a third of London's Dominion Theatre and had a management contract, I had the privilege to meet up with the owner of the other two thirds, the legendary American producer and theatre owner Jimmy Nederlander. When Jimmy introduced me to other members of his team he would just say "This is Sam the booker" at least that is what I think that he said!

At the time I was Chief Executive of the Apollo Theatres and I somewhat lamely corrected Jimmy on a couple of occasions but this was to no avail and I have been The Booker ever since to Jimmy. Later Jerry Katzman an American Lawyer, who is in charge of Jimmy's UK Theatres, explained that in America, The Booker was king and far more important than any old Chief

Executive. Maybe America had it right (You will not read that many times in this book!) and if that is the case Nicky was the star of the operation.

The skill of getting shows for all the theatres increased as we added new ones. With the demise of Glasgow Apollo we had desperately wanted to add a Scottish venue and Edinburgh Playhouse was the obvious one. We had put a bid in when the Council first decided to sell it and although ours was the highest bid and we were the most experienced theatre operator to be interested in it, we still did not get it. I think that this was on the basis that we were an English company.

Scottish businessman Norman Springford and promoter Graham Pullen operated it and then contacted us to offer it for sale. The deal was more protracted than normal with the result that Mike and I would keep going in to the theatre only to be kicked out as the deal was still not concluded. So we would pop in to say hello to Russ Abbott, who was starring in a ten-day run of his revue, and then return to the hotel and prop up the bar, something at which we were both quite talented.

Eventually after we had been In Edinburgh for four or five days we were allowed in and the fabulous Edinburgh Playhouse was ours. Whilst we had been trying to get the theatre we were regularly contacted by a Scottish manager called Gerry Tait, who was very supportive of our efforts. Gerry was a top theatre operator as well as being a fantastic bloke. He became the manager of the Playhouse, went on to be a Divisional Director, Director of Southport Football Club and a close friend. Mike did his usual and stayed in Edinburgh until he had got the theatre running in the style that we wanted. Under Gerry's guidance the theatre was a massive success and a very important addition to Apollo.

Quite early on in our tenure of Edinburgh Playhouse we were involved in The Commonwealth Games when we hosted the weight lifting. You may remember these were the Games that were savaged by withdrawals following New Zealand's decision to play rugby against South Africa during apartheid. As a result of this they would have gone bankrupt had it not have been for that wonderful man of the people, Robert Maxwell, through his Daily Mirror, promising to save The Games by paying its debts. You will be shocked to know that it did not quite work like that with a paltry sum being offered after the Games with a take it or leave it proviso!

In my busy life of show business glamour I had no intention of visiting Edinburgh Playhouse to watch people lift up weights until I was sent there to represent Apollo for The Queens visit. The system for visits from Royalty was that Paul chose the ones he wanted to do and then I was next in line. This resulted in me meeting Princess Margaret on 15 occasions (it may have been less but it seemed like 15 times!) whilst Paul seemed to spend his whole life meeting Princess Diana!

I was particularly pleased to have this opportunity to meet the Queen for the first time as I was somewhat vainly hoping to get a full set of the Royal Family meetings with photos to prove it! So I arrived at the theatre in my best suit (also my only suit) with a camera that was to be entrusted with my good friend Gerry Tait to ensure that the all-important photo was taken. There were five of us in the Royal line up and I was stood next to the head of Commonwealth weight lifting. When I suggested that Her Majesty would not be stopping very long to watch the weight lifting I was quickly informed that she was very keen on weight lifting and at the last Games had thrown her whole schedule out by staying 2 hours! The great moment arrived and she went down the line shaking hands with each of us without saying a word. She then went to her balcony seat, put her glasses on and leaned over to watch the proceedings with great interest. She then noticed some muscle bound guys who were in the audience but were up for the Highland Games. Word was sent that the Queen would like to meet them and so the second line up of the day was formed with her chatting merrily to them for 20 minutes.

None of this mattered as I had my photo with Her Majesty enabling me to tick off the Queen on my Royal list, or so I thought. Gerry had insisted that he had a great shot of us shaking hands and he probably would have had if there had not been somebody standing between us resulting in me not appearing on the photo!

As the years went by I managed more or less a full set of Royals, with the notable exception of the Queen. This all changed in 1999 when I was contacted by her Private Secretary, Mary Francis, to arrange for Her Majesty to visit our Lyceum Theatre to meet our staff and the members of the cast of the National Theatre's production of Oklahoma produced by Cameron Macintosh. The visit was a PR exercise overseen by Dickie Arbiter who had been brought in to improve her profile following the death of Princess Diana.

The Queen spent the whole morning with us before returning with Prince Philip to see the show at night. As we took her round, Dickie did not miss a photo opportunity with such things as Ma'am a photo with the popcorn machine would be really good! She was an absolute joy throughout the visit and when she visited the box office Dickie said it would be a good photo opportunity for her to hold her two tickets for the night performance. Tickets in hand she turned to me and said "if I do not come does this mean that I get a refund!" She also captivated the cast and production team with her interest and questions about the show. It was a most enjoyable visit for all involved and I got my photo which now has pride of place in our downstairs loo!

Chapter 14

THE LOVELY LIVERPOOL EMPIRE

I was delighted when I realised that we were also to take over The Liverpool Empire. This was a very special theatre to me having been taken there by my Dad to see Frank Ifield and Helen Shapiro and also to see one of his favourite acts – The Clancy Brothers.

The Empire was owned by the Council and run by a Trust that included Sir Philip Carter, who had a massive football influence on both Everton and the then Football League, and Terry Smith who was head of Radio City. They had contacted us as they had financial problems in the operating of the theatre but the final say on its future lay within the hands of the Council.

At the time Derek Hatton was the leader of the Council and there was a concern that politically they may want to close it. A close colleague of Derek Hatton, Keva Coombes was the person that we had to deal with as he had the final word on its future. We went up for a morning meeting and came to an agreement with The Trust for us to manage the theatre, but we were not very hopeful as members of The Trust kept saying that whilst they were happy with the deal they did not expect Keva to agree to it.

After arriving three hours late for the meeting he agreed to everything, much to the Trust's surprise and within a very short time had left the building. There was no subsidy included in the deal so it would have been hard to argue against our involvement as the alternative would have been to put the chains on it. I was absolutely thrilled to add this wonderful and historic theatre to the Apollo circuit and it is fair to say that we did it proud as it did us. Angela Hinchliffe, who had managed Scarborough and Coventry, took over as manager and Mike did his usual in getting the theatre to work

144

in the style we worked. They had a great team of staff there already and they could not have been more welcoming in the knowledge that we loved the Liverpool Empire as much as they did.

Being asked, which was my favourite theatre was a bit like being asked which of your children you loved most. I loved all the theatres and concert venues and they were all special in their own way but if I had to choose one, it was Liverpool Empire. It was my home gig and a large and very beautiful theatre.

I am sure this opinion would be shared by Britain's most prolific producer Bill Kenwright. I was acutely aware that we would have no theatres if it was not for incredibly creative producers touring great shows. Bill was the top of the list and of course Liverpool was also his home gig. His Mum, Hope, used to always come to his shows at the Empire and he always worked on the basis that nothing but the best was good enough for her.

When he decided to tour Blood Brothers he filled loads of dates in our theatres but would not go to the show's home because it had to be at its best before he and Willie Russell would allow it to come to Liverpool. When it eventually did I watched every second from the back of the stalls and also watched Bill and Willie walking backwards and forwards ignoring each other. It was a magical night as the Liverpool audience joined in with most of the songs and then at the end gave it a ten minute standing ovation whilst Bill and Willie hugged.

All provincial theatres, not only just ours, would have been much poorer places without the phenomenal output of shows from Bill. On top of that he was an absolute joy to spend time with and in my case football was always the number one topic when I visited his office. He was a proper fan of Everton and always revered the old players and in particular Dave Hickson, the legendary Everton centre forward My friend Brian Dixon used to bring Dave to Southport from time to time and he would always talk about how good Bill was to him. As the foreign money poured into football, Everton fans should have been thrilled to have a Chairman, who had supported them man and boy and was as big a fan as anybody on the terraces. When I left the American Owner of Clear Channel, Bill along with Jim Davidson kindly offered to say a few words at my leaving do. When everybody had gone home I sifted through the incredibly kind words that many people had written and I came across a wonderful letter from Bill.

BILL KENWRIGHT LTD.

BKL HOUSE
106 HARROW ROAD, LONDON W2 1RR
TELEPHONE: 020 7 446 6200 FACSIMILE: 020 7 446 6
e-mail: info@kenwright.com

Sam Shrouder
Chairman
Clear Channel Entertainment
35/36 Grosvenor Street
London
W1K 4QX

28th November 2002

Dear Young Sam

So I thought to myself...

After all those years of support and friendship Sam is departing to that wonderful playing field by the sea in the North West. What then could I give him that shows how much his friendship and support have meant to this company over the years?

I thought – "Wayne Rooney".

But then I decided that that was a little bit over-the-top.

And then I thought to myself that during the time Sam and I have been friends, I have only ever asked for one autograph. And if I passed my prize possession on to Sam, then he would be able to carry it with him all the way to his beloved Wembley with his beloved Southport. (I mean Cardiff!!!).

So as Wayne said to Bill – Sam, this "one's on me!" In the absolute knowledge that your departure from Clear Channel will only be another road on our personal friendship, and your friendship with this company.

Thank you for the dates, the support, the understanding, the laughs – but most of all the joy of working with a man of honour.

Yours ever

Bill

DIRECTOR: W. KENWRIGHT
REGISTERED OFFICE 843a FINCHLEY ROAD, LONDON NW11
REGISTERED NO. 1820115 VAT REG NO. 235 7951 39
MEMBER OF THE SOCIETY OF LONDON THEATRE

Lovely letter from Bill Kenwright

146

As I read it the odd tear fell – I was of course drunk and emotional! But that was the quality of one of the greatest producers of all time.

Bill's main man was Rod Caton and he was one of my closest friends in the business. We lunched once a month at Kettners, had the same meal and drinks and sorted out all the deals and still had time to put the world right! Rod was a special and very loyal friend.

One of the joys of Liverpool Empire was that I was able to invite the Southport players and their partners to a show every year. This worked well with usually nine or ten players coming along with their ladies. On one occasion one of them felt inclined to make a speech and his subsequent career would suggest that he was better at talking than playing football so thank you John Bishop!

One year it changed dramatically when our Southport manager, Ronnie Moore insisted that all the players must attend and he then chose the show which was one of Bill Kenwright's Elvis' Shows. This show had the incredible moment when completely unbilled P J Proby walked on stage and sang "Somewhere" – one of those theatre moments that you never forget. Great though the show was it was probably not the right one for our teenage players, most of whom had never been in a theatre in their life. Our 18-year-old midfielder came to shake my hand at the interval to thank me, but was somewhat taken back to find that it was not the end and we had the second half to come. His final words to me were "Was there ever anybody called Elvis?"!

There were many great nights at Liverpool Empire including a visit from the Queen when we reopened it after a major refurbishment to enable us to house Les Miserables. However, easily the most emotional was the Hillsborough Disaster fund raising show. I was slightly concerned what Evertonian Freddie Starr might say when he closed the first half but he was both brilliant and sensitive. The biggest problem was getting someone to close the show as they would have to follow Gerry and the Pacemakers whose set would finish with "You'll Never Walk Alone". In the end Stan Boardman volunteered and did a fabulous spot, which was followed by the whole cast and audience joining together for "You'll Never Walk Alone".

Somebody once said that Liverpool do grief better than anyone. I think that they were mocking but they were spot on and we were proud of it and this show was the perfect example raising money and profile for the victims' families.

Apollo was a very lean company with a very few middle management and all of us chipping in to make different areas work. One of my jobs was to negotiate the deals for ice cream, house programmes and drinks. I performed those tasks with great zeal being fully aware of the impact that they would have on the venues' bottom line. The ice cream deal was typical of the unethical way I went about getting the best result for the Company. We started with Walls and then changed to Lyons when I got them to agree to a sharper deal. The deals were annual and every year I would go back to Walls to see if I could get an even better deal but they would just say that my deal with Lyons was ridiculous and they would be losing money if they sold to us at those prices. So for a number of years I would go back to Lyons and lie that I had received a very competitive quote from Walls and that they would have to sharpen up their quote if they wanted to keep the business. This they did for three years until they, like, Walls refused to quote. However, a saviour was at hand in the form of Lewis Ice Cream from Morecambe.

They were represented by an entrepreneur called George Basnett, who had invested in them. George was involved with Crewe Alexandra Football Club and was a lovely guy, whom I always enjoyed meeting. We would talk football and then he would agree to sell us ice cream at a price even cheaper than Lyons. There was an added bonus in that with Walls and Lyons our patrons could compare our prices somewhat unfavourably with their local shop. However, with Lewis there was no such comparison and I was able to justify our prices as we were selling an International Award Winning Ice Cream – we obviously were not but it sounded plausible!

Having reread this part I realise that it does not show me up in a very good light, indeed unethical might even be a kind description. My only justification was that I was desperate to keep the theatres open and obviously got a bit carried away and anyway it was all done with a smile!

For the brewery deal I negotiated for many years with Stephen Spencer-Jones at Courage and he always came up with a quote that kept the business. I was very fond of Steve and to this day we still meet for a game of golf and a chat. He was a sporting nut. Both he and his father Pat were MCC members and they hosted my first visit to Lords.

I had been invited previously by one of our suppliers but it had poured down all day and I only made it to their hospitality suite in the hotel opposite. I was the only guest who turned up for the start and was therefore in the company of their cricketing celebrity who had been brought in to mingle with us. So he and I stood together forlornly watching the TV advocate that there was unlikely to be any play today when they described a new system to evaluate who were the best players in the world. I was even more interested when they announced that currently the greatest batsman in the world was Dilip Vengsarkar of India. The player next to me was probably marginally more interested as he was indeed Dilip Vengsarkar! When I asked what he was doing over here he explained that he was playing for Hanging Heaton in the Bradford League as one does when you are the best player in the world!

With Apollo's growth both with more theatres and the Hutchinson venues the need to bring in young enthusiastic Assistant Managers became even more crucial. To achieve this I had a tried and trusted formula which commenced with an advert in The Guardian. We would get in the region of 300 applications, which Gill would reduce to about 50 from which I would pick 15 to interview in the knowledge that I normally had two vacancies.

The system was not fool proof as on one occasion Gill queried why I was not going to interview some guy from Crewe who had applied on red note paper. Gill worked on the basis that as nobody else had ever applied on red paper that he must be a bit of a character and as such would fit in with our style of management. Had I not heeded her wise thoughts we would have failed to employ somebody who was to end up the most important person in the whole of the European music industry as Head of Live Nation Europe!

As well as that Paul Latham played a crucial part in Apollo's history as he maximised the potential of a number of our most important theatres and Arenas. He was great fun to work with and a great advert for job applications on red paper (possibly in the current bizarre world of HR Departments not a good idea for those seeking future employment).

My interviewing style was probably not out of the text books, I would allocate 15 mins per person and would normally make my mind up within a couple of minutes. Sometimes one answer would ensure that they would not be offered a job and in that case I would stop the interview there and then and tell them whilst explaining the reason. I would normally start by asking why they wanted the job and one applicant answered that he saw it as a stepping stone to a career in the Arts. Wrong answer and end of interview after 30 seconds as I only wanted people whose ambition was to build a career with us and nobody was going to use Apollo as a stepping stone!

I did not care what qualifications people had or what they had done unless it was in the entertainment industry. I just wanted young, sparky, hardworking ambitious people. Our track record would also show that, unlike the theatre industry in general, we employed as many females managers as male. I also worked on the basis that I only employed people that I liked. Strangely the system worked and we probably put together the finest group of managers the theatre industry had ever encountered, which sounds a bit over the top and probably is

Not all of those interviewed saw my style in quite the same light! Andy Lyst, who went on to be a top manager at Edinburgh Playhouse recalled his interview in slightly different terms when he kindly wrote a few words to be included in a book put together by Nicky Monk to mark my departure from the joys of Clear Channel. He wrote -

"I suppose the beginning was way back in July 1986, when answering an ad in the Guardian for "young, enthusiastic Assistant Managers", I was confronted with what I perceived to be a rather over-enthusiastic maniac conducting an interview in the Board Room at The Apollo Theatre Oxford.

However I was soon caught up in this man's love of the business and came out with the promise of a second interview realizing that for over half an hour I'd been listening to him enthuse, and that he still knew nothing about me!! I shrugged this off expecting to be probed deeper at the second interview.

I duly received an invite from Sam's secretary for said interview and trekked back to Oxford about two weeks later. Once again I sat in the Board Room listening to Sam regale many humorous stories about the industry, when suddenly after about 10 mins he stopped abruptly and asked "Haven't I seen you before?"

"Yes about a week ago" I replied, "this is my second interview". After a quick shuffling of papers I was asked if I'd rather work in Oxford or Edinburgh, and within the week I found myself in Edinburgh commencing my career with Apollo at Maddison's Night Club."

Another top manager who survived the Shrouder interviewing technique was Debbie Garrick, who applied for a management job whilst operating the Manchester Apollo bar under guidance of Paul Latham. I was in the theatre for a Tom Jones concert and after a brief conversation Debbie was appointed Assistant Manager at Edinburgh Playhouse. It might all seem a bit haphazard but it worked.

In this case Debbie went on to be one of Apollo's top managers as she went on to be General Manager of The Lyceum, the West End's top theatre, before doing a magnificent job in having a Mike Adamson type approach when we took over Sunderland Empire and getting it to both run in the Apollo way and making it profitable.

Other superb managers, who worked their way up included Lisa Chu, who started as an usherette at Liverpool Empire and went on to manage it as well as the Southport Theatre, David Pearson who went on to manage The Dominion, Jackie Hinde who did a great job managing Liverpool Empire; Cormac Rennick who went on to manage The Dublin Point; James Howarth at Birmingham Alexandra and Rachel Miller who managed Manchester Palace and Manchester Opera House at the same time! It is impossible to do justice to all the young managers who played their part in making Apollo the success story that it became.

I still pop in the Princess Theatre, Torquay when I am in Devon to catch up with Wendy Bennett and it is always a joy to see her and her great team with their enthusiasm undiminished. Wendy would undoubtedly have been promoted many times if she and her family had not decided that Torquay was the place for them. Graham Gilmore was another great character to come through the system and is now running the Olympic Stadium and Graham Bradbury, who started as a trainee in Edinburgh and went on to manage Apollo Victoria.

One of my interviews that did not quite work was when John Drury came from the theatre in Chesterfield and didn't accept my offer of a job in Bingo! We were able to rectify this in later years when he joined to work with Nicky in programming the theatres. He then married Leigh one of our valued members of the theatre bookings team and went off to manage Wembley Arena.

Another star manager who came through the ranks was Ian Sime, who managed York Grand Opera House for us. We had artistes demanding to play the theatre on their tours because the young manager had made them so welcome. He was my sort of manager and he went on to be the General Manager of the prestigious Leeds Grand. There was also Andrew De Rosa, who did a magnificent job when he ran both Manchester Palace and Manchester Opera House. I was immensely proud of the team of managers that we put together and was always very protective of them as to me they were the heartbeat of the company.

We did bring in a few experienced managers with Stephen Murtagh,

Peter Evans, David Gray, as well as Gerry Tait, all becoming Divisional Directors. However we remained a company that relied on the enthusiasm and ambition of youth. My apologies to all the really good managers that I have not mentioned, please put it down to my advancing years!

As Apollo continued to grow Paul and David took the view that they did not want to have non-working shareholders and embarked on a strategy to buy out the Isle of Man members of the Board. Lionel Becker had by now based himself in Gibraltar for reasons I never fully understood and Julian Harper, Ken Paul and Robert Sangster were up for doing a deal. I was not involved in this but was delighted with the result as the ownership was now in our hands with Paul and his family owning the vast majority of Apollo. This certainly remotivated him to drive the company forward and as usual David had drawn a hard bargain in doing the deal.

Domestically we had bought a house in Shrivenham. Andrea and Stephanie were doing well and Ben was having great fun at a a place called the Garden House, whilst telling everybody that the best place to go on holidays was Scarborough. Other children there seemed to go to Barbados, Florida or Greece and were probably not convinced by Ben's tales of Scarborough's slot machines!

Chapter 15

FUN IN DUBLIN AND A SAD GOODBYE TO LES

As I have said, Apollo still existed because of the staggering success of Starlight Express, which had been built on by the acquisition of top theatres. We were also in the golden era of musicals and they were to play a crucial part in the company's dramatic growth.

Cats was the first and Paul Gregg achieved a massive break through when he got Andrew Lloyd Webber and Cameron Mackintosh to agree for it to play a run in the North, Scotland and Ireland concurrently with its continued success in the West End.

Historically West End shows only ever played the provinces in a pre-West End tour or a post-West End tour but never at the same time, so it was a brave move by all concerned. When a six month summer season at Blackpool Opera House was announced, many people in the business were very sceptical believing that holiday makers in Blackpool would much prefer a traditional summer variety show. Wrong! Cats broke every conceivable box office record and undoubtedly could have run for much longer.

Its success was not down to the holiday makers but rather that people came specifically to see it from all over the north of England. Just as importantly, its run in Blackpool in no way affected its business in the West End. Indeed I believe it helped it, because when people who had seen it in Blackpool went to London to see a West End show I can imagine that with more than 50 shows to choose from that one of them would suggest that they went to see Cats again as they had so much enjoyed it. There would also be a mistaken belief that in some way the London production would be better. This was not the case as Cameron, Andrew and Paul ensured that the production was of the highest standard.

It was obviously very much in our best interests that the other two legs of the tour were housed in Apollo run theatres. This was simple in Scotland as The Edinburgh Playhouse was the natural habitat for the show. Not so easy in Dublin on the basis that we did not have a theatre there! Paul was not the sort of person to be daunted by this small matter and David and I were sent to Dublin to buy The Gaiety Theatre!

We were having a very positive meeting on this until as an afterthought, I asked if there were any restrictions on the licence that we should know about and if there was any future work needed to be done to the building to comply with licensing regulations. We were both somewhat shocked to be told that they didn't have a licence but not to worry as the President himself often came to shows.

After we left the meeting David and I went for a drink and both agreed that we could not possibly buy a theatre without a licence. Locally run, it may get away with it but there was no chance of a British company with such a high profile show as Cats being ignored. When we reported this back to Paul he was a bit miffed and, on the basis that if you want a job doing properly do it yourself, he went to Dublin to find a venue. He met up with Harry Crosbie, an Irish entrepreneur and one of the great characters in Dublin. Harry owned and had opened The Point Depot, an old railway shed (you probably guessed that!) and with a capacity of over 8,000 was the start of creating one of the finest arenas in Europe. Paul and Harry were both mavericks and it was no surprise that they got on famously and a deal was done. We bought half of The Point and agreed a management contract to run it.

So Mike and I went over to take over the management of it. The Point, like the Gaiety, had no licence but having Harry as a partner was a protection in this area. The first show under our management was Ireland's 1st Country Music Festival with Tammy Wynette and Waylon Jennings. It was absolute chaos with tickets being sold for areas rather than seats with the result that people just sat in the best seat available regardless of what they had paid for. Mike and I valiantly tried to direct people to where they should be whilst asking people to move out of seats that they were not entitled to be in. A hopeless task, with Mike on his way to becoming more Irish than the Irish, saying what the hell and I agreed so we went to the bar!

We also had the Licensing Officer in, who issued the immortal words "If you had a licence I would not let this show go on!" The joys of not having a licence! In terms of health and safety it was amusing to note that next to the fire exits were railway tracks and I always envisaged doing an emergency evacuation, everybody being run over by the 7.10pm from Cork!

I absolutely adored the venue, Dublin, the people that we worked with and especially Harry and Rita who were enormous fun and knew just about everybody worth knowing. Mike was the same and indeed he loved it so much that he has never left! My change in job titles at Apollo was entirely down to Mike. We would have a board meeting and David supported by Paul, would say that Mike really should be Operations Director. When I feebly pointed out that I was Operations Director they would say that I could be something else, so never one to lose an opportunity I would promote myself to Managing Director!

A couple of years later we would have the same scenario with them saying that Mike should be Managing Director resulting in me becoming the Chief Executive of the Theatre Division!

When we took over The Point Mike was Managing Director of the venues, but conveniently bought himself a house in Dublin and never budged. He would travel to the UK during the week and return home at weekends. This used to really aggravate David but he did such a fabulous job that I could only be 100% supportive and anyway he was a mate and seemed genuinely happy in Ireland. It was the only venue that he stayed to sort out that I wished there had been a role reversal. I would have loved to have lived there and had the day to day involvement with such a fabulous venue. I did, of course get there at every excuse.

The Point needed a major refurbishment and this was duly overseen by Steve Lavelle. It was done in a style that would enable it to house the very best productions touring the world as well as the top gigs. We had hired a stunning production of the Bolshi Ballet's Spartacus to reopen the venue. In advance we were doing a tour of the venue and admiring what had been achieved when I noticed a mosaic in the foyer with The Point logo. Except it was not the full logo as at the end of it, it just had wiggly lines. It turned out that the logo had been sent by fax and as was often the case it had ended up being crumpled hence the wiggly lines. I thought that this was a wonderful story and should be left like this for posterity, Paul thought differently and it was replaced!

I have many happy memories of The Point including a New Year's Eve when U2 came on at midnight. It was at the time that the Iron Curtain was collapsing and the show was being recorded in such countries as Romania and Hungary. Bono did a great introduction saying hello to all the countries getting the show before saying that above everything they were thrilled to be back home in The Point, Dublin. The reception they got was unbelievable and as was always the case in Dublin there was a party to follow. Freda and I left at 5.OOam, which would have been ok if I had not booked us on a 7.30am flight to the UK!

We also had a special night there when Dire Straits played it. My brother Simon and his wife Michelle were massive fans of Dire Straits and it was great that I could invite them over and even better that Harry and Rita had a do the next day and invited them giving them the chance to meet Mark Knopfler.

As always with Harry and Rita's events the room was full of Irish celebrities. When I was over for shows I would often go to Harry and Rita's for a drink before a show, which would inevitably turn into several drinks and much laughter. On one occasion we were there at lunch time and there is a knock on the door on their lovely converted warehouse home on the river and in came Terry Wogan, sat himself down and joined in the conversation.

It was during the period that Ireland seemed to win the Eurovision Song Contest every year and following their success we got to house the next one at The Point. Freda and I took Ben aged ten, over to see it, only to discover that there were strict rules that nobody under the age of 14 was allowed to be in the audience. In every other country this would have been the end of Ben's chances of seeing the show but this was Ireland and Mike sorted it with Ben getting a pass that said he was 14!

The show was interesting but the interval was magnificent! A guy with long fair hair, white shirt and black leather trousers bounced on the stage and started tap dancing and bit by bit he was joined by 80 girls who were also tap dancing, it was a fantastic spectacle and we were mesmerised. You have probably got there before me but the guy was, of course, Michael Flatley, and we were seeing the very beginnings of the massive hit show Riverdance. It was to go on and play many of our theatres as well as being a hit worldwide.

There were many memorable nights in Dublin, including the joy of seeing Bob Dylan from backstage. As I was standing there, I had a brief conversation with a guy who seemed somewhat nervous as he was about go on stage to join Bob Dylan. I had not recognised him but it turned out to be Van Morrison, who you would never describe as nervous (well obviously I just did!)

Within 12 months of taking over the management of The Point, Paul and David were able to bring about one of the biggest coups of all when we bought Manchester Palace and Manchester Opera House. It was a major vote of faith in our ability to run theatres considerably more successfully than any other company.

No provincial theatre had ever been sold for more than £750,000 and we paid in the region of £7,000,000 for the two Manchester Theatres. The deal was completed on New Year's Eve in 1990 and the three of us had to sign the necessary paper work. We were all thrilled with this acquisition as it really gave us control of the provincial No 1 theatres touring circuit.

It was perceived by many to be a gamble and indeed, had it gone wrong, it could have jeopardised the whole company, but we were supremely confident that it would be a great purchase. The two theatres were run by Bob Scott, known as Mr Manchester for his attempt to get the Olympic Games to Manchester and then his success in getting the Commonwealth Games. He was a lovely, larger than life, character with an extremely high profile and obviously a very hard act to follow.

When I went up to The Palace to see all the staff from the two theatres there was a great (large!) turn out with more than 300 people sitting in the stalls. Bob said that he would talk first and then introduce me. I am sure that he was hurting from losing these two great theatres and I did not expect any favours from him when he chatted to his team of people. However, he could not have been kinder, saying that Apollo was the only company that he would be happy to see take them over and in introducing me, that I was well known throughout the industry for my love and passion for all theatres and that they could not be in better hands.

He was a top bloke in many ways and I very much enjoyed his company and friendship. We also kept him on as a consultant and he was to go on and be a great help in many areas.

Because of Bob's profile I wanted Andrew De Rosa to take over. Andrew was a guy of great style, brilliant with the media and the perfect person to get involved with the Manchester scene. I knew that he would do a great job but even I was astonished by what he achieved. He was very much the acceptable face of Apollo in Manchester and every show opening night he seemed to have an endless list of celebrities to make the occasion special.

This list included just about everyone who had ever appeared in Coronation Street, who seemed to be his personal friends. It was always very important to me that we were never seen as a faceless company and following my mantra that each theatre was an individual jewel to be cherished, that our managers were characters that were very much in the public eye and Andrew did this very handsomely.

With the addition of Manchester Palace and Manchester Opera House we were in a wonderful position to make the most of this golden period of magical musicals. After the success of Cats outside of the West End, Cameron Mackintosh agreed to put Les Miserables into Manchester Palace for an open ended run. This caused great problems for Nicky and I as we had to juggle contracted shows from The Palace to the Opera House and it would be fair to say that the Arts Council were particularly difficult. However it was gloriously worth it as Les Mis ran for an unheard of 14 months, smashing the record of the previous longest running provincial musical by 11 months!

As always Cameron and Nick Allott and their team, including Sue Ewing and Robert Noble, were a joy to work with. For the opening night, Andrew De Rosa had put together a star studded audience and with my sporting connections we also had most of Lancashire Cricket Club's top players as well as household names from Southport Football Club!

The first half went like a dream, but it turned into a nightmare when the barricade stuck and whatever was done to rescue this situation it was not budging. I went backstage and stood looking at it as useful as everybody else who did not have a screwdriver. Eventually there was no choice but to cancel the second half.

Cameron fronted up and went on stage to explain what had happened and had quickly organised for the cast to come on and sing some of the numbers from the second half. As Cameron explained how the barricade could not be moved a very loud voice from the circle shouted "Can you tell us how it ends", which brought the house down. Trust Les Dawson to get the biggest laugh of the night!

When Les and his lovely wife Tracey came back to see it, Paul and I went out for dinner with them and to discuss future projects utilising Les. They were both great company and in very good form but sadly Les was not to live to see these projects through. I was very upset when Les died and was very grateful to Tracey for not only letting Andrew and I know about his funeral, enabling us to pay our respects but also inviting us to his memorial service at Westminster Abbey, which was a fitting tribute to comic genius and the most likeable of men.

The funeral was held at the White Church Fairhaven Lancashire and featured readings from Michelle Dotrice, Mo Moreland and Roy Barraclough with a tribute to Les from Edward Woodward. There was also a haunting version of "Wind Beneath my Wings" from Jacqui Scott.

At this service and The Service of Thanksgiving for the life of Les Dawson" at Westminster Abbey there wase laughter and there were tears. I was particularly moved by a reading of a passage that Les wrote immediately following the birth of their daughter Charlotte.

"They say the age of miracles is passed but on Saturday 3rd October 1992 at 2.35pm in the delivery room of Saint Mary's Maternity Hospital in Manchester I saw such a miracle when I witnessed the slightly premature birth of our daughter, Charlotte Emily Lesley, who struggled into the world a tiny 5lb 6oz to enrich the lives of us both. By doing so she has welded a ring of happiness that will enrich our destiny until the end of time. She arrived fourteen days ahead of schedule and thus gave us an extra fourteen days of joy. This clown will cry no more."

Chapter 16

THE STARS KEEP COMING

The unique first-half-only of the Les Miserables was followed by one of the greatest after show parties that I ever attended. Cameron and Paul were kindred spirits as far as parties were concerned and no expense was spared. By the end of it our celebrity guests were all talking about how brilliant the first half had been rather than the lack of the second half – so object achieved!

The show was my favourite musical of all time and whenever I was in Manchester, be it at The Opera House, Apollo or Tameside Hippodrome, which we had taken over, I would always end at the Palace with Les Mis being a late finishing show, to catch the end. Every night the audience stood as one at the end and I always reminded myself what a lucky boy I was having a job that enabled me to be a small part of giving so many people the special experience of this show.

Les Miserables had exceeded our wildest dreams in its length of run but it was to be surpassed by Phantom of the Opera, which astonishingly ran for two years. This was followed by Grease starring Shane Ritchie, which ran for 49 weeks.

I was particularly thrilled with the success of Grease as it was produced by David Ian and Paul Nicholas, two of my favourite people in the business. They had done a brilliant job producing the show and had a fabulous run in the West End at the Dominion Theatre as well as the triumph in Manchester. I dealt mainly with David and he was a real fun guy, who was just as pleasant when things were going wrong as he was when it was non-stop success. Little was I to know then just how closely we were going to work together in the future.

With the success of Manchester and the knowledge that business for these shows in the West End was not adversely affected, they, in time, played our

Edinburgh, Bristol and Liverpool Theatres. We also benefited from other top quality products including Bill Kenwright's smash West End hit Blood Brothers. Producers were clamouring for dates in our theatres and Nicky and I had the luxury of choosing which shows to take, which was a far cry from the early days when I visited producers' offices trying to persuade them to bring their shows to us.

We were incredibly indebted to the many producers, who raised the money or invested their own money to put quality shows on the road. Almost without exception they were a pleasure to work with as we jointly took responsibility for selling the tickets. Amongst my favourites were Pola Jones with Andrew Fell and Andre Ptaszynski. Andre and I would lunch in Oxford on a regular basis and I loved his company, and was thrilled when he became Chief Executive of Andrew Lloyd Webber's Really Useful Company. In my later years he brought me in as a consultant and I always regarded him as not only one of the top people in the theatre world but also as one of the nicest. We were also indebted to Martin Dodd and Peter Frosdich of UK Productions, who were prolific in their productions of musicals.

I was also very fond of Vanessa Ford who I first met at a meeting in Oxford to discuss a Shakespeare production. I have forgotten the show but will never forget how she smoked a very big cigar during the meeting. She went on to produce many shows including "The Lion, The Witch and The Wardrobe" and to play many Apollo dates in a wide range of our theatres.

We would also have shows from Ambassador's Howard Panter, who was to go on and run more than 40 theatres. I best remember him for coming to Southport football matches when we played Woking. He was fantastic company and once he worked out what colour we played in he would bellow his support!

We were also indebted to Ellen Kent who was bringing into the country top quality Eastern European Opera and Ballet Companies. She was a great show person and some of her Chisinau Opera Productions (Moldova's National Company) were incredible spectacles with eagles, dogs and horses featuring regularly. I particularly enjoyed her Rigoletto, which as well as featuring animals also seemed to have quite a lot of naked ladies!

Her incredibly long tours were a godsend in playing successful dates in a large range of our theatres.

I was always fond of the old theatrical producers and none more so than Charles Vance. He would describe himself as the last of the Actor/Managers and would regale with me wonderful stories as we lunched at The Kennel Club, where he was someone important. He knew everybody and would invite me to meet all sorts of other people. I remember him inviting me for lunch at The Ivy with Adam Faith and, being Charles, he insisted that we had our photo taken. I may not have mentioned this but I was star struck from the start to the finish and at such moments would have to pinch myself to ensure that this really was happening!

Mark Furness was also a lovely producer to work with and had lots of productions that played our circuit. I particularly remember his production of "Some Like it Hot" starring Tommy Steele. It was a fabulous show although it did not quite do the anticipated business.

I enjoyed Tommy Steele's company both before and after this tour but for whatever reason he was quite difficult at that time. There were a number of disputes and I made sure that I appeared at all of the tour dates in our venues and would always pop in to see him before the show in the knowledge that if he was unhappy about something there was a limited time that we could discuss it before the curtain went up.

We were very lucky that we had one of theatres top PR people in Janey Sargent handling the tour. She was great fun to be around and defused many a potential problem. My abiding memory of the tour was at Manchester Opera House going with Mark Furness to say hello to Tommy before the show. We knocked on his dressing room, then saw a "do not disturb" sign, looked at each other and ran so that he did not know it was us!

A couple of years later Tommy was doing a workshop for a new musical "Chaplain" at our Oxford Old Fire Station and he came out to our offices to say hello. He was as nice as pie as he was every time I met him afterwards but "Some Like it Hot" was not his finest moment and without the humour of Janey Sargent and the diplomacy of Mark Furness, I do not think that the tour would have been completed.

I also very much enjoyed the company of Nick Thomas, who became the King of Panto and theatre owner but never changed from his self-depreciating humour. Nick was from Scarborough and when I was up at The Futurist we would often meet up for lunch and he was just a very funny guy.

On one occasion we both ended up on a judging panel at The Scarborough Spa Theatre for the final of a competition to find a star from one of the UK's resorts. Fatefully we both had a few drinks before we were deposited in a box with our clipboards and a glass of champagne. We were in a bit of a giggly mood anyway but we tried to put our serious face on as we listened to the first act, a serious ballad singer from Rochdale (which I know is not a seaside resort!). Unfortunately Nick picked up his clipboard, which resulted in his full glass of champagne being deposited onto the hair of an elderly lady in the audience. We just collapsed and burst into uncontrollable giggling. Just as one of us would just about get some self control, the other would start off again. This was all very unfair to the singer from Rochdale, who in the unlikely event is reading the book, I apologise profusely on behalf of Nick and myself!

Some of the producers would put their shows with a booker to plot the tour. I would do a lot of dates with Greg Ripley-Duggan who was a pleasure to work with but the doyen of this art was Renee Stephan. Renee was more theatre than theatre and could count many of the greats as her fiends and would regale us with tales of the time she worked for Bernard Delfont. For whatever reason both Nicky and I had a fabulous relationship with Renee and she was a massive help to us when times were tough.

In 1991 we entered into partnership with legendary American producer and theatre owner Jimmy Nederlander to buy The Dominion Theatre. The deal was that we owned one third and had a management contract. We had previously run the Dominion on lease from Rank.

We had had mixed success with the low point being when I booked the musical "Bernadette". Andrew De Rosa was the General Manager of the theatre and we both worked hard to ensure the show, which was known as the people's musical as a result of the Daily Mirror doing a scheme enabling people to invest in it, got to opening night. This took a lot of juggling but we managed to get to the opening night knowing that the show could only survive if it got good reviews. Freda and I were sat with the actress Liz Fraser and a lady who was the head of BBC's Radio 4.

As always I loved the show and both Liz and her friend were full of praise and belief that the show would be a hit. Naively I actually believed them until we got the reviews, which somewhat predictably all said that this show needs a miracle! It turned out to be the shortest running musical in the history of the West End with Andrew and I having to pick up the pieces as it gave notice after two days! So what do I know about shows!

Luckily, in association with Jimmy Nederlander, we had a lot more success. As previously mentioned Grease was a massive hit there as was Disney's Beauty and the Beast. At one of the opening charity galas for Beauty and the

Beast we had the Queen Mother as our Royal guest and, stood in the line-up, I had one of the longest conversations ever with a Royal.

She wanted to know all about the show and what age would most enjoy it so she would know which members of the family to bring. She was everything that you would expect of a Royal and charm personified.

On another occasion we had taken Ben to see the show, when Stephen Murtagh the General Manager of the theatre, asked if we would mind sharing the hospitality room with the Duchess of York and the two princesses. At the time Ben was into magic tricks and he spent the whole of the interval doing tricks for the two girls, whilst I chatted to their mother. it gave me an insight of how difficult it was to marry into the Royal Family. The press were being very horrible to her even by their low standards, with headlines such as Duchess of Pork. She was great company but obviously very vulnerable and I did wonder how the members of the media who hounded her and also Princess Diana ever slept at night.

Our relationship with Jimmy Nederlander and with his representative in the UK, Jerry Katzman, was always great and when in New York I would always go to Jimmy's office. On one occasion David and I dropped in to discuss air conditioning (its non-stop glamour this show business!) Jimmy had a desk full of paper and every time he needed something he would call Nick, who ran the office, to come and find it and Nick would go straight in the pile of paper and come up with the required document. I was in awe of Jimmy knowing that he was one of the greatest people in world theatre.

Luckily we also had a great relationship with Jerry Katzman, which ensured that The Dominion was the success that it was. We did a number of Royal Variety Shows there as well as the Children's Royal Variety Show, which we took Ben to and we were sat directly behind our Royal guest Princess Margaret. His behaviour to our surprise was impeccable, which was not the case with Princess Margaret who talked to her aide through a number of the acts.

The Dominion was also the scene of my last Royal Variety Show just before I left Clear Channel. This was kindly arranged by Laurie Mansfield and Peter Elliott, who were the inspired organisers of the show. I was delighted that Ben could manage to desert his academic studies at Cheltenham College to be part of the occasion. I should point out that Ben had no problem deserting his academic studies at the slightest of excuse! When I had said to Ben that it was a special occasion for me as it would be the last of these sort of events for me and that I would love him to be there, he wanted to know if he could bring a friend. I so much wanted him to be there that I was more than happy for him to bring one of his mates. I assumed that we would have the pleasure of the company of one of his pals such as Kit, Naser or George but he fooled us all by saying that it was a girl from Cheltenham College.

Whilst Ben had been given the day off the young lady had been told she could only go after lessons so Ben had to go to Paddington to pick her up at about 6.00pm. He arrived back at the hotel with a very attractive girl with a small bag and dressed with a top that left her with a bare midriff in the middle of November. I was anxious that we should not be late (I should point out that I am always anxious that we are not late!) so I pointed out that we have to leave in ten minutes if that is OK.

My experience of females is that ten minutes is not OK to get ready to go to the Royal Variety Show or indeed to go to the local pub. However on this occasion, within ten minutes a vision of beauty appeared with a very stylish black dress with a bare back. We did the show and eventually ended up back at the hotel bar and she was very good company. She was to go on and spend seven years as the girlfriend of Prince Harry but I like to think that Chelsy Davey's interest in Royalty begun that night!

Of all the shows that we had at The Dominion none of them gave me more pleasure than the success of "We Will Rock You". By the time that the plans to bring the show in were being discussed my star was very much on the wane but I was pleased to be able to encourage and help the producers reach a deal. For me it was the perfect ending as Phil McIntyre, with Paul Roberts, and the guys from Queen embarked on a massive hit show.

If you have been paying attention you will remember that one of the first shows that I did all those years back in Blackburn was Showaddywaddy with Phil McIntyre. We had done many shows of Phil's over the years and there was nobody I would rather have had the success that We Will Rock You was.

I also really liked Paul Roberts who worked with Phil and was a partner in the show. Paul was a great promoter but also a lovely guy to do business with, he also was one of a small band that, as my role in the business subsided with my departure from Clear Channel, always found time to meet up as we still do this day. He also arranged for a note from Brian May, Roger Taylor and Ben Elton to be sent to me thanking me for the gig. He and Phil also presented me with a disc celebrating 60,000 sales of The We Will Rock You album and also Paul arrived at my leaving do with a guitar from Brian May.

Looking back at my career I enjoyed a special relationship with a number of people but very much to the fore were Phil and Paul.

One of my favourite Dominion memories was when we did panto there starring Michael Barrymore and with Frank Bruno. Michael was at the height of his stardom and the show was a big hit. At the traditional bringing up of young children on stage Michael's routine included asking what their Dad did for a job. There was a period over a couple of years that Ben would always end up as one of the kids. I should point out that this was nothing to do with me, just kind managers arranging it.

For this show Ben was about six and an experienced panto kid on stage. When Michael got to Ben and asked what does your father do he answered "He owns this Theatre". This was obviously incorrect as in reality I owned about 1% of it and when I asked why he had come up with that reply he explained that the usherette who took him up to the stage had told him to say it. It brought the house down although Michael got the last laugh by asking if his mother cleaned it! After the show we popped up to Michael's dressing room and he was being his usual kind and hospitable self when Ben announced that he was bored and could we go home!

I loved the pantos that we did and ensured that I saw every one which at the end would be in the region of 15 shows. We had some incredibly spectacular pantos in our big dates but I also always enjoyed the productions in our smaller theatres with Duggie Chapman and Simon Barry being two of the producers who always put on fabulous shows on a low budget.

With Barry Clayman we had our own Panto Division headed up by Barrie Stead and he would produce such shows as Peter Pan with Brian Blessed and Anita Harris in Manchester and them with Michaela Stracham in Bristol. Brian was a fantastic character who was just as loud off the stage as he was on it.

On one occasion, with Gerry Tait and John Wood, the excellent General Manager of Bristol Hippodrome, we took him and Michaela out for dinner and he took over the whole restaurant. There was an affectionate couple in the corner and I am sure that the guy was about to propose to the young lady when the peace was shattered by Brian saying in his trademark booming voice, "Michaela, when you come down that rope you are fucking shaggable!" We had an incredible night out with one of the greatest theatrical characters. His wife Hildegarde Neil chose not to come out with us for dinner and by the end of the evening I fully understood why!

Ken Dodd did a massive hit panto for us in Manchester and the likes of Joe Pasquale, Jimmy Cricket and Bernie Clifton also did some memorable shows. What I learned about panto was that the story was the most important thing for the children in the audience. On one occasion in the Dominion panto, Michael Barrymore was ill and his agent Norman Murray said that we must cancel the show. I said that was not acceptable and we could not have a situation where young children had been looking forward to the panto only to be told there was no show.

The Director rejigged the show with Frank Bruno doing more including the children on stage and we had a notice in the foyer saying that if anybody wanted to swap their tickets for another performance to enable them to see Michael, then go to the box office. Norman Murray insisted that we would have chaos with all the people wanting to change their tickets but the reality was that not one single person asked to change their tickets. This was because the story was the biggest star and as I noticed the show getting a standing ovation it emphasised to me that no matter who the stars were they were always less than the story.

As big musicals took over, our major theatre Christmas productions changed. Firstly we got the rights to produce Scrooge, which starred the wonderful Anthony Newley along with Stratford Johns, and Jon Pertwee. It was a magical production that played The Dominion and then our provincial theatres.

I remember receiving a letter from one time Dr Who star, Colin Baker, much more talented actor than simply being the good doctor and also great company. Having watched Scrooge he wrote to me saying, "What a stunning show! It actually rekindled in me the excitement of going to the theatre and Mr Newley certainly has that special something that makes you want to watch him even when he has his back to you. I suppose star quality is the word!"

My thoughts entirely! Anthony Newley was fabulous in the show and it was always a great pleasure to chat to him, but he also had an aura round him that made me realise that I was in the company of a real star. Scrooge was the perfect Christmas Show but was very hard to follow without reverting back to panto.

When Scrooge played Oxford Apollo it was a great help to be friends with Hedda Beeby and Trish Francis who ran the very successful Oxford Playhouse. We often lunched and were always available to help each other's theatres. On this occasion I rang them as soon as we decided not to run a panto to enable them to take over the mantle. It was obviously good news for the Playhouse but it also helped us to demonstrate that Oxford would still have a panto as well as having a fabulous Christmas Musical.

The answer came in the form of Harry Secombe and Pickwick. When I am asked who were the nicest stars I ever worked with, Harry would be right up there. I should point out that actually nobody has asked me that question but if they should...!

I first met Harry at the age of six (me not him!) when my Dad was invited by his jazz friend Leslie 'Jiver' Hutchinson to a cricket match in Blackpool between Geraldo's Orchestra and one of the summer shows which starred Harry. Apart from the one ball that he faced he spent the whole of the afternoon playing cricket with me and two other youngsters.

My Dad was also happy as the singer Jill Day was serving teas and for some reason he seemed to have numerous cups!

I also had a great time with Harry when he won a life time achievement award from the Institute of Arts and Entertainment Management, when I was the President. It was known as the Waterford Crystal Award, which may have had something to do with the fact that they supplied a splendid crystal vase to the winner! Modesty should prohibit me from letting you know that in 1993 I was nominated for the award but as you will have ascertained by now I am not very good with modesty!

My nomination said Sam Shrouder (obviously!) "Outstanding work in entertainment operations, the success against free competition and the dedication to duty. The vast knowledge and encouragement that is passed on via Sam's Seminars are indeed an example to all and he remains a jewel in the entertainment crown. The recognition of his efforts is long overdue"!

Would you like me to repeat that? No? Oh well....Thanks for that anyway to the very nice editor of Encore, Peter Foot. I would love to end this little tale by inviting you to pop round and see my very nice crystal vase. However life is not like that and as the other nominees were Ken Dodd, David Kossoff, Cleo Laine and John Dankworth, Humphrey Lyttelton and Norman Wisdom you will not be surprised that I came last. Indeed I doubt that I received a single vote. I did not even vote for myself as I felt that Ken Dodd was slightly more deserving than me!

None of this has actually got anything to do with the massive success that was Pickwick. Harry was a lovely man who always greeted me with a big hug and made any guests that I might have with me extremely welcome. He was magnificent in the show as well as being very generous with the rest of the cast in allowing them their moment of glory. Scrooge and Pickwick broke the mould in our long provincial dates with musicals replacing panto even when they had no Christmas theme. For instance there is not a lot of Christmas cheer in Bill Kenwright's Blood Brothers but it still played to record business over the festive season.

The fact that Apollo was having an incredibly successful time was highlighted when in January 1990, Paul took The Stage newspaper's centre pages to announce that in the last week of the 1980s, 171,978 people had visited an Apollo Theatre, an Apollo Production, or co-production in the UK and Ireland grossing in excess of £1.8 million.

Some of the shows and admissions were Michael Barrymore in Aladdin at the Dominion Theatre, 19,092; Cats, Playhouse Edinburgh 18,075; Starlight Express at the Apollo Victoria 10,442; Sue Pollard in Dick Whittington at Bristol Hippodrome 15,772; Jim Davidson in Cinderella at the Alhambra Theatre Bradford 15,232; U2, The Point Dublin 22,000; Dana in Snow White at Theatre Royal Nottingham 12,081; and 42nd Street at Manchester Opera House 12,003.

Within the advert it read "Paul Gregg and Sam Shrouder would like to thank all the artistes and people involved in making this a great week". It also pointed out that the first week of the '90's was even better! Heady days indeed.

Chapter 17

PARADISE AND THE CIVIC HALLS

As well as working hard we also played hard and we were very much indebted to the generosity of Paul and Nita. For many years we had an annual holiday in their fabulous apartment in Marco Island. We had great times there, normally with friends Colin and Claire. For Ben it was like a second home with the highlight being going to Stan's at Goodlands on a Sunday lunchtime. There were bands, dancing and some very dubious Polish jokes from Stan who owned the venue but always compered the show – remind you of anyone?! – obviously not the dubious Polish jokes! On top of their kindness in letting us use their apartment they also masterminded the most wonderful of works outings. The trip to Venice, staying at the Cipriani and returning on The Orient Express was an incredible experience particularly for somebody who spent his childhood holidays at St Anne's on Sea! There were lots of mind boggling trips including when Paul said to David and Julie and Freda and myself to turn up at Heathrow for a surprise trip and to pack for cold weather! When we arrived and picked up our tickets we discovered that we were flying to New York on Concorde! The trip did not go quite as smoothly as intended as when we arrived, and I was heading in the direction of a yellow cab David pointed out that as part of our package we were entitled to a helicopter ride into the centre of Manhattan. I did not fancy this at all but I was outvoted by 3 to 1. I felt ill from the start and my peace of mind was not helped by the guy next to me informing me that recently a helicopter had crashed whilst trying to land on the Pan Am building! When we arrived at our swish hotel

Paul and Nita were already there as well as our head of productions Adrian Leggott and his wife Jackie. The itinerary was a trip to the Russian Tea

Rooms before seeing "Grand Hotel" on Broadway (This was our official reason to be there as we were considering bringing the show to London). My popularity declined considerably as I announced that I could not go anywhere and took to my bed! After 3 hours kip I felt great and ready for the trip to Grand Hotel. The musical had no interval and after 10 minutes I was the only one in our party of 8 that was still awake! That remained the case for the whole of the show, which in my opinion would not work for us, however those who slept through it, thought differently so it was brought into The Dominion, where it did not work! Paul and Nita were forever handing out treats and on one occasion he asked if I had ever been to Las Vegas, which obviously I had not, so he gave us two tickets for the flights, accommodation at The Mirage and somewhat bizarrely 2 tickets to watch Mike Tyson fight at Caesar's Palace. It turned out that he had bid for the package at a Variety Club auction. David and Julie got a trip to Sardinia plus tickets for a World Cup game.

Paul and Nita loved a party and a special effort was always made for the Managers Christmas Party. In my first year there were just 12 of us at the Bear Hotel in Woodstock, by the end there were around 250 crucial members of Apollo and their partners at the most lavish of parties. Paul, David and I all had our specific roles at these events, with mine being calling the bingo – so not much progress there then! The prizes would be on the lines of a weekend in New York for a line, with a full house winning an all-expenses paid fortnight in Barbados. I have never called a game of bingo where people concentrated so much! It was always an incredible event and was massive for the morale of the Company as well as enabling us to mix with people from different parts of the business. One of the old stagers, who joined about when I did, was Chris Smith from the Accounts Department. He and his wife Brenda had a son Michael about the same age as Ben and we would annually compare notes as well as in the early days sharing Calpol – for our children, obviously not for ourselves! Paul also insisted that every member of the staff got a Christmas bonus of a week's wages. Even in our very tough early years this was non-negotiable. No wonder we all loved our jobs.

Birthdays in our office also never passed without a major celebration. Work stopped, the phones were switched off, a banquet provided and the drink flowed. However Paul did go somewhat over the top for my 50th. Freda, Ben and I were picked up by a chauffeur and driven towards London and I remember thinking that I hoped that we were not on our way to a formal dinner. I need not have worried. As we arrived at Hammersmith Apollo, the front of house sign shone brightly with "For I Night Only Celebrating 50 Years — Smiling Sam Shrouder"! The theatre was also covered with posters featuring the same slogan plus a photo of me in my DJ-ing previous life. Across the road in Deals Restaurant they had arranged the best party imaginable with friends from all sorts of areas in my life as well as within the business. There was a great band, speeches were made, Paul presented me with a Cartier watch, and many fantastic gifts, the guests were all given a tie pin with a cricket bat and 50 years not out on it. I had the most wonderful night. It was made even better by having ten year old Ben there with me. Graham Gilmore, one of Apollo's top managers was General Manager of Hammersmith Apollo and he later told me that somebody passing the theatre and seeing all the posters had gone to the box office to try and buy tickets! Someone else said that when their taxi dropped them off the driver looked at the posters and said "I suppose he is another of those bloody alternative comics!" My 50th also included a surprise party in the village organised by Freda and our lovely neighbours Stef and Diana, and a family visit to Thurlestone in Devon so I was one very spoilt 50 year old!

But of all the incredible works outings that Paul arranged the trip to Richard Branson's Necker Island was still special. Along with 6 year old Ben we were in a group of 20 or so friends of Paul and Nita invited to spend 10 days on this paradise island. We had our own huts but enjoyed a wonderful community space where we ate, drunk, danced and above all laughed. Needless to say the sound system and selection of music was of the highest quality. As well as David and Julie, among the guests were Barry and Linda Clayman, Leslie Rose and Jan, who shared a box at Spurs with Barry and were great friends of Paul and Nita's, and Harry Crosby with Rita. They were all funny people and very enjoyable company. Harry and Rita added even more to the joy of the holiday when they agreed to get married – I am not sure that this was how they would have planned it! However it was a special day with the ceremony on the beach, a great band and a drunken limbo dancing competition. The staff were very friendly and lots of fun. Wherever you went on the Island there were cool boxes with drinks in and if you were in the sea somebody would arrive with Pina Colados for you. St Anne's on Sea it wasn't!

For the first part of the holiday Ben's behaviour was impeccable as he just joined in whatever was happening. There were activities planned for every day including an infamous sand sculpture competition which some took rather too seriously! However things were about to change with the unannounced arrival of a helicopter with Richard Branson, his wife Joan and children Holly and Sam. They had built their own Bali style house on the edge of the Island but did not visit it when they had rented Necker out. There had been some confusion but they were welcomed with open arms by most of us. Sam Branson was the same age as Ben, whose eyes had lit up when he saw him climb out of the helicopter. They soon teamed up and the very well behaved Ben was no more. Climbing on the roof and firing water pistols at the sunbathing ladies resulted in Sam being banished back to the family home. Ben would go there to play with him and when Freda and I went to collect him we would enjoy a drink and a chat with Richard and Joan, who were both witty and very entertaining. On our last evening there Richard joined us and we all ended up fully dressed in the swimming pool. It was somewhat surreal to spend over an hour stood in the pool chatting away to Richard. By the time that we left there was no doubt that he was my new best friend and he had given me his phone number so we could arrange to meet up. The reality, of course, was that he was an incredibly gregarious guy who obviously behaves like this with everybody and I actually never met him again which meant I had to reinstate my previous best friends! A very special experience to have visited this incredible Island with such great company and thanks to the generosity of Paul and Nita.

Apart from me other people also seemed to have birthdays and celebrations! One of the artistes, whose company I always enjoyed, was Danny La Rue and we went to his house Walton Hall near Strafford upon Avon for one of the finest parties of all time. His partner Jack was also a lovely guy and their hospitality was unbelievable. Danny also introduced us to two Canadian guys who were his new business partners and who had plans to develop Walton Hall. Danny was really bubbling with all the ideas and was naturally devastated when during his "Danny's Dazzling Roadshow" tour the two guys were arrested. It turned out that they were conmen and had fleeced Danny. Upset as he was the show went on and with his audience aware from the media what had happened, he got an incredibly warm reaction at every show. It was an indication of the affection that people had for this great showman. I also got on very well with Russ Conway but was still surprised to be invited to an EMI lunch to celebrate his 40th year in Show business with his 40 best friends. As everybody brought their partners I worked out that I must be in his list of 20 best friends! Billy Cotton made a great speech and we all had to come up with an anecdote. If you are anticipating what witty and amusing story I came up with you will have a long wait as I have no idea what I said but you are right in that it will obviously have been very amusing!

Whilst all this fun and socialising was taking place, we continued to build the Apollo empire. We had a big breakthrough when we were entrusted with the contract to run Torbay Councils Paignton Festival Theatre and Torquay Princess Theatre. David did the deal which enabled us to receive a subsidy which was a considerable reduction on what it was costing them to run them, yet was still enough for us to make a reasonable return – so everybody was a winner. Torbay Council were a pleasure to work with epitomised by their Director of Tourism, Bob Sweet. Bob did a brilliant job for Torbay and he and I developed an immediate rapport and established that our meetings to discuss our progress and crucially summer season programming, should take place over lunch or an evening meal. He had firm views and was very knowledgeable about all levels of programming and any differences in our approach were sorted out over a glass of wine. We became great friends and I particularly admired his ability to create wonderful exhibits to display at Chelsea Flower Show where they always won a gold medal. After many years of working together he asked my advice during our "working" lunch. He had been offered three jobs and was unsure of which one to take. One was as Chief Executive of a major council, another was to run a prestigious venue and the other was to work for the Royal Horticultural Society. My advice was "Bob you are a gardener so the RHS is the only job for you!", which is how he became their Show Director masterminding Chelsea and Hampton Court as well as many other flower shows. He had a brilliant career there as one of the top experts in the world.

Within our deal with Torbay Council there seemed to be an unwritten agreement that we would sponsor an event each year. These included the firework display on the Paignton front, a Starlight Express exhibit atChelsea and much more interestingly, a cricket match at Torquay between the Minor Counties and South Africa. This I was not going to miss and it was great to take Ben along and have him introduced to the South African players. Those not picked for this game were sent to mix with the sponsors so we had the company of such as Brian McMillan, David Richardson and the friendliest of them all, Fanie de Villiers for a large part of the day. The free booze may also have had something to do with the time that they spent with us! One of the Torquay players was telling me that Fanie De Villiers, who was a fast bowling legend with South Africa, had played as a Pro for Torquay for a season and that the night before our game he had walked in torrential rain from his hotel to the ground to see his old mates there. When he was there he asked to pop upstairs to the dressing room to see where he used to change and when he got there he found a sign saying "Fanie's Corner" and that he was genuinely moved.

The Festival and The Princess were both 1500 capacity theatres and in the early years were easy to programme for summer season. Jim Davidson was our favourite in every way. He loved Torquay and always wanted to do The Princess whilst living on his boat moored in the harbour. He always did great business and was very popular with everybody involved at the theatre including me. The pattern for both theatres would be the summer show Monday to Saturday for 8 to 10 weeks with another act doing all the Sundays. For one of Paignton's Sunday spots we had The Barron Knights, who not only did good business and a great show but were also always good value to spend time with. I particularly got on well with Pete Langford, who became a great mate, meeting regularly on the golf course including being part of a foursome that won Encore Magazines Roy Castle Classic Golf Tournament – I knew that you would be impressed! Pete also went on the play at Wychwood Festival for me as well as more importantly bringing The Barron Knights to play at my wedding.

Sadly as summer season business started diminishing throughout the UK, David got great encouragement from the Council to close Paignton Festival Theatre and replace it with an Apollo 8 Screen Cinema (another area that we were expanding in). While it was impossible to argue with the logic I found it very hard to support. I had great memories of the theatre and would always support live theatre against any other art form. Unfortunately I was in a group of one (not including the local amateurs!) that was opposed to the change and when it went to a Council vote it got unanimous approval. After this The Princess went from strength to strength. A number of our top managers had spent time in Torbay learning their trade. But Torbay got lucky when Wendy Bennett went there to be General Manager, got married to Mark, had daughter Lucy and Charlotte and decided to stay there. She was a top manager and artistes and shows would go there because they knew that they would be well looked after. She also had a great team who she was fiercely loyal to including Brenda and Rona who had worked there forever running the front of house. It was always nice to visit the theatre and get a kiss from both of them. In getting the shows into The Princess, the theatre was lucky to have Martin Jenkins an extremely talented Stage Director. The theatre had a very small stage and very little space backstage. I would frequently book musicals into The Princess in the knowledge that there was no chance that they would fit in and then go there in trepidation to see the show. Miraculously he will have got the show on, often in a reduced state, and would ensure that it looked a million dollars. To this day I cannot believe that he got Starlight Express on stage. He was poached to sort out problems all over the country but there was never any doubting where his loyalty was focused.

Torbay was the start of a campaign for us to add Civic owned theatres, where we would receive a subsidy that was substantially below what it was costing the Council to run them. Our next acquisition was The Beck Theatre in Hayes, Middlesex. The Beck was a fabulous 650 seater theatre, where we were able to present an exciting (well I thought so!) mix of shows.

One of my highlights of The Beck was when Sir John Mills, who lived in nearby Denham, approached us about trying out his one man show there. He was in his later years and had planned a show with film clips and him reminiscing about the films and his life. It was agreed that we would do a mock-up of our suggestions for print and that we would then meet up at The Beck to discuss the show and how to sell it. I arrived early thinking how incredible to be meeting Sir John Mills on a one to one basis and talking about his career. When he arrived in the foyer, I met him with great enthusiasm and suggested that we went up the stairs to the office, had a coffee and then show him our suggestions for the print. He declined this invitation explaining that his legs were not so good. So I immediately commandeered a table in our coffee bar and asked a nice young lady to bring Sir John a coffee and pastry, whilst I went up to the office to get the said print. I explained this to him and he responded by saying that he was rather deaf and that I would have to speak up. When I arrived back he said that he could not see very well so could not comment on the print. We had a brief and very pleasant chat and then he asked me what the time was. On hearing it he said, with a very large smile, that he would have to go now as he was playing golf at 1.00pm! I rather felt I was had by Sir John and I liked him the more for it.

We had some very good young Managers at The Beck as they learnt their trade and moved on to bigger theatres. One of them was Stephen Levine whom we adopted as an Assistant Manager when we took over the York Grand Opera House. He had followed the usual Apollo management pattern going to Tameside Hippodrome, Birmingham Alexandra and Hammersmith Apollo as Assistant and then Deputy Manager before becoming the General Manager of The Beck Theatre. He was later to recall that on the day that we took York over the staff were full of trepidation and all ready to find fault. It was obviously one of my better days as he kindly said that following my usual speech, which obviously included the Joan Littleton and steps story, that I got a round of applause, and that it helped the team there to feel that they were now part of Apollo. He also stated that he heard the speech many times, which must have been incredibly boring! On this particular day I arrived at The Beck for a meeting with Stephen and there was a lady polishing the steps. I had a good old chat with her and she explained that she was doing this because someone important is coming. When she later saw me in the office she realised that she had got that wrong as it was only me! I think it would be fair to say that our theatres, always had the cleanest steps in the business!

The next local authority theatre that we acquired was the Swindon Wyvern Theatre. This was a strange one because before Ben was born Freda had worked there in PR and had loved every minute, and when asked I had dutifully joined the Board of the Wyvern. It was lots of fun with some great characters including Terry Court who was on a mission to get everybody into the Arts, Charles Savage who was its artistic director and Alan Lord who ran it and controlled the finances.

All went well for a number of years as they spent their £500,000 budget on worthy Arts projects. However, it all unravelled when the leader of the Council, who was on the Board, rang me and asked if I would come in and see him. The conversation was simple in that the Council could no longer afford to fund it to the current level and what was the lowest subsidy we would need to take the Theatre over. I told him that we would do it for £200,000 giving them a saving of £300,000 and enabling us to make a £100,000 profit, which was the minimum that David insisted we make when taking over a theatre. Sadly some of my friends on the Board saw this as a massive betrayal as we took The Wyvern over. My rationale was that if we had not stepped in the plight of the Council was such that they could have closed it.

We achieved our projections by in the main, not paying any guarantees for shows and using our power in the market to bring in some shows that otherwise would never have gone there. We were also able to centralise some of the costs, as well as reducing some of their artistic content in the community. I loved going there and it was the only theatre that we had that I could see a show and still be able to be back in the village pub before closing time! They also had the best amateur shows of any theatre that I have ever been involved with. They had two stalwarts in Sheila Harrod and Mollie Tanner, who both put on weekly shows of the highest quality.

We also did a fabulous youth theatre project in the summer when we would take in around 300 children for a fortnight and put on a wonderful production using a top director and hiring great costumes and sets. These shows were incredible with all the children being found a role, including backstage and front of house. I never missed these shows from the first one which was Bugsy Malone. 42nd Street was my favourite and was one of my most magical of theatre experiences when they came to "The Lullaby of Broadway". It started with one boy on stage and ended with 270 children (I obviously counted every one!) on stage and down the aisles. The audience were blown away I just cried (I seemed to have done quite a lot of that!) I was so proud of what was being achieved, and these were not just kids from drama schools, they were youngsters who had just come along and given it a go. When we started we would do three performances and by the time we did Joseph we were doing 11 shows such was the projects popularity with the public.

We had also taken over Tameside Hippodrome for the Council. Jim Burns their Director of Recreation had been at a seminar where I was explaining why every local authority should let us run their theatre for them, and as a result approached us. We did a deal, making it our fourth theatre in Greater Manchester.

We were lucky that when we had taken over Manchester Palace and Manchester Opera House we had also acquired a bright Assistant Manager called Karen Jones. Karen was the ideal choice to take over as General Manager at Tameside Hippodrome, where she did a great job managing a challenging theatre. With our position in the industry we were able to provide a satisfactory programme for the theatre and Karen did well to squeeze the maximum business she could from the shows.

With the range of theatres we now had I was seriously indebted to Nicky

Monk and the great team that worked on the programming at the theatres. Nicky was very much in control and when she came to tell me that she was expecting her lovely daughter Lizzie, I said all the right things and was delighted for her and Doug but I was also thinking what a problem this left me with. I need not have worried her assistant Fiona Brent took over and did a magnificent job. Although she was about to send out a contract for Snow Shite to her least favourite Panto producer!

It always made me feel really proud when people like Fiona stepped into a difficult situation and with lots of hard work and dedication came up trumps. We also had a great back up team with Alison Whitefield taking charge of all the contracts and ensuring that none went out with the word shite on them! We also had Karen Jacob and Amy Marshall, who were a great support. Within our office attached to Paul's house, he also had some great PAs, none better or nicer than Annalise Dobson, whose husband Dave was a fine fellow who came to a Southport game with me. The office was a fun place to be but more importantly, was responsible for providing shows for all our theatres.

In my domestic world we had moved house a couple of times with Freda adhering to Paul Gregg's advice of always buy a house that you cannot afford! Freda was very talented artistically and had a great eye for improving houses, which was just as well as I had zero talent! Andrea and Stephanie were having more fun than we probably knew about and Ben had ended up at St Hugh's School, which he very much enjoyed. He was very good at sport and despite not finding time for much else outside of work (obviously apart from cricket!) I always ensured I was there for the school matches. As the school's first team goalkeeper he was a bit flash, but good to watch and he was also a good rugby player, including being joint captain on the school's Scottish tour. We went up to watch the games and the parents undoubtedly had more fun than the kids. I particularly enjoyed watching his cricket and was far more delighted than he was when he became the first choice wicket keeper for Oxfordshire Under 11's, 12's and 13's, and I hardly missed a match of the 28 county games he played (I know it was 28 because I kept a scrap book – now that is sad!) Unfortunately at 14 he dislocated a shoulder and despite three operations he was never able to play these sports again – so if anybody would like an 80% empty scrap book I have got one spare!

I had many very enjoyable hours watching the games normally with Ted Sandbach, whose son Chris also played in the team and when they went on tour along with Ted's wife Sue, we had lots of laughter and alcohol – not necessarily in that order! I also got on really well with the team's manager Nick Mills who was fascinating company. I was devastated both for Ben and myself when his injury curtailed his sporting life. He twice had keyhole surgery and when they failed he was opened up for the operation that would definitely sort the problem out. We lived in hope, but then his shoulder came out again, which took away his hope of getting back on the sports field. Ben has always been the most positive of souls and he moved seamlessly into his next interests of drinking, girls and flying – obviously a bizarre combination. He had always been interested in planes and he wanted to learn how to fly, so when his mates were playing rugby I would come over to Cheltenham and take him to Staverton Airport for lessons. He had a natural aptitude for flying, which is just as well as he now flys Jumbo Jets for British Airways! I carried on very much enjoying playing for Shrivenham and on two occasions got selected along with Chris Sugden for the Oxfordshire League team, which was obviously not the same as playing for Lancashire!

However, somebody who was playing for Lancashire (how seemless was that link?!) was Kevin Hayes and he contacted me to see if Apollo would sponsor Lancashire. They did not have a Commercial Manager and the Chairman had arranged a deal for the club to be sponsored for £2,000. The players were on a percentage and the great West Indian and Lancashire captain Clive Lloyd, had worked out that his and the players share would be less than £2 and on behalf of the players complained to the Chairman who responded with a, if you think you can do any better you find a sponsor hence Kevin's call. I chatted with Paul and we agreed that we would offer £4,000 plus an agreement that whatever sponsorship we could obtain for the following season, we would keep 50% of everything over £4,000. I mentioned this to Kevin and was duly summoned to Old Trafford to meet the Lancashire Head Coach Peter Lever, of Rochdale lecture series fame. After a quick chat with Peter, he explained that this had actually got nothing to do with him and I needed to meet two of the players, Paul Allott and Graeme Fowler, who were representing the player's interests.

They were both England players and I was delighted to be able to meet two of my heroes – I obviously did not tell them this as it would not be very cool or good for negotiations and anyway I am not sure you can have heroes who are much younger than you! They were both great characters and we got on really well, resulting in the three of us going to the Club

Secretary Chris Hassall's office to discuss the deal further. Whilst talking to Chris I did explain, as a supporter and nearly ex player, that this was crazy as what they really needed was a top Commercial Manger like Jim Cumbes. of Warwickshire. It was probably coincidental but they then went and appointed Jim, who then went and got them a far better deal than we were offering – so there's gratitude.

Jim Cumbes was one of the nicest people I have ever met. He was one of the last people to have had both a top cricket and football career. As a fast bowler he had played for Lancashire, Surrey, Warwickshire and Worcestershire. His football history included Tranmere Rovers, Aston Villa and West Brom, but his career really hit its pinnacle when towards the end of it he signed for Southport. My Dad thought that he was wonderful and used to comment on how he would stand with the ball under one arm as he organised the outfield players. There was a very obvious flaw in this in that it was the season that Southport got kicked out of the Football League! I am not saying it was totally his fault but I have mentioned it every time I have introduced him at Sportsman's Dinners which has been often. Coming to think of it he is probably quite bored of hearing it. I got to meet him when he was playing for Worcestershire and guest pro-ed in the Ribblesdale League for Baxenden against Cherry Tree. After the match we had a few beers and a great chat resulting in us becoming close friends. Jim was to go on and become Chief Executive of Lancashire and was instrumental in creating the new Old Trafford.

Paul Allot and I kept in touch and he was responsible for a special moment in my life. When his cricket career finished and before he took up his very successful media career, he worked as an ambassador and fund raiser for the Marie Curie charity. With the kindness of Cameron Mackintosh we were able to get the charity a Gala Charity Performance of Les Miserables, which raised around £50,000. He later contacted me to say that he had been invited to 10 Downing Street, where Norma Major was holding a reception for the charity. He had been told he could bring two guests and I snapped up the chance of being one of them. His other guest was Julie Walters and it is probably fair to say that he spent more time looking after her than he did me and who could blame him!

Chapter 18

RIVERDANCE AND THE CHANGING TIDE

As Apollo continued to grow the next big acquisition was Hammersmith Odeon, which we bought from Rank. It was a legendary concert venue and certainly one of those that you would never wish to change its name. However, that was not possible as Rank owned the name Odeon and they insisted that we could not use the name. Hence it became Hammersmith Apollo. This was to change again as a result of a phone call I received from John Giddings, a top promoter, head of Solo, and now best known for running the Isle of Wight Festival. John's question was would we put a sponsor's name in the title for the right fee and if we would, he had somebody lined up and we agreed a fee to John of 10%. He did a great deal for us. hence Hammersmith and Manchester both became Labatt's Apollos.

The purchase of Hammersmith further advanced our position in the concert world and this was helped when we decided to have the flexibility to take out the stalls seats for standing only as we also did with Manchester. This increased the capacity to approx. 5000 making it able to compete with the new Arenas that were opening and, in London, Brixton Academy. It was quite a complex change to be able to make, with storing seats an art form. This was masterminded by Terry Carnes, one of the great characters of Apollo, and the man we went to, to keep our theatres in working order.

As a seated venue we also had some great hit shows with Riverdance, Cliff Richards' Heathcliffe and Philip Schofield starring in Joseph. When Riverdance opened at Hammersmith it was to feature above the title the two major stars from the outset in Michael Flatley and Jean Butler. As I stood in the foyer, as the audience entered I was near a board stating that due to injury Jean Butler would not be appearing in the show until further notice.

Then came the bombshell that Michael Flatley would also not be appearing. He had got in a dispute with the producers, which resulted in them axing him. I anticipated that we would have major problems with the audience but the show was so cleverly recrafted that people just adored it. For the producers it was a master stroke as it took Riverdance from being a star headed show to an ensemble piece with nobody featuring above the title. As such they were able to run productions all over the world simultaneously.

Another great show there was Stuart Littlewood's "Oh What A Night", starring Kid Creole but with the extra standing capacity for concerts, Hammersmith reverted more and more back to the fabulous concert venue that it always was.

I loved the concert side of our business and we were lucky that there were some great promoters, many who had started out at the same time as me, responsible for a really vibrant touring scene. Although our interest in promoting tours in our company was directed through Barry Clayman, we did dip our toe in the water and as Apollo, promoted the biggest single act show of all time in the UK!

This followed Barry's tour of Michael Jackson, which had been a sell out of major stadiums. With the success of the tour, Paul suggested that we should go to the well one more time, but Barry felt there was no point taking a risk after the success of the tour. Paul and risks went together so we promoted the final date of Michael Jackson's tour at Aintree Racecourse with a capacity of 100,000. The tickets flew out and with people desperately wanting to be there, I am sure another 10,000 found their way in one way and another!

I was delighted to be able to take Andrea and Stephanie and for them to be included in the VIP area. I had seen Michael Jackson earlier in the tour at Wembley Stadium but this was something else. The Liverpool audience are always special and it was a sensational event to be part of as well as triumphant vindication of Paul's gambling instincts!

As well as getting great concerts I was the lucky boy that could be on the road going to see them. One of my favourites was when Barrie Marshall, one of the most delightful promoters to deal with, rang to get my opinion on his proposal to bring Tina Turner over to the UK to do her first solo tour after her break up with Ike. I was very enthusiastic, if only because I really wanted to see her show, which obviously is not a very good reason in itself for Barrie to tour her.

In the end he decided to test the market with a few shows starting at Oxford

Apollo. I fancied it that much that I persuaded him to do the show at 8.30pm so that we could add a 5.30pm performance if the business demanded it. Well the business did demand it and Barrie also added lots of extra dates as the clamour for tickets increased. Once he went on sale with the tour he used to ring me at home every Sunday to discuss how sales were going.

I decided that I would go to the Oxford 5.30pm show so that I would see her very first solo performance in the UK. Oxford's audiences are great but not known for being the most demonstrative and at a first house even less so. However this was the exception as they stood the moment Tina Turner came on and just went crazy. The show was sensational with that incredible voice, fabulous stage presence, and superb dance routines with sweat flying everywhere. I was privileged to see this fantastic show and Barrie had a sell-out tour, which became the first of many for him with her. No wonder he was always nice to me when he saw me!

I also got the chance to house and meet my favourite singer of all time when Paul Fenn from Asgard booked Joan Baez in to London's Dominion Theatre. I had always pestered Paul for a date when he started touring her and I like to think that being the nice guy that he is, he put her into one of our dates to shut me up. In the highly unlikely event that he reads this he will no doubt think – stupid fool I put her in there to make money! Her show was great and when I chatted with her after the show I was mesmerised by her and decided that she was my new best friend!

I should have left it there but when she played Manchester Apollo we went to see her with a couple of friends in the knowledge that I could take them back stage after the show and get a great welcome. However this was not to be the fine occasion that I anticipated, as from the moment she came on the stage she complained about how cold the theatre was and she then asked the audience if they were cold and after they roared their agreement she went off stage and returned wearing a great big coat and proceeded to play the rest of the show in it whilst continually complaining.

When I asked Ian Coburn, the Apollo's General Manager, about the problem he explained that they had taken a very long time getting the gear in resulting in the Dock Door being open for longer than normal, on what was a very cold winter's day. Needless to say I steered well clear of going back stage after the show and she was relegated in my affections being replaced by Tina Turner!

There were so many memorable concert nights with the added bonus of getting to meet many great stars and we were indebted to the promoters who brought their shows to us. These included Tim Parsons from MCP, Harvey Goldsmith, Danny Betesh, Barry Dickens, Derek Block, Pete Wilson, Mel Bush, Jeff Hanlon, Nick Leigh, Phil McIntyre and Paul Roberts, Simon Moran, Paul Walden and Derek Nichols for Flying Music, Barrie Marshall, John Curd and of course John Giddings.

They were all great characters, and we certainly did not agree on everything, particularly our rental deals, but they were a massive part of our success and I enjoyed working with nearly all of them!

Also crucial to us were some of the promoters, who had shows that could also play our smaller theatres. One of my favourites was Dudley Russell, who is married to Pam Ayres, and he would bring some of the Irish Acts, Postman Pat, Fireman Sam as well as Pam herself. These shows could play all sizes of theatres and he and Pam were a couple whose company I always enjoyed.

Another great character was Alan Leightell, who had the best Queen tribute act called Magic. They were massively successful and he looked after them brilliantly and always gave me lots of dates as well as plenty of laughs. We operated a no-censorship policy, which meant that I had no problem having such lady pleasing acts as The Chippendales, promoted by Carl Leighton-Pope, and they played to massive business. I went to see them at Oxford Apollo where they did 4 sell out shows. It was an astonishing spectacle with the all-female (apart from two blokes!) audience going absolutely crazy. They were all fired up and after the show a few of them rushed in my direction and then past me to a Chippendale who was stood behind me! We also had to make all the Gents Toilets into ladies (Don't ask!), which must have slightly inconvenienced the two blokes!

The no censorship gave us a very difficult few moments when we booked Bernard Manning, who had recently been filmed secretly by Granada TV doing a show in a Police Club. The show was unpleasant and racist and deservedly drew a lot of criticism. My take on Bernard was that I enjoyed his company but disliked his humour from the day Linda and I had been to see him with Brian and Mitzi in a Birkenhead Club.

There were only about 20 people in there and when he picked on a black guy in the audience he lost all of us and he walked off after 10 minutes just before I was about to walk out. The show at Oxford was his first since the TV exposure and he was subjected to death threats. I, having booked the show, was also targeted receiving a number of threatening phone calls plus some guy who I thought that I was having a reasonable conversation with, explaining our self-censorship rule, which enabled people to exercise their own standards and just not come. However that ended with him telling me that he had taped the whole conversation and would be giving it to the papers, he then issued a number of unpleasant threats presumably after he had turned his tape recorder off. I, of course, went to the show and I went to see Bernard beforehand. He was undoubtedly extremely worried. The result was that he left out the most offensive parts of his act, went down a storm and was very funny.

This was a rare situation and did not deter from great nights watching and meeting the likes of Tom Jones, Rod Stewart, Elton John, Meatloaf and Chris De Burgh, who is included because when we met up for a drink at his hotel he personally queued up at the bar to buy his round, whilst the money is normally handed over to the Tour Manager to get the drinks! I should also add that he is also included because he did a great show. Meatloaf's music featured heavily in my life as Ben always insisted that we put his CD on when I took him to school. Invariably as we arrived surrounded by parents and staff he would simultaneously put the windows down and turn the volume up to maximum, with the sounds of Bat out of Hell drawing disapproving looks from all and sundry. To this day when the drinks are flowing and the sing song starts Ben will invariably include a bit of Mr Loaf for us!

The smoothest concert that I ever went to was Daniel O'Donnell at Liverpool Empire. He had the capacity audience eating out of his hand, particularly when he invited an 88 year old lady to have a cup of tea with him, not because she was old, but because she had more years of wisdom!

During his last number people started forming an orderly queue to meet him after the show and the Empire's General Manager, Jacqui Hinde, explained to me that he would not just sign autographs but he would chat and have photographs taken. When I went back to thank him for the show I asked him what time did he expect to leave and he estimated 3.00am so I made my excuses and left.

One of the best shows for glitz was Gary Glitter, who was a fabulous showman that I once saw in a tent performing his Rock n Roll Circus to about 50 people before his career, under Jeff Hanlon's guidance, took off again. He was brilliantly innovative in that show. He was also one of the nicest people to visit in his dressing room where he always had time to chat. His incredible downfall from grace is a great sadness when you consider the joy and pleasure his shows gave to so many people.

The next two theatres to be added to our roster were the York Grand Opera House and Birmingham Alexandra for which we did a deal with Paul Elliott. I had always liked Paul Elliott but Paul Gregg was not so keen so I was surprised and delighted when he told me that he and David had come to an agreement to take the theatres over. I was less delighted to be told that part of the deal was to give Paul Elliott first choice to do the pantos at all our theatres. My annoyance was not as a criticism of his shows, which were always excellent quality, but rather it would be very disloyal of me to take the dates from the current producers.

Along with his partner in the pantos, Chris Moreno, we met up at The Waldorf, as one does, to discuss the deals. This had not been part of the discussion between the two Pauls so was virgin territory for me. I insisted the deals would be the same as the current ones. They said they could not work to them and needed improving, Chris Moreno got quite excited and I stuck to my guns. For a while it got vaguely unpleasant until Paul Elliott just said, "Sam we will walk away from them". Gaining my eternal respect he got up, shook my hand and wished us well with Birmingham and York.

They were two lovely theatres with Birmingham Alexandra, although the number two theatre in the city behind the Birmingham Hippodrome, a strategically important venue for us. With the strength we had with most of the top touring dates we were able to persuade a lot of shows to play the Alexandra.

Despite a lot of staging space restrictions we still squeezed shows in. I remember persuading David Ian and Paul Nicholas to bring Grease there and I think that they and the musicians were somewhat surprised when we had to base them in a bar displaying the wonders of technology. The General Manager of the theatre, James Howarth, was the son of friends, but appointed by Mike Adamson. He was a most likeable guy and a very good manager.

He also worked with Terry Carnes and Daniel Gidney, another top guy in the Apollo set up, to arrange our one and only Apollo cricket match. The opponents were to be a Cameron Mackintosh and Les Miserables team, and to keep me quiet they made me captain. I was in the Alexandra Theatre having a meeting with James, when the subject turned to the cricket match.

I explained to James, probably in a somewhat condescending way, that to have a game of cricket we would need a ground! He had obviously worked this out for himself and somewhat stunned me when he informed me that he had arranged for us to use Edgbaston! We did not get to use the main pitch as we were on the practice ground but we did get to use the main pavilion.

To add to my enjoyment Ben was also included in the team and Daniel's brother took some great photos of him batting and looking a proper player. Daniel so enjoyed his day that he went on to be one of cricket's top administrators as Chief Executive of Lancashire. Obviously far too late to get me into the team!

York Grand Opera House was a super theatre with a great team working there with the only weak link being that it was near a river and got flooded from time to time! Again we came up trumps with young managers showing what can be achieved by sheer enthusiasm and love of the job with both Lizzie Richards and Ian Sime doing a great job. The theatre had a capacity of 1,000 and with no subsidy it was a tough task making it work. I remember trying to get a producer to put a musical in there starring Barbara Dickson but he just would not go for it. Talking to Ian Sime, he said that last time she had been there he had invited the whole cast to his house after the Thursday performance for a curry and he was sure that Barbara would want to play York. He was spot on and when the producer mentioned the date to her she immediately remembered her last visit and insisted on playing York.

This was a great example of how a manager could have a positive influence on their theatre's programming. Ian was not only great with the artistes, who played the theatre, he was also very good with the public as well as the media. He had the sort of presence that as soon as you walked into the theatre's foyer you would know straight away that he was in charge and at the end of the show he would always be there chatting to members of the public and checking that they had enjoyed their evening.

This made it even more astonishing that as a result of some HR driven two day course, when Apollo was under American ownership, they assessed him as being not very good with the public. When I rang the head of HR to explain what nonsense this was and how on earth had they reached this bizarre conclusion she explained that it was as a result of a story Ian had written. She went on to tell me that the management training consultants were very good. I went on to tell her that any person who could have come to this conclusion was a complete idiot and that I was astonished that the company now had so much money that they could afford to waste considerable sums on a complete waste of time.

My love of all things HR was compounded when I visited Manchester Palace and went to enter through the box office. I always went into theatres either through the stage door or the box office as I would always be able to have a good chat with the team working there and learn about how things were going. On this occasion the box office door was locked. The time was 10.30am and displayed sign confirmed that the box office opened at 10.00am. I then found another sign that announced that the box office would be closed until 11.OOam for staff training!

As I explained, somewhat excitedly to the gentleman taking the course, that the first item on box office training was to ensure that the box office opened on time – seemed pretty obvious to me! The meeting was brought to an abrupt halt with the members of the box office telling me that they had told the man that they should be selling tickets rather than listening to him.

I also had an unhappy experience when under pressure from Ben, I agreed to join the rest of the world and cease to be the only person not to have a computer. As far as I was concerned I operated very well without one as I had Nicola Tailby, a great PA and lovely person, who humoured me and just printed off any emails sent to me and I scribbled a reply to the ones that were not complete nonsense and she sent it back.

However Ben persuaded me of the error of my ways and I duly contacted the IT department and ordered a lap top. I also asked if one of their experts could teach me how to use it. The lap top arrived, as did a very young man, who was the requested expert. For my first lesson we agreed it would be good to access my emails. I diligently took notes of all the wise things that he was telling me ready for my next lesson in a week's time. Unfortunately my enthusiasm was somewhat dented by two setbacks, in that I discovered that I had got confused in my notes writing and could not do any more than turn it on and then came a slightly more serious setback when somebody stole the said lap top. I took this as a sign that God did not want me to have a computer and I very happily reverted to my previous ways!

Unfortunately two other members of the team also had their computers stolen and I was told that HR were going to send them warning letters for not putting the lap tops away when they left the office, which seemed similar to the demise of mine. I pre-empted that by contacting the head of HR to ensure that she arranged counselling for these poor young ladies who were distraught at having their personal space invaded! This seemed to do the trick! By now you will not be surprised to know that after a few drinks in the pub I can do a very boring 30 minute rant on the evils of HR!

However amongst the many there was one shining light in Denise

Aldridge, who actually understood the theatre industry and always seemed to be on the side of the people trying to make the business work.

So back to the plot! The next Civic venue to be added to the chain was particularly special as it was the Southport Theatre and Floral Hall. David did brilliantly in negotiating with a hung Council, who could not agree on anything. It required lots of patience, not David's strong point, and I hope that I was able to help as a home town boy with a vision for its future. As with Torbay and Scarborough it had been hit by the decline in summer tourists and as a result also in the summer season shows. We were able to improve its all-round year and to bring concerts that would not otherwise have played the theatre. Lisa Chu who had started with us as a 17-year-old usherette at Liverpool Empire, took charge of it, having also managed The Empire, which was a great story in itself. She worked very hard to improve its Conference and Exhibitions trade and once it had been given a major refurbishment she took the business to a new level. The only weak link was that I was never able to persuade her to come to a Southport home game!

We then took on Felixstowe Spa Pavilion. I must have caught David on a good day for this one as when we did our presentation it was against a background of very few shows going there, although it did have a nice sea view restaurant. I, of course, fell in love with it as I did with all our theatres but I knew that we would struggle to make the required £100,000+ from it. David and I stood on the sea front to discuss whether we continued with our application and in the 40 minutes we chatted we did not see one single human being. That did not help my cause, with David asking if anybody actually lived in Felixstowe! In the end having dismissed my rather pathetic claim that it was strategically important he said that as long as we would make some money from it let's go ahead. So hello Felixstowe Spa Pavilion!

Next was Folkestone Leas Cliff Hall, which was a great multi-purpose venue with the capacity for stand-up concerts of 1400. That made it a major attraction to us. Another of our young managers in Jo Barnes did a stunning job there. I went to a sell-out Bluetones concert there and she was rushed off her feet but everything was done with a smile and cheerfulness. On this occasion I ended up checking tickets with her as the punters arrived as she needed a bit of help. The show was a great success with record bar takings (no doubt due to us putting the prices up!) The theatre was a great success and Jo played a major part in achieving this.

Our smallest theatre was the Old Fire Station in Oxford, which had been paid for by Cameron Mackintosh as part of his involvement with Oxford University's Drama facilities. It was used by the University for their own theatre groups whilst also being used as a venue to try out future shows for the West End and touring.

On one occasion they were doing a workshop for Chaplain The Musical starring Tommy Steele. I was taken by surprise when the receptionist at our office buzzed me to say that there was somebody called Tommy Steele asking for me. We had a coffee and a good chat and I was really appreciative of him going out of his way just to say hello. So if I have been slightly critical of him earlier in the book please disregard it! Afterwards I asked the young lady if she knew who Tommy Steele was and she looked at me blankly and said that she had never heard of him. I sang Little White Bull to her and she looked at me as though I had just dropped in from Mars!

The most remarkable of our theatre acquisitions, which was to be the jewel in our crown, was The Lyceum. It was owned on a long lease by Brent Walker, who at the time were in serious financial trouble. It was seriously run down and they were facing all sorts of dilapidation clauses, which if not dealt with would require them to surrender their lease to the Theatres Trust. The other establishment West End theatre owners were just sitting back waiting for this to happen before putting their bid in to operate it.

In a stroke of pure genius Paul said that we should buy the lease from Brent Walker and he and David went on to negotiate this at a knock down price. For Brent Walker it was very much the case of everything must go so, whilst they were at it, Paul and David bought Cardiff International Arena!

The Lyceum deal took the industry by surprise and even more so when the Theatres Trust realised that as the new owners, we were not subject to the dilapidation process that they had instigated and that they would have to go back to square one. They need not have worried as with a budget in the region of £12,000,000 Steve Lavelle set about creating the finest theatre in the West End. He undoubtedly achieved this and we were all justifiably proud when Prince Charles came to re-open it.

In advance of that I suffered from one of Paul's "What are you doing tomorrow" jobs. As The Lyceum was nearing completion and we reached the moment to announce that the opening show would be Andrew Lloyd Webber's Jesus Christ Superstar, Paul arranged a press launch to feature The Lyceum in all its glory and the opening show. The theatre was still being worked on and its gimmick was that the 26 media people plus Andrew and

Paul as hosts, would have to wear hard hats for the launch lunch.

The day before the event, Paul decided that he had something better to do so I was drafted in as a late substitute. Paul explained to me that it was agreed that Andrew and I would not do interviews before the lunch but would both make a presentation and then field any questions. I turned up with my speech prepared eulogising Andrew, and the importance to Apollo of Starlight Express, whilst pointing out that the big story was the re-opening of this incredible theatre.

Unfortunately Andrew was working from a different script and chatted with the journalists beforehand and then when asked to speak at the lunch just said a few words about the show and that he had spoken to most people, but would be available to do interviews. I considerably revised the eulogising in my speech and concentrated on The Lyceum. Afterwards the media had the choice of interviewing Andrew Lloyd Webber or Sam Shrouder. You will be surprised and disappointed that they appeared to focus on Andrew. He did an interview with all 26 journalists, whilst I did 4! One of my four was with BBC Radio Hereford, not quite sure what they were doing there although I was very grateful to them for bothering with me, and in another interview the young lady stopped half way through because she saw that Andrew was available! This was not my finest hour! However the reopening of The Lyceum was undoubtedly one of Apollo's greatest achievements and after housing a number of shows it became the long term home to The Lion King.

Cardiff International Arena was also a great addition, and having been awarded the contract to manage Sheffield Arena took our Arena's to three. Paul Latham did a great job with Cardiff, which was also a World Trade Centre. It became very successful thanks to Paul's guidance and an excellent General Manager, Graham Walters. I loved going there and was always royally treated by Graham and his team.

My best night was going to see Tom Jones, who being in Wales seemed to take his show up to another level. When Freda and I arrived we were taken to a hospitality room with drinks and a buffet. I was very impressed but was about to say how unnecessary this was when I saw that we were sharing the room with The Stereophonics and Cerys Matthews, who were the obvious recipients of the hospitality. The night got even better when Cerys and The Stereophonics joined Tom on stage. It was another of those nights, when it was an absolutely privilege to be there.

There were many of these special nights and I never lost sight of how lucky

I was. By now I was very focused on getting the best shows in for all the theatres on the best deals and ensuring that we sold the maximum amount of tickets. Nicky's great theatres booking team was further strengthened by the addition of John Drury, who apart from supporting Chesterfield, was an excellent addition. John was to go on to run Wembley Arena as well as taking with him another of our fine team Leigh and it was a delight to be a guest at their Torbay wedding.

Also in the team we had Sarah Godfrey and Hilary Wells. It was a massive task to keep all the theatres booked but we all bonded together, whilst having lots of fun together. Every morning wherever I was I would receive the box office figures for every show in every theatre. I would visit the theatres, meeting up with the managers, marketing team and head of party bookings to painstakingly go through each show and what we could do to increase the business. I am sure everybody else thought these meetings were a waste of time but I loved them, we had so many great people full of energy and great ideas.

It also enabled me to pass on these ideas to other theatres to ensure that we used the collective knowledge we had in the Division.

It also helped when talking to promoters and producers to not only know how their ticket sales were but also our plans on how to improve them. As part of this I ensured I saw as many of our shows as possible, always popping backstage to say thanks to the artistes, which also was a great help when dealing with the producers of our shows. Mike continued to do all the proper work of running the theatres and would liaise with David on such matters as spend-per-head and budget overspends. I had created the perfect job for myself and if nobody had been kind enough to pay me for it would have done it for nothing, – I obviously never said that at the time!

As a company we had spent so long fighting the Industry's establishment that we probably failed to notice that bit by bit we became a crucial part of it. As well as being a Fellow of the Institute of Entertainment and Arts Management, I served the Government's Working Party of Best Value in Theatre (Letting Apollo run them all was the obvious answer to that one!) as well as being appointed to Board of the Theatres Trust by the Minister for Culture, Margaret Hodge.

The Theatres Trust had the potential to be a bit boring had it not had a great Chairman in Rupert Rhymes. Rupert was very amusing and spent most of the time telling us things that would be followed by a "do not minute that". The two Chief Executives Peter Longman and Moira Samuels, who served during my involvement were also good value. Simon Callow and Penelope Keith were also on the Trust. For a period I was a monthly columnist in the Trade Magazine Encore courtesy of Peter Foot, its editor and inspiration. On one occasion I did an article on Showmanship, which I include in this book despite it covering a number of things that I have already mentioned. (I am working on the basis that you will have long since forgotten them anyway!)

Sam says ...

THE Sam Shrouder COLUMN

WHAT EVER HAPPENED TO SHOWMANSHIP?

A few years ago I hosted a 'marketing' meeting for all the Arts Council sponsored companies that played the old Apollo circuit. It was a dispiriting experience as one expert after another explained that marketing was mailing everybody who had previously booked to see the company, remailing those that did not respond, sending a reminder to those who still had not booked and finally sending a 2 for 1 offer.

After explaining that I felt to mail people four times was a lazy and negative way of selling tickets as well as ensuring that nobody buy tickets in advance as they would wait for the 2 for 1 offer. I asked about publicity, promotion and showmanship. It was explained to me that this did not come under the heading of marketing so I changed the title of the meeting to 'How can we sell more tickets?' I then explained my vision of making the show seem desirable, exciting and unmissable and that you have to buy your tickets immediately because the show would soon be sold out. It was also imperative that we create new audiences because if we just rely on past attenders the art form will not survive. We did not make much progress and as I drove home I remembered that the meeting had been called because of dwindling audiences!

JOHN WADE

After lunch...
After dinner...
On stage...
In cabaret...
In close-up...

"THE PATTER OF MAGIC FEATS"

(020) 8994 0511
E-mail: jwmagicadvisor@dial.pipex.com

'OUTDATED CONCEPT'?

When I had a similar conversation a few weeks ago I asked the person I was chatting to to give me his thoughts on showmanship. He told me that in this high tech age it was an outdated concept. I spluttered, took another sip of my beer and decided to bore you dear readers (if you have not already turned to something more interesting) with my memories of Showmen.

I started my career with ABC in Ten Pin Bowling and ABC insisted that all their management work to earn a Showmanship Star. This entailed sending in a publicity campaign which was judged on media coverage and public profile. I was lucky to have a great showman as a manager in Graham Schofield (later to run Sheffield City Hall) and he taught me the first tricks of the trade. Graham always ensured that we had a tie up with a local store, which gave them coverage in the Bowl whilst we were able to utilise their shop for a window display. Next he would take a photo of the display, write an article explaining the tie up, which usually included prizes for our customers, and take it to the local paper. He taught me that if you handed it on a plate to the paper they would often use it whereas if you rang them with details it normally did not warrant coverage. He also always invited stars, who were in the town, to come and bowl in a charity event and, needless to say, he always had a photographer there. I well remember Graham organising a charity challenge with Frankie Vaughan, Norman Collier and Mike Yarwood. Great publicity for the Bowl.

NUMBER ONE SUPER SHOWMAN

The greatest showman I ever worked with was Francis Lee, who was Entertainments Officer for Rochdale, when I was Manager of Middleton Civic Hall and Deputy Entertainments Officer. Francis set out single handedly to change the image of Rochdale from dour northern town to a place of fun, excitement and entertainment. He taught me that, above all, showmanship was about opportunism. Whatever took place should be examined to enable as many publicity stunts as possible to be pulled. Francis had his car painted with 'Britain's Number One Super Showman' and he was.

He appeared more regularly on television than the News – normally in fancy dress! One day whilst dressed as a tramp with a billboard advertising a show he

was approached by a Councillor who told him it was degrading for a council official to behave in this way. Francis explained to her that he was an entertainment officer not a public health officer! He put a smile on people's faces not least when he offered £1¼ million for the Loch Ness Monster dead or alive to go into Rochdale's Hollingworth Lake. The two television companies thought that it was a great stunt and were on their way to film him, when he got a letter from warning for offering council money without permission! Greenpeace wrote to complain about the dead bit and 'Disgusted of Rochdale' wrote to ask why if the council could afford this sort of money they had not mended her guttering. The rest of us laughed. His showmanship not only changed the image of Rochdale, it also ensured that we sold tickets for the very ambitious programming in the theatres.

As Blackburn's Entertainment Officer I worked with John Garforth and John Jardine who were both brilliant publicists capitalising on situations to get maximum exposure for events. I well remember that when we were looking for a fire eater to publicise a festival, David Green, a young YTS lad in the office, volunteered. We immediately rang the paper to sent a photographer down, whilst David ostensibly went home to get his equipment. The weak link in all this was that David had obviously never done it before and just went to a shop to buy the equipment. Whilst practising he was half decent and we named him the Great Flambeau. Unfortunately, when the time came to do it for the press he went for the big one resulting in a burnt ceiling, singed hair and

eyebrows, all the fire alarms going off, three fire engines and a wonderful front page picture advertising our festival.

WATERMAN'S SALTY TONIC

Sometimes showmanship helps in adversity. The story is often told of Don Waterman, who was a larger than life Tourism Director of Scarborough, and of how he reacted when the first publicity came out about the sea not being fit to swim in at a number of resorts including Scarborough. Don is reported to have arranged for both television stations to meet him on the beach, where he had a gentleman dressed as a butler with a silver tray and glass and he was in his swimming trunks. They both waded out to sea, the glass was filled with sea water, handed to Don who drank it and said 'That is how confident I am of the safety of swimming off Scarborough'. That is showmanship. Incidentally, I believe that it is not true that Don spent the next two weeks in hospital.

In the present day I see very few inspired examples of showmanship. One exception is Ellen Kent, who always has some stunt to publicise her operas. Recently she has had a horse that taps in time to the music in Carmen; eagles, falcons and dogs in Rigoletto; and a stunt double who did a 25 foot death leap in Tosca. All ensuring massive coverage in the media.

Showmanship and stunts advertise shows for free as well as creating a buzz about the events. If it is now an outdated concept the industry is not only a sadder place but also we must ask ourselves whether Showbusiness has now become just business.

You, of course, may not agree. Do let Encore know your thoughts.

13 years on - now with the industry's most comprehensive **database** ...and that means targeted distribution for ads and inserts

...the always good value *Encore* subscription

the *Encore* website: www.encorextra.com

Sam writing for Encore magazine

The subject of Showmanship was the theme of my talk at the IEAM AGM and astonishingly was the sole topic for the Stage's editorial that week. I reproduce it in all its glory as you will no doubt enjoy that this is a popular theme among those long past their best, who prefer to wallow in golden ageism!! It was obviously their case that the only reason anybody could take the old fool seriously was because of his position with Apollo. So in a roundabout way we had truly arrived!

At home we had moved for the sixth time to an incredible property, Sherborne House in Lechlade. The house with an outdoor swimming pool, large orchard and William and Mary style (not sure what that means but it is what the estate agent told me!) was beyond my wildest dreams.

It fully justified Freda's changing house on a regular basis policy and Lechlade, a 5 star pub, three restaurants, Londis and tea shop type of village was a great place to be. The New Inn, run by Nicky Sandhu and his family, was a friendly meeting place, which I very much enjoyed, particularly with Ben. Ben and I also got to play four games of cricket for Lechlade at the end of one season before his cruel shoulder injury put a stop to our blossoming caught Shrouder (B) bowled Shrouder (S) act.

Sherborne House was also the venue for two great weddings when firstly Stephanie married Richard, which was to result in sons Patrick and William, and then Andrea's to Simon, which sadly did not last the test of time. On both occasions I was in charge of entertainment and alcohol – so not much change there! We also made some great friends in the area with Charles and Christine Eatwell being close friends with whom we enjoyed some unforgettable trips to Portofino as well as others. Next door there was a Doctor and Nurse team of John and Vivienne Bestwick, who were always great fun to be with and tended to our ailments as well!

We also combined with Charles, Christine and their sons Matt and David to host a Millenium party. With the cost of bands and disco being prohibitive, we did our own enterianment with Charles putting together a family and friends band and Ben and I doing the disco. The disco was such a roaring success that we got two more bookings over the next twelve months!

One of them was for Christmas Eve at The Swan in Southerop. We were paid £50 which I am sure I declared on my tax return. Of course, everybody had come to dine and then went home! At the height of the evening we had seven dancers on the floor so we finished at midnight and loaded our equipment into the car. As the last item went in, a group of people arrived with a lady asking where the Disco was which is how we nearly did a show for Kate Moss and her friends!

So all in all, life could not have been better but the storm clouds were gathering both in business and domestically! That is obviously a bit dramatic but if you are bored with this book hopefully it will entice you to keep going!

Chapter 19

SFX AND CLEAR CHANNEL

By the end of the 1990s it was obvious that the very close relationship that Paul, David and I had was slightly diminished. Whilst my friendship with David has remained rock solid to this day, Paul had embarked on a different agenda. His first priority in life was undoubtedly Nita and their son Simon and Nita had become less enamoured with the Apollo life.

This first manifested itself when she told me that she no longer wanted the theatre bookings team to work from her house and gave me two weeks to move them. It was their house and I fully understood that their life might be better without us there, although I was slightly surprised as she had always got on so well with everybody that worked there.

The move was not a problem as our team was integrated into the Apollo Head Office in Cowley. Indeed there were many advantages as we were able to mix with the other departments. The disadvantage for me was that instead of working in the office next to Paul and being able to discuss many varied subjects, we now saw a lot less of each other. It then became obvious that Nita wanted the company sold and that Paul wanted to make this happen.

Paul and his family owned 83% of Apollo with David, Julie and myself being the only other shareholders. The fact that things were not as sweet as they were probably made the sale more attractive to all. Nita, wishing her interests to be independently looked after, got family friend John Jarvis, of Jarvis Hotels, to represent her. This was fine with us as we all liked and got on with John and he was undoubtedly going to be a major asset in assisting with the sale.

We initially looked at a stock market flotation and David led a team of us to make a presentation to the City. I found this to be a bemusing experience as I looked at a table of 20 plus analysts, who looked to me as though they had just came from the local junior school. There was an array of multi-coloured glasses, braces and bow ties and what was very evident was that not one of them had a clue about the theatre business so I got a very easy ride. For some of the rest of the team their questioning was both aggressive and unpleasant.

Afterwards when David and I left in a taxi with our adviser, he told us that they had agreed to a float but with a 25% deduction to our proposed value. David was very blunt and said that there would be no deal as Paul would never agree to it and as it turned out neither would David. I marvelled at how this bizarre gathering of business "experts" could come up with a value in something that they were pretty clueless about. This was somewhat supported when Apollo was sold for a figure nearing double the value that they gave it.

The first serous interest for the company came from the American Company SFX and Paul, David and John Jarvis concluded a deal with them to buy Apollo Leisure and Barry Clayman's BCC. I was not much involved in the negotiations but David loyally kept me fully informed.

Shamefully there was something quite attractive about receiving a large cheque and a 5 year contract, which they insisted that Paul, David and I signed as part of the deal. In hindsight the three of us were later to agree that it was by far the worse decision of our business life. As the deal looked like happening, David and I agreed that there were others who had been crucial to the Apollo success story that although not shareholders deserved to be rewarded and top of that list for both of us was Mike Adamson.

Whilst Paul was ok with this idea, Nita was adamant that it should not happen. When David and I said that we would pay out of our share it caused a certain amount of unpleasantness. It was very sad to think that we had all stuck together through the many difficult years but when we hit the jackpot both David and my relationship with Paul was tarnished. I like to think that part of this was because deep down we all knew that we were making a dreadful mistake.

I cannot claim any moral high ground because I too was excited about the money I was to receive. At the conclusion of the deal with SFX David rang me to say a large sum would be in my account by the close of business and to ring my bank to request that it was put on the money markets over night. To this day I have not the slightest clue what the money markets are but I obviously followed David's advice.

I had a somewhat fractious relationship with the Nat West Bank, which commenced in my early days when they sent me a letter to tell me that I had no money and charged me £10 for telling me! I have always found this to be a most obnoxious trend as the sheer logic of it is flawed as you cannot pay £10 to anybody to tell you that you have no money when you have no money to pay it!

Years later when things were going well I received a call from Nat West with a gentleman telling me that he was now my Personal Bank Manager and he would like to meet me. At the meeting he asked me what Nat West could do for me. My reply went along the lines that all banks were thieves, rogues and vagabonds. (This was later to prove most visionary!) and what the bank could do for me was to stop charging young people for telling them they had no money.

He was not impressed and asked what services could the bank supply for me and the answer was none until I had to ring him to carry out David's advice. I explained that I had a bit of money coming in and I wanted it put on the money markets, when I told him how much he said that he did not call that a bit of money, indeed that was the sort of money that he would take me out for lunch. I pointed out that it was the sort of money that I could buy my own lunch and that he should have bought me lunch when I had nothing!

A couple of years ago I received a photocopied letter from my Personal Banking Manager at the time stating that I now did not have enough money to justify a Personal Bank Manager! After 50 years of banking with Nat West it was the last straw and on the advice of my cricketing and now swimming friend John Smith, I went to see a very nice man at Santander, who painlessly switched my account. When I set out to write this book I decided that I did not want to upset anybody so if there is any vaguely pleasant and honest person working in our banking system I apologise. Indeed while I am at it I also apologise to any worthy person working in HR!

In my case the money did not change my life but it did did enable me to do a number of things, which included buying a home in Thurlestone, in Devon, which Freda found, and more importantly help Andrea and Stephanie buy the houses they wanted and put money aside to ensure that we could buy Ben an apartment when the time was right. It also enabled me to help with projects that I was to go out and see with World Vision. This was good news and thank you very much the kind people of SFX. Less good news was that I was now employed by them!

What we did not realise at the time was that they were building the company up so that they could sell it on. They bought in a number of top promoters including Tim Parson's MCP, John Giddings and Solo and Barry Dickens' ITB. They also, with Paul's guidance, split the music and the theatres with the arenas Hammersmith and Manchester Apollo joined by the music promoters and then a Theatre Division to include the Theatres, Backrow Productions and crucially David Ian Productions.

The ramifications of this for me was that I lost responsibility for the music venues, lost my job as Chief Executive of the theatres to David Ian and became Chairman of the Theatres Divison. The only part of this that was good news was David Ian, who I had always liked, but was to go on and find out what a fantastic guy he was. He was very funny, self-deprecating and although his star was rising and mine was disappearing he always made me feel important. We laughed a lot together and really bonded.

When all the Divisions were told that they had to make a presentation to SFX's senior management we held a meeting where there was a lot of talk of power point presentations, professionalism and impressing them with our preparation. It was agreed that everybody would forward their presentation on the Monday for other people's view to ensure that we had a high quality meeting on the Tuesday.

David, bless him, said that he and I would not be doing that as we were in theatre and we would split the 20 minutes allotted to us and do it off the cuff without any presentation aids or power points. The others were outraged as they explained the level of professionalism expected by our new employers. We stuck to our guns and the level of professionalism of our new owners was such that they cancelled the meeting!

In fairness. SFX were just building the company up to sell it on to Clear Channel, a Texas based Company. This is when it really kicked in that we had sold our souls and that we were about to be exposed to a completely different style of running the company that we had lovingly built up.

The Clear Channel senior management were in awe of David Ian, who would wander into the office after a three-hour lunch having tied up crucial deals with Andrew Lloyd Webber or Cameron Macintosh and they would look at him open mouthed. I became convinced that Clear Channel – or Muddy Waters, as they were known in the theatre world – were not for me when David Ian came to me and said that they wanted to make Gerry Tait redundant.

Gerry, as well as being a close personal friend, was also magnificent at his job. He would get shows to finish the week when they had gone bust on the Thursday. This was a great skill of negotiation as all the money would be in the last two days of the week and he would get the cast on stage and do a deal with them, which was to everybody's benefit particularly the audience. He would also be crucial to dealing with Becta, the industry union. Above everything the managers that he was responsible for loved him and would do anything he asked to improve their theatres.

David Ian was again brilliant in this, as he was also a great admirer of Gerry. He left it with me in that if Gerry left now he would get him a year's salary as he knew that there was money in that fund, but if I wanted him to stay David would fight and win the battle but if he was made redundant a year later they would only give him the statutory amount.

I desperately wanted Gerry to stay but felt I had to make him aware of the situation. Once I had spoken to him, I knew that, as a very proud Scottish man, he would leave. Paul had already negotiated his departure and taken our Cinema Division as part of the deal and the day after Gerry received his redundancy deal he started work for Paul running the Cinemas.

Gerry and I stayed close friends and I was part of an incredibly happy day when he married Agnes and I think that I got to make a speech – I probably was not asked to but did one anyway! Nowadays Gerry and Agnes spend half their time at their French home, which is in a fabulous situation and was partly paid for by his Clear Channel redundancy – so there was only one winner there!

As I was coming near to completing this book, Gerry lost his battle with lung cancer. He was a special pal for more than 25 years and I very much miss him.

Gerry was Jewish and his funeral was only a couple of days after his death but despite this there was a good turn out of the old Apollo team. On this sad occasion I was asked by Agnes to say a few words and was pleased to pay my own tribute to him.

On the way up to Glasgow I received a call from Ellen Kent who was very fond of Gerry. She toold me that she was dedicating the whole of her Nabucco tour to 'Darling Gerry'. I thought this a lovely gesture to a lovely man.

The changes were happening thick and fast with the Theatres Booking Department being moved to London, with some of the team leaving and

David taking Nicky out to dinner to persuade her to move. Being a real charmer he is probably the only person who could have achieved that. This left me isolated in the Oxford Office and even more so when they brought in a Managing Director of a Division to support David. Katie Callender was from Nike and very capable and very sensitive to my situation but she had no theatre experience, which to me was important.

Just as I was about to be deserted by my Theatre Bookings team 9/11 happened and I remember watching it at the Stage Door at Liverpool Empire having had lunch with Bob Scott and I remember thinking at the time that if America's response results in more than 3000 innocent people losing their lives that they would lose the moral high ground. At the last count it was over 400,000 innocent people – sorry being a bit political here!

We received an email from the President of Clear Channel saying that most of their American team were asking for a percentage of their salary to be deducted to help the families who lost someone in the tragedy and would any of us like to make the same gesture.

This incensed Hilary in our Theatre Bookings team who wrote an aggressive response explaining that America was a rich country and would be able to help these people unlike some of the third world countries where people were dying of starvation. She included a number of expletives and then went to press the delete button, however she pressed send instead! She managed to send it straight to the President himself and all hell broke loose.

I came in the next day with Nicola handing me a list of emails culminating that she had to be dismissed immediately and that the head of HR had to be involved in this and to then march her off the premises. I explained to the head of HR that she could not be present when I talked to Hilary. She did not agree but I insisted that nothing would happen until she left my office. I then saw Hilary, who was most apologetic, but I explained that as she was leaving anyway because she could not transfer to London she now had the best story ever on how she handed in her notice! I also told her that the team and myself would meet her in the nearby pub for a farewell drink. The HR lady then stood there as she cleared her desk and marched her off the premises.

My career's down turn was accelerated when I was invited to a Clear Channel Theatrical Conference in Key West. I flew via Paris and got slightly confused and missed my connection, resulting in me only arriving at the Conference as a few hundred delegates were in the middle of dinner. There was no bar to lean on and I was just about to abandon the evening when Adam Kenwright, Gary McQuinn and Liz Coops from Backrow Productons spotted me and kindly rescued me with a place at their table. They and the rest of the table were good fun as the evening went from disaster to enjoyable. As it turned out I was only postponing the disaster to the next day.

In the morning I attended a marketing master class from some guy from Calvin Klein, which was a long way from being very stimulating. My moment of destiny arrived when I was part of an International Panel discussing and taking questions on how to sell show tickets. As far as I could gather there were only five non Americans at the Conference so it was no great achievement being on the International Panel.

Once I got going I explained that with due deference to the gentleman from Calvin Klein selling theatre tickets was not the same as selling underpants! This was my first mistake as it turned out that the said gentleman was a close friend of the President of Clear Channel! As I warmed to my theme I pontificated that every show was special in its own right and that they needed to be nurtured by marketing focused on the potential audience. When asked from the floor if I did not feel that shows could be marketed together and sold as a package I told the large gathered audience that that was nonsense. For instance you would not try to sell a performance of The Chippendales to the same people who might want to see a Shakespeare play. I again emphasised that you must take each show in isolation and target its potential audience.

There were more questions on similar lines but I felt that my one show focus routine was going down very well indeed there was quite a buzz in the audience. It did occur to me at the time that perhaps Clear Channel would want me to come over to the States and explain how to sell shows. As the day progressed numerous people came up to me to say how refreshing it was to hear my views, one or two also commented on how brave it was of me which I didn't understand.

Late in the evening I was having a drink with an American theatre owner, who told me that what I had said was exactly what a lot them thought but they did not have the courage to say so at this event. When I asked why not, he looked at me incredulously and after a moment said "You do know what this event is". When I explained that I assumed it was just a bit of a get together to discuss some new shows coming out on the road. Wrong! It was to launch Clear Channel's Subscription Series where you lump a load of shows together and sell it as a package! So I had upset the President of Clear Channel by labelling his friend an underpant seller and had then spoken against the whole purpose of the conference. Not a great career move and probably explained why the head of Clear Channel Europe did not even bother to come and say hello. Thankfully I had to miss the next day as I was flying back early for a family event.

Despite the changes, I had maintained my role in trying to bring acquisitions to the company. I was really thrilled when we managed to get the contract to run the fabulous Sunderland Empire. It is a spectacular four-level Frank Matcham theatre and I fell in love with it on first sight. (Once a luvvie always a luvvie!) The question was, who would manage it or rather how to persuade the perfect person to move from the West End glamour of our top theatre The Lyceum.

Debbie Carrick was from Sunderland and ticked every box as the perfect appointment. If you have been following the script you will remember that Debbie started out with the company working the Manchester Apollo bar and it was a massive compliment to her that she had got the Lyceum job. However she trusted Mike and myself that Sunderland would be a good career move and it was. As an attractive local girl the media loved the appointment and were massively supportive and she was to go on to do a superb job. We also added Grimsby Auditorium to our list of venues. It was a multi-purpose venue, to which we were certainly able to bring a far better level of shows.

However under the Clear Company I was slowly losing the plot. At one of our Theatre Division meetings, which David Ian and I joyfully jointly chaired, we were told that we had to be particularly respectful to some finance guy who was going to talk about our weekly reporting system and life does not get any better than that. David knowing my aversion to finance people that I have never heard of, suggested that it might be best if he introduced him.

Ever the showman he gave him a great build up only for the guy to then wander round giving out papers and losing everybody's focus – obviously not a theatre person! David Rogers had formulated our weekly and monthly reporting system and it was hard to see it being bettered, and certainly not by the guy addressing the meeting. David Ian showed me a note saying that this is so dull and would anybody notice if we nipped to the bar!

The questions from our managers showed that they did not see his plans as an improvement. When it came to questions it became more and more obvious that he had not thought this out. Eventually I stopped him in his tracks and asked anybody in the meeting to put their hand up if they thought what was being suggested was a good idea. Not one hand went up, including the people from his own department so I said that we would continue with the current form and move on to the next part of the agenda. It was not kind but he was talking a lot of rubbish!

Things went from bad to worse, when another very important member of the new regime emailed me (via Nicola!) from the office next door to say that Southampton Guildhall, which my team, led by Neil Sharma, were negotiating to run did not fit into the company's synergy. This resulted in me losing the plot completely and storming into his office, going into a rant along the lines that he was here to add up and I was here to decide which venues we took on and as we were forecasting a £200,000 profit, this was one we would take.

He responded that in his opinion, but did not get any further as I explained I was not interested in his opinion and that once he had been in this business for 40 years and knocked on my door with his opinion, I would still tell him to piss off. This was made worse by everybody in the open planned office hearing it. It was at that moment that I realised that I had to let go, it was no longer our company and I could not treat people in a manner that I would never have done in the Apollo days.

Fortunately, David Ian came to the rescue at one of our many lunches when he asked me what in a perfect world I would like to do, and this memo is the result of that conversation.

(See Press Release and Memo next page)

The resultant press release and memo reflected David Ian's kindness and diplomacy.

A year later David rang me with, what he hoped was good news, in that Clear Channel wanted to get rid of me. Not only that, they wanted a swift settlement and for me to leave within the fortnight. It was not quite how I envisaged my 20 year journey ending and I had actually no intention of leaving by the back door. I needed longer and a big party to go out on. David agreed to this and the wheels were set in motion.

I was visited by a very pleasant lady from the HR Department. Sadly I have forgotten her name otherwise I would have added her to my list of one of pleasant HR staff! Their enthusiasm for getting rid of me was reflected in the deal. When I went on a three day week my salary was reduced by 40% and I was gearing myself up to insist that they pay up my current salary till the end of my contract which had 20 months to run. But before I could make this demand, I was told that they would pay up my original salary in full! When I asked about my company car she said I could keep it and likewise with my mobile phone and number. It did occur to me that I must be particularly bad at my job as they were paying me considerably more not to come to work than they would have done if I had continued.

The only sticking points were an issue over my shares, which I did not fully understand and they wanted me to go on a year's gardening leave. A ridiculous expression as I neither liked or had any aptitude for gardening! I insisted that neither of these conditions were acceptable to me. David Ian was massively supportive and asked me which of the two issues mattered most. I explained that I was not bothered by the share issues but I was not going to accept not working for 12 months.

David told me to leave it with him but to write a letter saying that the share issue was non-negotiable. He then told the company that he could probably persuade me to back down from that stance as long as they agreed not to implement the gardening leave. They thought that David had done a great job solving this and I thought that David had done a great job getting me what I wanted! Throughout the negotiations David Rogers had been the true friend that he is with advice and support.

Clear Channel Entertainment – Theatre

Company Announcement

Sam Shrouder

I wanted to take this opportunity to announce that Sam Shrouder will be leaving Clear Channel Entertainment as of November 30, 2002.

We want to thank him for his more than 20 years of dedicated service, during which time he has not only overseen an unprecedented period of growth starting with one of the first venues to join the group, the Apollo Victoria Theatre in 1980, but also operated one of the finest Theatrical operations in England. I hope you will join me in thanking him for his incredible achievements, and wish him the best of luck in his future endeavours.

Steve Winton
Chief Operating Officer
Clear Channel Entertainment
Europe

Sam company announcement

The Company Announcement was made by Steve Winton and The Stage featured the news on its front page. It included the quote "Insiders have said that his personable style – a mark of the Apollo old guard was at odds with the corporate mentality of the multinational Clear Channel" and one source said 'The Company is now run by accountants and I do worry about how it will end up now that Sam's gone". So that was it, this incredible journey was over and all that remained was for David Ian to arrange a decent farewell party and boy did he achieve that!

With no regard for financial restraints David raided the Christmas hospitality fund and put on an incredibly lavish party at Balls Brothers in the West End. With the help of Nicky Monk, Nicola Tailby and David Rogers I was given the best possible send off. I was moved to tears (again!) by the thought, generosity and overall kindness of the organisers and everybody else, who came and also those who wrote to me. Not many farewell parties actually get reviewed but thanks to Peter Foot this lovely review appeared in Encore.

"LOVED SAM THE THEATRE LOVER

'What a way to take this one out' to quote Barry Manilow. Sam Shrouder's farewell party to mark his departure from the Clear Channel organisation was indeed a fun punched send off. I was honoured to be among the hundred plus invited friends, all of whom were greeted personally by Sam as they packed into the basement lounge of Balls Brothers in London's West End.

How did he remember everyone's name? Thereby lies the reason behind the great popularity of the man in theatre-land circles. Clear Channel's David Ian spoke of learning much and receiving sound advice from Sam – a sentiment frequently endorsed by the company's theatre managers. Bill Kenwright spoke on behalf of many of the producers present, illustrating his complimentary tributes to 'a true friend' with much humour. Jim Davidson's mischievous grin hinted of 'bombshells' to come but he actually started with an embrace and a whispered 'Relax' to Sam before delivering a very complimentary speech.

In response Sam Shrouder stressed that when he joined Paul Gregg and David Rogers in the early days of Apollo they wanted to achieve many goals in the theatre market but, most of all, they promised each other that they would have fun. Inspite of some desperate situations caused by bad decisions – `I thought every show I saw was good' Sam admitted – and some great successes created by brilliant decisions it had nearly always been fun.

As with all the speeches Sam's included some good natured swipes at the new Clear Channel regime. He claimed the directives received – not only on office efficiency but also on how to conduct your private life were 'most useful'! The roars of laughter that greeted such remarks may have coloured the cheeks of the American top brass had any of them been brave enough to attend. The unscheduled tirade from Clear Channel's Chief Operating Officer was the icing on the party cake however. Delivered in the style of the Chairman of the Wheeltappers and Shunters Club, Paul Latham urged his brothers to unite for the fight. Very, very funny. A memorable evening and Pete Langford of the Barron Knights whispered to me that the speeches had provided him with the most entertaining 60 minutes or so he had witnessed for many a year. Hear hear

I was incredibly flattered to have David Ian, Bill Kenwright, Jim Davidson and Paul Latham entertain the gathering with their humour and from time to time the odd pleasant comment about me! Paul's flat cap act had lit up many an Apollo do and I was delighted that he made an unscripted appearance. David Ian presented me with a Golden Ticket entitling me to see any show in a Clear Channel Theatre for the rest of my life. A great gesture and I do not blame David for them selling the theatres making my golden ticket worthless! Nicky had organised an engraved glass bowl with Sam Shrouder Apollo Leisure Sept 1980 to Nov 2002. Passionately yours with 48 venues that I had been responsible for all engraved.

These were fantastic gifts and I received many many more including the famed Brian May guitar from Paul Roberts and the Producers of We Will Rock You, and a sketched picture of me on the Decks of Blackburn from Phil McIntyre with 'Sam it must be a comfort to have something to fall back on".

It was a night that I will remember for the rest of my life and I was honoured to be able to share it with so many people that I loved and cared about, particularly Freda and Ben (who later disappeared to Stringfellows!)

When we got back to the Hotel I found a book that Nicky had organised, full of letters and cards plus stacks more that had arrived after the book had been completed. To say that I felt humbled by the kind comments people had made does not even begin to justify the emotion that I felt.

I realise that it is somewhat immodest to record some of the comments made but as I had just been sacked I hope that you will forgive me reminding myself that some people thought that I was ok.

From David Rogers there was The Great Escape – so there is light at the end of the tunnel!" Nicky Mark wrote me a very moving letter reflecting on 17 years of working together and of great friendship. Paul Latham made a number of very kind comments, needless to say on red paper and Mike Adamson's included "In all of the 22 years I have worked with Sam, he was always the same as the first day I met him in 1980, one of the greatest positive thinkers I have ever met with an overwhelming passion for his work, a guy in love with his Theatres and a superb morale booster". Mike also queried how in our good cop/bad cop routine he always got to play the bad cop!

Gerry Tait remembered his interview 16 years earlier and the journey that we both travelled, which included his 12 years as a Director of Southport FC as well as a special friendship. I will also treasure a card from my PA Nicola, whose life was also affected by my departure. She had protected me from technology, as well as the corporate world going on around me and without her my last couple of years would have been considerably less bearable. These were all people that I cared greatly about and had been a massive part of my life.

I was also grateful to receive cards from other people, whose paths I had crossed. John Holmes, head of SFX Sports Group and agent to multiple International Sporting Stars remembered the horror I displayed at a board meeting, when he insisted that the future of cricket was about to change with the game played under floodlights, with limited over games being the priority and a tournament for areas rather than counties. How ridiculous! Roger Bottomley was Chairman of the Division which ran all our Recreation Centres and gyms and was a lovely guy. He remembered me for a smile and a funny story every time we met. He also recalled that with the new navigation system in my car I went a different way to Scarborough which saved 20 minutes and that I had worked out that because of the many times that I had driven there, I had wasted three weeks of my life going the wrong way!

There was also a kind letter from Sir Philip Carter, who chaired the Liverpool Empire Trust whilst Jerry Katzman with Dominion Theatre commented that we have both made and lost money together and that is always a true test of friendship and trust. Little did Jerry know that we would later be involved in another venture where we lost money and still remained friends! I heard nothing from any of the Clear Channel hierarchy apart from Catie Callendar, who, to her credit, sent me a card with a promise to look after all the wonderful people who work in our theatres.

There would have been no Apollo story without the people who booked our theatres, so I was also gratified to hear from many of them. Ken Dodd and Anne wrote "You have always been so kind and understanding over the years. Sam Shrouders are very few and far between in this whizzkid ww/ dotcom world". I was very touched by this as Ken had always been a massive help in my career. The letter from many promoters and producers seemed to be summed up by Bill Kenwright's words "Thank you for the dates, the support, the understanding, the laughs but most of all the joy of working with a man of honour". There was also an overriding sentiment that the fun was going out of the business. Cameron Mackintosh wrote "Your style will be very sorely missed. I am afraid far too much `wing and a prayer' has gone out of our business and though the theatre always has a knack of surviving, it certainly is not as much fun as it was." I cannot say that all these numerous letters said that I was any good at the job but they did seem to think that I was a pleasant enough bloke!

What touched me most was the response I received from all the people I had worked with over the years. I was immensely proud of the achievement of the many people who had joined Apollo and gone on to do great things. To watch people join as young trainee managers and to go on to manage some of the greatest theatres in the country was a real joy. Even with my lack of modesty it would be too self-indulgent to bore you the reader with the many incredibly kind things that my friends in the Apollo Theatre team wrote but I hope that you will forgive me just a few.

Debbie Carrick wrote "The most important lesson that you taught me is that the Entertainment Industry is fun. It is about people having a good time, both on and off the stage."

From Jackie Hinde, "No matter what the circumstances you were always calm, courteous, supportive and found the positive in every situation".

James Haworth in a very humerous letter wrote, "He has the absolute respect and indeed admiration of the promoters and venue staff alike. The fact that he made the effort to communicate with everyone within the theatre, whatever their supposed status, spoke volumes and his enthusiasm for theatre and its people has been truly infectious. When the news filtered through about Sam's departure the disappointment of the Birmingham

Alexandra's staff was quite tangible and I think that is a wonderful testament to a true theatre man".

From the Princess Theatre, Torquay Wendy Bennett said, "You have touched so many lives. Your passion for your work, your loyalty and support and the fact that you genuinely care about the people you work with are all things that make you unique! Also from Torquay Roma, who, along with Brenda did a brilliant job running the front of house, wrote "Who am I going to kiss now?"?

Ian Sime recounted the story of collapsing seats.

"Dear Uncle Sam

BARNUM at the Oxford Apollo in the November of 1992 was not just a Hit, but a MONSTER HIT? An all too rare creature: a total sell out! Paul Nicholas portrayed the Greatest Showman of his age. And was, as the story goes "The Master of Humbug".

The production was a total joy and it exceeded even the most optimistic forecasts and obviously everyone was really very happy. On the Saturday Night, the gentleman many of us consider to be The Greatest Showman of Our Age – (that's you Sam) came to see the show with his family.

Well, you arrived in time and after pleasantries, had a wander round the theatre, as you do, whilst Freda and Ben took to their seats. Three minutes before Curtain Up a call came over the Walkie Talkie. A seat had collapsed in the stalls, could it possibly be fixed? Well, just guess who's seat this was? That's right – Freda Shrouder's.

Making my way down to the front of the Stalls, I hoped beyond hope that I could fix the seat before the Overture, as on this particular night there wasn't a single available seat in the house. So there I was on my hands and knees, pushing and shoving and praying for the damned thing to slot back into place, but no it simply wouldn't connect.

Obviously I didn't wish to draw attention to this incident. And so with a fixed nonchalant grin I struggled to repair the seat. But to my horror, one of the Cast members had seen my dilemma. The fellow was only supposed to crack jokes and distribute funny shaped balloons to younger members of the audience. But he couldn't resist the temptation.

"What have you done to this lovely man's furniture Missus?" he shouted.

Everyone looked around to see a young man (then with hair), struggling like anything to fix the red velour pad. I was mortified and livid. But still I tried to fix the chair. Now sporting a fixed panicky grimace wishing for the Clown to

212

simply disappear. On and on he went. By now, I was absolutely determined to fix the chair. I pushed and shoved and the sweat was trickling down my arms and then ... WHOOPS, the flipping nylon whatsit completely snapped off!

Being the gentleman that you are, Sam, you had already discretely disappeared to the rear of the auditorium. I scuttled away just as the Band started to play.

I couldn't believe it! We had done so much for the show: Trekked around Oxford dressed as Clowns in the Lord Mayor's Parade, painted the building in red and yellow stripes, ... oh heaps of stuff. But on the Big Night itself, a chair collapsed and you couldn't enjoy the show, with the family, as intended. As soon as I made it back to the Foyer, I found you all smiles and totally understanding. The first thing you said was I should be grateful that it was your chair that had collapsed, and not a member of the public's.

You always taught us to treat our patrons as our personal guests. They are our lifeblood. And this we all know is not "humbug". I knew you were right. But then you usually are."

Jo Barnes, General Manager of Folkestone's Leas, Cliff Hall wrote, "Sam was my mentor, he was passionate, inspiring and motivating, always teaching by example. Telling me very early in my career that the minute the hairs on the back of my neck did not stand up at a good performance or a capacity crowd's applause, it was time to get out of the business. Thank you Sam for helping me to achieve my dreams".

Peter Evans, who had progressed to be a Divisional Director wrote, "I've learnt from you just how kind a boss can be, always think of everybody and how passion can be a skill not just an emotion. Thanks for the fun that we have shared, such a lot of laughter and good conversation".

I had tried throughout my career to make sure that I appreciated everybody who made the theatres the magical places that they are so I was pleased with a letter I received from Roz Thomas, who ran the party booking department at Oxford Apollo. Roz wrote "You never forgot the true meaning of working in the theatre and knew that being friendly to the cleaner was as important as checking in on the Box Office Staff, and not ignoring the stage door keeper. In short you respected people and they all adored you for it – especially Eileen, the cleaner, who was quite difficult to please!"

From my special Theatre Bookings team also came many undeserved compliments. From Ali came, "I think the first time we met was my first day at Apollo and you came into the office wearing a tinsel tiara and carrying a silver wand ... Not your usual office wear admittedly but you had just come from the launch of the Oxford panto and as you always told us this is `showbizz'! You were always great fun to work with and always helped the day along with jokes(!) and comical tales of car-related disasters that we really tried hard to be sympathetic to. You were always there with a comforting word if things didn't work out as expected either at work or personally and I know that meant a lot to everyone that worked with you".

Fiona remembered the incredible loyalty that we had all shown each other in the team and Leigh remembered my office with "An office decorated with framed pictures – shows, faces, names, messages, autographs and memories detailing years gone by – a credit to you that barely a scrap of wall was still showing. I used to enjoy stealing a look for famous faces and stifling a giggle at the variety of Shrouder hairstyles! You always go the extra distance to ensure an individual feels valued – that is why your reputation in this business is as incredible as it is – well deserved and inspiring.It later occurred to me that only the people who liked me would have bothered to write and that all the people who disliked me and thought that I was a complete waste of space would not have seen this as an appropriate time to let me know! However as I read these and many more incredibly generous, and in many cases over the top tributes in the hotel room after one of the most incredible nights of my life I just crumbled with emotion. The book that Nicky had put together had lost some of its letters and as I started to put it away in a box, so that 15 years later I could embarrass lots of people by quoting what they said(!) a note that I had not seen lay on the floor. It quite simply said.

To Dear Sam

The warmest smile in Showbiz

Love and Kisses
Paul Nicholas

It really lifted me and I thought yes that will do me! The warmest smile in showbiz" is how I wish to be remembered. This was somewhat spoilt by David Ian saying that anybody that can do false sincerity is laughing! However it was a perfect end to a fantastic period of my life.

Chapter 20

LIFE AFTER CLEAR CHANNEL

I did not die overnight but did wake up with a hangover, unemployed and a feeling of immense sadness and loss after the euphoria of the night before. It had all happened so quickly that I had had no time to plan for the future.

My feeling of abandonment was not helped by seeing the Jack Nicholson film "About Schmidt". The parallels with the film were pretty horrific, in that his character was retiring from a company that he had been with for many years and he had this wonderful retirement dinner, with great speeches with the head of the company telling him that he was so much part of the fabric, that he was not sure if the building would survive his departure. He was also invited to drop in anytime that he was passing as they would all love to see him and get his advice.

After a month he decided to pop in, help them with any problems and see all his old friends and colleagues. The visit lasted about five minutes, with everybody too busy to see him and the boss having been horrified that he was coming in, told his secretary to bring him into his office and then ring him two minutes later to remind him that he had a very important meeting for which he must leave immediately. The final humiliation for the poor guy was when he saw all the boxes that he had carefully prepared with all the information they would need, had been thrown unopened into a skip.

The film was probably nothing like this but it is how I remember it! It reminded me that the cricket and football dressing rooms I had occupied were not the place for you if you were not playing. There was no going back for me, I was not in the team and I had to create a new working life. The similarities were even worse as Schmidt took to telling his sponsored child all his troubles in his regular letters. I had Jatuparn, whom I sponsored in Thailand through World Vision but there was no point telling Jatuparn of my woes as whatever I wrote to him and whatever questions I asked, I always got the same reply about how he enjoyed fetching water!

The lead up to Christmas was difficult as it had always been the busiest of time as I ensured that I got round all the theatres to see their shows, the team running the theatre and the cast of the panto or show and often take them out to dinner to thank them. In the kind letter that Lisa Chu, General Manager of the Southport Theatre and Floral Hall, wrote to me on my departure she alluded to this with "I always marvelled at how you could sit and watch the pantomime in every theatre. As managers we are all proud of our own show but to watch five performances of Cinderella, four of Snow White and three of Aladdin one after the other is pretty impressive. I am not sure if anybody will willingly follow in your footsteps with this one Sam but if you ever get withdrawal symptoms then you know where we are!"

Despite Schmidt I took Lisa up on this and received a great welcome but it was not the same any more. I had always worked up to Christmas Eve and visited a theatre with any members of the family not bored by panto, on Boxing Day.

I was now destined to spend the Christmas period like normal people do and with Freda being a very sociable person there were lots of events to go to that she had manfully previously gone to on her own. The first was somebody's Christmas Drinks Party at which I dutifully appeared.

Most of the people probably had no idea who I was and one lady with glass in hand asked me what I did and to my horror I answered that I used to run the Apollo Theatre chain. I was mortified and within 48 hours had set up my new company, Theatrexperience, for which I could have any position I wanted depending on who was asking. There was obviously a weak link if the conversation progressed to what clients I had, but despite no clients I felt a bit better having a business identity!

A week or so later, life got a whole lot better when I received a call from Ellen Kent who specialised in bringing the top Eastern European Opera and Ballet Companies to tour this country. Ellen said that she was sure that I had had many offers but she would be delighted if I would consider acting as a consultant for her and also become a director of her company.

As it was the only offer I had received I was incredibly grateful and delighted to be part of her team. I was always very fond of Ellen, whose tours had filled many dates in the Apollo diaries, and who was a great character with an eye for the spectacular in her productions. So now I not only had a company, I also had a client. The new life was already looking up.

It was also a chance to see more of family and friends. I had two grandchildren with Stephanie and Richard's boys Patrick and William. Patrick, as the older, I was particularly attached to and when he came round he would either ask me to sit under the table with him or play shop during which we sold the same football to each other hundreds of times!

I also had the joy not only of Ben's company, but also to often have drinks with some of his friends. Ben had become a dayboy for his last year at Cheltenham with the result that we spent quite a lot of time in the New Inn in Lechlade. Despite this he passed whatever exams he needed to, to enable him to go to University in Leeds, obviously after a gap year!

The change in my working circumstances enabled Freda and I to have more holidays, and we had a great trip with Colin and Claire to Longboat Keys and then on to New Orleans. I adored New Orleans and Bourbon Street and we all spent long hours listening to bands and drinking. We also revisited Portofino with Charles and Christine and as always loved every minute, particularly the nightly sing song in the hotel bar. Music and alcohol seems to be a recurring theme!

We were able to spend more time in Thurlestone with the family. We also saw lots of our neighbours John and Vivienne, who would wander round and in the end they and their children Tom, Hannah and Jack were so nice to our dog Sasha, that she went to live with them! We went to lots of shows, with the golden ticket still valid and we also saw a number of performances with Dudley Russell and his wife Pam Ayres, who were both really good fun.

Sadly during this time my Dad died having spent a number of years at a lovely home just outside Lechlade. For many years following a stroke, he had been unable to communicate or walk but despite that I felt that I got closer to him.

As Dad was reaching his final moments I rang Ben to ask him to come to the Home, which he did, with his friend Kit. When they arrived my brother Stephen, his daughter Emma and the vicar were already there. The vicar explained that he had recently lost his father and that he had found it a great comfort when everybody held hands round the bed and said a prayer.

This solemn moment was re-enacted with the vicar taking my Dad's hand and then mine and we all dutifully held hands. I was obviously very moved by this until I looked up and got an uncontrollable fit of the giggles. Why? Well, at the end of the chain, holding my Dad's other hand was Kit. He had set off to go to the pub with Ben and ended up holding hands with a dying man that he had never even met before!

My Dad had a very dry sense of humour and I have no doubt that he would have found this strange situation highly amusing. It goes without saying that nobody else was amused and that my giggling was deemed highly inappropriate!

My Mum had died ten years earlier. She had Alzheimer's and it was tragic watching a woman, who had got an honours degree at Oxford, steadily decline. She had been a very outspoken character, which could be somewhat embarrassing for us children. In my case this was highlighted when I went to Denstone College at 13 and my future house master took children and parents on a tour of the school.

Most parents were seeking his attention with such questions as was there a chess club that George could join, and untold joy that the club met twice a week. My mother never spoke during the whole tour until there was a lull in conversation and she said "Mr Nash are you a homosexual?"! Not great for my school career! Freda's mother Ruthie, who was also a great character, had moved down to our area and she too spent some time in a home nearby before sadly passing away.

Working with Ellen Kent was fascinating and it included a trip to Moldova, from where she regularly toured their national Opera company the Chisinau Opera. As well as meetings with them we also met with the Minister for Culture, who spent a lot of time telling us how beautiful the Moldova women were. This theme was continued when we met the United Kingdom's Assistant Ambassador for dinner. I, of course, did not notice!

The Assistant Ambassador was a very impressive fellow, who came from Birkenhead and having left school with no qualifications, had worked his way up. He was an expert on Opera, Ballet, wine and spoke many languages and he also supported Tranmere Rovers, but he was such great company that I almost forgave him for that!

Ellen also won me over to Opera with her production of Rigoletto, which I saw at Sunderland Empire. It was a most enjoyable evening with Debbie Corrick, the General Manager of the Theatre, ensuring that we were extremely well looked after, and watching a performance that had two naked ladies on stage for the first 20 minutes as well as eagles and some rather large dogs!

Theatrexperience then became a two client company when Craig Morgan, who had previously run Apollo's Leisure Division contacted me. He was now working for Leisure Connections, who not surprisingly ran Leisure Centres! However they also had a contract to run St Albans Arena as well as a deal with South Beds District Council to run their as yet, unbuilt Grove Theatre in Dunstable. They needed a consultant for this project and Craig, who I always liked, remembered me and who could resist being involved in Dunstable again!

In St Albans they were lucky enough to have an outstanding manager in Paul McMullen, who was later to be tragically killed in a dock door accident when tour managing Port Isaacs Fishermen Friends. What became evident very quickly was that apart from Paul and Craig, there was no appetite to run the Dunstable Grove Theatre within the Company. Indeed many of the conversations that I had, convinced me that they had no sense of theatre at all.

However the answer appeared to be at hand when Andre Ptaszynski, Chief Executive of Andrew Lloyd Webber's Really Useful Theatres contacted me to see if I would come in as a consultant to work with him to build a provincial theatre group to go with the 12 West End Theatres that they controlled. I liked and respected Andre enormously and this was a fabulous opportunity. Also in the team was Vanessa Stone, another consultant, who added to our ability to make presentations, documents and overall knowledge of the business. The Stage took this all very seriously with their flattering coverage again making the editorial and saw that as my second coming!

The potential was massive and Andre had agreed that if we built a provincial division I could come in and run it, which is everything that I wanted. Vanessa put together a great presentation for the Swindon Wyvern Theatre to take it over from Clear Channel who had David Ian leading their presentation. With my history with the theatre I thought that we were in with a good chance but in the end neither of us got the theatre as it went to Nick Thomas, who we were told had put in the cheapest bid. So at least it went to a good guy. When Craig left Leisure Connection I lost my only ally and in meetings with their hierarchy it became increasingly obvious that their best option was to let Really Useful Theatres run it and to share the profits with them.

Andre also saw this as a way to get started so we met up in their Soho offices with representatives of Leisure Connection. The deal was just about done, when Andre was called out of the office and ten minutes later he called me out to tell me we could not go ahead with the deal.

He told me that the front page headline of The Standard that evening was that Andrew Lloyd Webber no longer wanted to run theatres and that he wanted to concentrate on productions. We had to go back in to tell Leisure Connection that there was no deal. It is one of my greatest regrets that I never got to run theatres with Andre as I think that we could have built up a considerable presence in the provinces. As far as Dunstable was concerned it was back to the drawing board.

During this time my stepdaughter Andrea, who was to have an outstanding career in film and TV, asked me if I would see a friend she worked with at Spire Films as he was interested in starting up a festival and that was how I was to meet Graeme Medfield.

As we sat round the kitchen table in Sherborne House, Graeme explained how he wanted start a music festival. I was very dubious about the project and would explain that he would have to do lots of things before it could even be a discussion.

A week later he was back having done everything that was asked and more. Slowly I warmed to the idea of working with Graeme to deliver the event. I was impressed both by his vision and his determination that no obstacle would stop it taking place. I remembered when I was young how so many people had showed faith in me and my ideas and it was now time to repay that faith by helping Graeme achieve his ambitious. As our talks progressed, Wychwood Festival was born, and after much discussion we approached Edward Gillespie, Chief Executive of Cheltenham Racecourse, to see if we could use his venue.

Edward was unbelievably supportive and so we now had a site and another hurdle had been jumped (Bit of a racing pun there!) We now needed to put a team together and quickly added Pete Allison, who was responsible for the production of the Greenbelt Festival, which also used the racecourse. Knowing my own weakness, I insisted that we could go no further unless we got a top financial brain to join us. We did better than that and got the best when David Rogers agreed to come in as Chairman and as an added bonus he persuaded Jerry Katzman to become a Director. So Wychwood Festival was happening and we all started planning for June 3–5 2005 and the birth of Wychwood!

Chapter 21

FEVER PITCH

I was now very excited by the prospect of Wychwood and added to my other working activities gave me a great balance of different projects.

On top of this I also had other activities that I involved myself in which were all part of my phobia of having to fill every minute in my diary. At the top of this list was Southport Football Club. My Dad had taken me to watch Southport and Scunthorpe in May 1955 and I was hooked.

When people ask me why I support Southport I have always answered that they were the first team that I ever saw and that in later years I would ask my dad why he had not taken me to Liverpool, Everton, or Man Utd as he was responsible for more than 50 years of misery! None of this was true as my Dad had been a season ticket holder at Everton and had taken me to games and I have also had some fantastic moments supporting Southport (obviously not many!)

Dad and I started going regularly and there was only ever one team for me, which enabled me to quickly live with disappointment. We used to sit with a band leader, a hangman and a male dancer, all of whom were loud and funny, whilst Dad was much more reserved. I remember one trip home after losing 6–1 to Hartlepool United and he was moved to say that he thought that we were disappointing, which is as critical as he ever got.

However, I just loved the team and always saw the positives so I responded that it was a fantastic goal that we got. He looked at me with disdain and said "Sammy it was a penalty!" to which I responded that it was a very good penalty!

There were not many great moments as we constantly fought, normally unsuccessfully, not to be in the bottom four and have to apply for a re-election. Indeed things must have been so bad that my cricketing friend Sandy Tittershill and I decided to apply for a trial. We wrote to Lem

Newcome the manager and were duly summoned to Haig Avenue.

He took us on to the pitch to show us how Eric Jones, our winger, had scored a volley against Peterborough. Then without seeing us kick a ball took us to his office and got playing registration forms out. We duly filled them in and he told me that I would be playing centre forward for the A team on Saturday. When I explained that I couldn't because I went to a Boarding School and was going back on Friday, he uttered a considerable number of expletives and ripped up the forms, making me undoubtedly the shortest signing in the whole history of the Football league and another reason to resent Denstone College!

I was quickly followed by Sandy who explained that he could not play centre half because he had to play rugby for Ormskirk Grammar School. In hindsight we probably had not thought this out!

In the mid 1960's, former Northern Ireland legend Billy Bingham was appointed manager and supporting Southport became a joy. In his first season we reached the 5th Round of the FA Cup after an epic run that included knocking out Halifax Town, Stockport County, Ipswich Town and Cardiff City (I knew that you would be impressed!). I saw all the games apart from the replay at Ipswich having drawn 0–0 at home. We won the replay 3–2 with a late goal from Colin Alty, who regularly attends games now with his friend, the legendary Eric Redrobe and it is always good to chat with them about these special days.

For the Cardiff game, Sandy and I decided to drink Southport dry before the match. We started in a pub in the centre of Southport, met two Cardiff fans and we spent the whole day with them including watching the game. We won 2–0 with goals from Ron Smith and Alan Spence, the club's greatest goal scorer of all time. After the game, the two Cardiff fans suggested that they joined our celebrations in Southport before catching their train. Those were the days, at no time did they want to fight us, shout abuse at us or our players, although there was lots of banter! A truly memorable day to be followed by a 2–0 defeat at Hull City in front of over 35,000 people. The following season we won promotion clinched by a George Andrew's goal against Southend that induced me to run on the pitch – I should point out that I was not on my own as there were several thousand success-starved Southport fans there as well.

The joy of the Bingham era continued when we were 8th in the Third Division, our highest finish ever. We also played Everton at home in the FA

Cup and were unlucky to lose 1–0 to a Joe Royle header from an Alan Ball free kick eleven minutes from time. The game was also memorable for our tactics. The Everton goalkeeper was Gordon West, who was the first keeper to bring a bag with him onto the pitch resulting in the Liverpool fans, to the tune of Georgie Girl, singing "Hey there Gordon West, you're a bigger tart than Georgie Best". He was regarded as being a bit temperamental so the plan was that from the kick off to get the ball to him just as big Eric Red robe arrived and flattened him. Eric did it perfectly and got booked so we had to revert to plan B! Billy Bingham was destined for much greater things and went on to manage Everton and Northern Ireland. He still lives in Southport and comes to some of the games – a true legend.

We, of course, then got relegated! However we were to have one more Football League season of glory in the early 70s when we won the Fourth Division Championship under Jimmy Meadows with our sensational strike force of Jimmy Fryatt and Andy Provan, who were suitably honoured by Linda and I naming our two cats after them! At the last game of the season we only needed to draw at home against Hartlepool United to be champions. But this of course is Southport so we entered the third minute of stoppage time losing 1–0. However for once it was to be different, we got a free kick and Alex Russell, the greatest player I ever saw at Southport, stepped up and sent a screamer into the back of the net and once again I ran on the pitch!

We were of course relegated the next season and in 1978 having finished second from bottom, above Rochdale, we were voted out of the Football League to be replaced by Wigan Athletic, who used to play in the same league as our Reserve team! Wigan now ranks with St Helens in my list of places not to revisit!

Now I appreciate that the fortunes of Southport FC are of no interest to the majority of people on this earth but there is more! The club entered the Northern Premier League, where they continued to struggle as the ground deteriorated. They were still my team but instead of celebrating FA Cup victories against Ipswich and Cardiff, I now celebrated such achievements as an away draw at Marine FC! There were constant calls for donations to save the club from closing down.

Then in the late 1980s a saviour arrived in the person of Charlie Clapham. He went to a game with his son Wayne during which the Club asked for volunteers to help run it. Only one person volunteered and Charlie's life was about to change forever. He rescued Southport and whatever has been achieved since has mainly been down to him. Our paths crossed when I wrote to him complaining that we only had three players from the previous seasons, in pre-season training.

He obviously gave my very helpful letter due consideration and filed it in the bin! But not being the sort of chap to give up easily I wrote an even stronger letter saying that it was typical of the way the club was run that he could not even be bothered to reply to my very helpful letter! His response to this resulted in a phone call and the ultimate result of this was that I gained a great friend and have enjoyed one of the great characters in football.

Apollo became the club's sponsors and I was to join the board before becoming Charlie's Vice-Chairman. It was a good time to become involved as Charlie had already done lots to improve the Club, whilst under Manager Brian Kettle the team was to go and win the Northern Premier League. This entitled us to be promoted to the Conference and into National League football, but only if our ground was up to the required standard. When we had the pre-inspection we were told it would be impossible for us to make the necessary changes within the time limit. But they did not know Charlie and, with help from Apollo, for whom Paul Gregg sent Steven Lavelle and his team to Haig Ave for a week to assist, we qualified and started the next season away at Dagenham and Redbridge in the Vauxhall Conference.

We had some great seasons ahead with some real characters as managers including Billy Ayre and Ronnie Moore but ahead of us we had the greatest moment of all, when under Paul Futcher we got to the FA Trophy Final at Wembley. Paul was our player manager and his ability on the field was a big part of our success, he was also the nicest of people. Never in my wildest dreams did I expect us to get to Wembley (This is not quite true as in my younger days not only did I dream of us winning the FA Cup I also always scored the winning goal!) The semi-final was two-legged against Slough and having won 1–0 there we just had to draw at home. But this was Southport, so, of course, we went behind 1–0 but to our astonishment we equalised with a goal that was about five yards off side, hung on and were on our way to Wembley to face the mighty Cheltenham.

The arrangements were first class with the players booked in to a Guildford hotel for the Friday, Saturday and Sunday after the game. Charlie also arranged for the players' wives, girlfriends etc to stay in London and I organised for them to see Starlight Express. Before the Final Charlie advised me to forget family and friends and to use this once-in-a-lifetime experience in the way I would most enjoy. I booked a coach to take family and friends to Wembley whilst I took Charlies' advice.

On the Friday night I went down to the players' hotel to have an evening with them before returning home to watch Ben play cricket for Oxfordshire. On the Sunday Ben and I went back to the Guildford hotel to enable us to travel to Wembley on the team coach.

What a day! Police outriders (probably only one!) led us to Wembley and as we got near we put on the record that we had recorded. Good friend Norman Prince from the Houghton Weavers had written a song to the tune of the Wild Rover. So as we entered Wembley Way we were singing away as thousands of Southport supporters waved and cheered. You will not be surprised to know that there was the odd tear! We drove into the tunnel and I was able to take Ben into the dressing room and then on to the Royal Box. We then played a game of football and lost 1–0 before the players joined us for a drinks reception provided by the FA.

Cheltenham joined us but being softy southerners did not understand the implications of a free bar. Most of our team came from Liverpool and knew that a free bar was to be utilised, which we all did in great style! By the time that they got rid of us we had forgotten the defeat and were in the mood to celebrate having got there. The ladies joined us at the Hotel and we had a fantastic party. Captain Brian Butler and goalkeeper Billy Stewart made speeches thanking the club (Charlie) for the superb way that they and their partners had been looked after and we all drank to that. Indeed we drank to virtually anything we could think of.

Around midnight I was having a drink with David Gamble, one of our longest serving players and Dave Thompson, when somebody remembered that we still had all the champagne that we were going to celebrate our win with, on the coach so that was duly dispensed to cap one of the most incredible days of my life made even more special by being able to share it with Ben.

Paul Futcher handed over his only ever Wembley medal to Charlie at the end of season party as he looked forward to taking the club further forward as manager only as he retired from playing. But football is a cruel game and twenty months later he was sacked with Southport in the bottom three. A lovely guy, who was the only ex-manager to come to the funeral of Jack Carr, the Club President. Jack was another great character with lots of tales and was famous for insisting that all the players sang "Onward Christian

PLAY IT AGAIN SAM

Soldiers" on the team coach! Jack's memory was suitably honoured by the Club naming our new stand at the home end after him.

While I was writing this book I received the sad news that Paul Futcher had died at the age of 60. Along with Charlie and Haydn, I attended his funeral in Sheffield. The fact that it was standing room only with so many people from the world of football was a tribute to Paul the man as much as Paul the footballer.

Paul was followed by ex-England and Liverpool centre half Mark Wright, who took us up to ninth and then third the following season. He brought in Mike Marsh, ex-Liverpool and West Ham and Shaun Teale, ex-Aston Villa and Southport(!). Before his first game in charge I shook Mark's hand and said let's have lots of fun. He responded "There will be no fun whilst I am in charge"! He left us to manage Oxford United and popped into the Apollo offices a number of times to say hello, which I appreciated. He also pinched two of our best players in Phil Bolland, and Scot Guyett, which I did not appreciate!

After that we had a poor spell and eventually were relegated back to the Northern Premier League. In our first season we had to finish in the top half to ensure that we were in the inaugural Conference North. We started badly and another manager bit the dust. The interviews included two ex-internationals, various famous non-league managers plus a 33 year old who was player manager with Runcorn. The 33 year-old did a brilliant interview and was the only person for the job. Liam Watson was to go on and become Southport's most successful manager of all time over nine years split into two spells and just as importantly he was to become a good mate.

In his first full season we won the first Conference North title by winning 5–1 at Harrogate and boy did we celebrate. I was due to drive home after the game but Charlie was having none of it and asked someone else to drive the car to Southport to allow me to return with the players on the coach. This was a fabulous experience and I was most impressed as we neared our ground when Liam got everybody to be quiet (not easy!) and he told them that moments like this happen very rarely in a player's career so celebrate well but make sure that you never forget that feeling.

Liam always generated a fantastic team spirit and had a team full of characters led by the captain Chris Price and including Dominic Morley, Big Earl Davis, Steve Dickinson, Farrell Kilblane and Steve Pickford. We also had great goal scorers with Steve Daly, Kevin Leadbetter and, astonishingly with 33 league goals, Terry Fearns. It should be remembered that we were part time and that Terry like the rest of the team had a career outside of football.

A couple of seasons later we went full time, resulting in Liam leaving as he had a very good job at Ashworth Hospital. The result of this was that we got relegated; Liam returned and got us promoted as Champions again. Another great night was had after we clinched the title at Eastwood, with the Grandstand Bar at the Club really rocking. Linda ended up on the pool table dancing with one of our greatest playing characters Kevin Lee and I just hugged and kissed everybody – well I was in Showbiz!

Characters in this side included Big Earl, again, Adam Flynn, Michael Powell and Alan Moogan, a lovely guy who was our Mr Nasty on the pitch. The goals were scored by Steve Daly, again, Ciaran Kilheeney, Matty McGinn and Chris Simm. Liam, as well as an outstanding manager, had a massive interest in promoting the club and was to become much more than a manager when he joined the Board to entertain us with his knowledge of football and humour – not necessarily in that order!

At the same time Southport's Board received another massive boost when Nigel Allen and Dave Barron joined it.

Liam also got on better with Chairman Charlie than any previous managers, which was crucial as Charlie, ably assisted by his wife Mavis, ran the club. He is an old style Chairman and as such should take the credit for everything that Southport FC has achieved in the last 30 years. As well as being one of my best friends he is also one of the greatest characters that I have ever encountered, with a merry quip for all occasions. Such as –

ME – I was looking back ... –
CHARLIE – last time I did that I walked into a lamp post!

CHARLIE – We were bloody awful –
ME – Were there any positives? –
CHARLIE – Yes we were positively bloody awful!

Charlie on a player – He is a very well balanced lad – he has a chip on both shoulders!

Charlie on Lawyers – It is like lending someone your watch so that they can charge you to tell you the time!

Charlie on a manager who could not keep things confidential – If you asked him about the spot on his dick he would get it out and show you!

Charlie on me when I missed games for a holiday – Commitment! You wouldn't know how to spell it! (which is actually correct – is it two m's and one t or vice versa or one of each?!)

In my 25 years of being involved in the running of Southport we have won three league titles, been to Wembley, played Derby County in the FA Cup in front of more than 20,000 people and lost to a 93rd minute penalty; played Sheffield Wednesday live on TV and equalised twice (we actually lost 5–2); have achieved FA cup giant billing status in knocking out Notts County 4–2 in BBC's Match of the Day and Dagenham and Redbridge (Don't laugh they were a league club at the time!). We have also won numerous Liverpool Senior and Lancashire Junior Cup competitions, which Charlie describes as Mickey Mouse Cups until you reach the final when they become pure Disney!

So there is more than enough excitement there for any chap! As well as Charlie and Liam I have enjoyed the company and friendship of some great characters at the Club including Hayden Preece, Ken Hilton, Big Wes Hall, and particularly Steve Porter, who as well as being a great mate is a massive help with Wychwood including being the official photographer. There are many more people at the Club who have made being there such a joy and I thank them all.

So do I wish that I had formed an allegiance with some flash Premier League Club? Not in a million years! I would not swap the ups and downs, comradeship and humour of Southport Football Club for any club on the planet.

For a happy ending the book should have finished the chapter on Southport as above!

But this is Southport so nothing is ever that simple ! The season of 2016–17 has been an unmitigated disaster on the field with us being relegated to the Conference North. The Board and the fans were unhappy but did not hold hands in their unhappiness with a section of the supporters making their feelings clear that they wanted change at the top. They got their wish when Charlie as Chairman resigned. I, as Vice Chairman also resigned, Haydn Preece, as Chief Executive in all but name, resigned and Dave Barron, who had only recently joined the board and had done wonders with sponsorship and hospitality, also resigned. This left Liam and Nigel Allen as interim chairman to put it all back together.

It was a very sad day particularly for Charlie who had been Chairman for 33 years and on the board for 35 years, which made my mere 25 years seem insignificant. Charlie had also put very substantial funds into the club, which again made my substantial funds seem insignificant ! He deserved a far better exit and as a close friend I hurt for him, Mavis and his family. I was also rather sad for myself ! I joined the board as a fan and I walked out of the door as a fan. So in future Linda and I will pay at the turnstiles which is a considerably cheaper option. I will find someone new to bore with tales of times gone by and Linda will not be able to kiss as many young footballers as previously ! So every cloud etc !

UP THE PORT!

Chapter 22

THERE BUT FOR.....

I obviously got a bit carried away with the joys of football, but my other major involvement was a lot more sombre. As I watched Ben enjoying the first years of his life I knew that I had been truly blessed and that I needed to give something of myself (I obviously had lots of spare time!) to people for whom life is a struggle. The easy bit was putting some money in the many envelopes for good causes that came through the door, but I was looking to do something that took me out of my comfort zone. So as the result of a chat with a guy on holiday I decided to become a prison visitor.

This was easier said than done as there were only 760 in the whole of the UK and you could not join the select bunch without being cleared by the Home Office which took forever. Eventually my debut arrived and I set off for the Oxford Prison with a visiting order for a gentleman, who was on remand. The way it worked was that a lovely fellow from the Probation Service would chat to prisoners who had no visitors and ask if they would like myself or one of my colleagues to come and see them. We were there as their guest and were not allowed to ask them what they were there for, although they normally told you and explained why there had been a miscarriage of justice!

We were also asked if there was any crime that they could have committed that would result in us not wanting to visit them. I said no to this. When I arrived at the prison, I was frisked by a warder, who made it clear that he did not like do-gooders. I was eventually ushered into the visiting room to meet my new friend, who was from Liverpool. He had wrongly been accused of burglary and we spent the whole time discussing the various merits of Everton and Southport over a cup of coffee and a Mars bar, which I was able to purchase. So not that difficult!

I saw lots of prisoners and quickly the system changed and we were allowed to go at any time and visit them in their cells, which the wardens hated even more. When the decision was made to close this horrible Victorian prison I was regularly visiting two long term prisoners. I promised both of them that wherever they were sent I would continue to visit them.

They were two very different characters with one being a very articulate man in his 60s, who had been given eight years for embezzlement and the other being much younger doing seven years for raping and assaulting a foreign student. The older gentleman ran the prison library, did the wages for the warders and represented the prison at a number of outside events. He was also a very talented painter, and great company and we could chat for hours, but never about his offences.

His long sentence could suggest that he was a consistent embezzler although obviously not very good at it! He was up for parole and had the support of the Prison Governor who was so confident that he would get it that he allowed him home visits. Astonishingly his parole was turned down and he went on a home visit and never returned.

There were those who said that it was the thought of me visiting him wherever he went that caused him to abscond but I am in no doubt it was the refusal of parole! Having never committed a violent crime in his life he had a slight career change and started robbing banks!

He was caught and sent to Strangeways before ending up in Leyhill Open Prison in Gloucestershire, from where he contacted me to see if I would come and see him. I regularly visited him and always enjoyed his company. At Leyhill he had a number of friends and had a bridge four that included the ex-editor of a national paper, a former mayor of a local town, and a surgeon. He was also particularly good with helping first time prisoners adapt, and indeed introduced me to a number that should never been jailed. He also did a lot of painting including a picture of my house, which he gave me as a thank you.

My other friend was sent to Nottingham High Security Prison and I was able to visit him, when I was going up to Scarborough's Futurist Theatre. He would talk about his offence, which he would put down to drink and drugs, but he would, not surprisingly, rather talk about football! The prison was very oppressive and even worse than Oxford to visit but he was a cheerful soul and seemed to get on well with all and sundry.

When he was released he got together with a lady who had been taking one of the educational classes, got a lorry driving job and they had a baby.

All of which delighted me. On the other hand the other gentleman left the flat that a previous prisoner had found for him and I never heard from him again, although I was later contacted by the police, who were looking for him! Now that I had got a taste for taking myself out of my comfort zone I was looking for my next challenge.

I had a sponsored child with World Vision so I contacted them and asked to meet one of their team and I got Neil Warwick, who was to become a special friend. We went for lunch and after discussing the fortunes of Nottingham Forest and Southport. I explained that I wanted to get close to one project and really understand the problem, and go out and visit it. Which is how in 1996 I ended up going to Rwanda two years after the horrific genocide when in around a million people were killed in 100 days. Neil and I were joined on this trip by World Vision's Lynne Morris who was also to become a special friend and the three of us really bonded.

The project that I had asked to see was child-headed households where despite the Hutu's policy of killing all Tutsis in some villages they had left young children alive. In these cases girls 11 years old or younger got together to look after the younger children and babies. With World Vision's support these inspirational young people formed a co-operative with hens, seed and goats and looked after the others. On this trip we cried a lot and laughed a lot.

The low point came when we were taken to a school in which over 30,000 Tutsis had gone to, having been guaranteed protection by the Mayor. On the third night the protection slipped away and the following midday there were only three survivors with over 30,000 people having been killed with Clubs and Machetes. The guy who took us round was one of the three survivors and as he showed us classroom after classroom full of skeletons he came to one and explained that his wife and children were in this one.

It was hard to take in what we were witnessing and shaming that in the worse act of genocide since the second world war, not one nation made any effort to stop it following America's veto of the word 'genocide' in the United Nations. The significance of this was that in the UN's charter, if genocide takes place they are duty bound to go in and protect the people but thanks to America, nobody did have to go in and help and nobody did. Bill Clinton was later to say that it was his single greatest regret in his term in office, which was probably of little consolation to the dead!

Without the company of Neil and Lynne I do not think that I could have coped with what I saw. However in the acts of reconciliation taking place in Rwanda there was the hope for the future. One person I met had been at Bradford University in 1994 and had lost every single member of his family and all his relations and he had just been told that the man who had killed his mother was in Kigoli Prison and wanted to see him. When he returned he told me that they both broken down in tears, and agreed that madness had overtaken the country and he forgave him. This was happening all over.

A year later we went to Kigoli Prison to meet some of the perpetrators of the genocide and there was just overriding emotion of remorse. Three of the prisoners had been ordained and we joined them in a service with over 700 others. Moving though this was there was a level of farce when Neil agreed to say a few words. On the basis he did not speak their language they could not understand a word of what he said. Realising this he resorted to shouting Hallelujah and punching the air and they all joined in. He obviously decided that this was the future as he went on to be ordained and the last time I saw him preach he was still punching the air and saying Halleluja!

I think that the trip was probably too much for all three of us as when we went to our Hotel it proudly advertised that it had got the very latest baths from Europe, which turned out to be sit-in disabled baths. We laughed non stop for the whole of the evening!

I came back from the Rwanda experience determined to help in any way I could, including going round giving talks to organisations and raising awareness and money. There was also no doubt that World Vision's work in Rwanda was making a considerable difference, as one lady told us that without them there would have been no hope and they would have been dead.

At the Charity's request I next went to Zambia, a country racked with HIV Aids. The project was focused on the Zambian/Zimbabwe border where at any one time there would be around 300 trucks waiting for clearance to come into the country which could take days. Whilst they were there with the most basic facilities there was only sex and beer to pass the time. We were working with the 300+ sex workers who were based there and trying to persuade them to go on training courses to obtain jobs in Lusaka. When we chatted with the girls, who were aware that the truck drivers, as well as their loads, were transporting HIV Aids, they either said that this is what they do and they knew it would kill them or if they had an alternative they would move away.

The fantastic World Vision team on the border rescued many girls and there was a fantastic success rate with those who left to train in catering, dress making and other jobs. World Vision were also able to reconcile many of them with their families who had disowned them. When I was on the border it felt like I had reached the end of the world but at least the Charity was once again making a difference.

I was also to visit Sierra Leone and a project working with girls who had been captured by the rebels to be used as slaves and had managed to escape. Their testimonies were heart-breaking as were the cases of boy soldiers, as young as six, and the many amputees who had suffered from the rebel's habit of chopping off a limb or two from innocent people.

The rebels' war could never have been sustained, of course, without the purchase of diamonds from the mines that they controlled, by the Western World, Some of the diamond merchants truly did have blood on their hands. Whilst in Sierra Leone I got friendly with our local guide as we had the common international language of football. We were in the middle of nowhere but he said he would take me to watch a game. We ended up in a village which appeared to have no electricity but there was this bar with a generator and a TV and we were able to watch Bayern Munich v Chelsea together. Bizarrely my mobile phone got a signal for the first time and I got a call from Charlie to tell me that Southport were beating Hucknall 4–2!

I was also privileged to go to an Aids project in Cambodia, and a massively successful campaign in Chennai, India getting street children into education. There was also a wonderful trip to Kissumu in Kenya to meet David, Linda's sponsored child. He was a bit wary at first and I noticed that in his class of 74 he was the only child not to laugh when I did my party piece of "Head, Shoulders, Knees and Toes" going faster and faster (Once an entertainer always an entertainer!)

However when we took him and his family out for lunch he was a different child once Linda had given him a Manchester Utd shirt. She first gave him and his brothers and sisters Southport shirts but for some reason this did not seem to have the same effect! We had also taken those tubes that you can blow bubbles from, which always worked really well.

My last trip with World Vision was probably my most scary, when I went to D.R. Congo. The attack from the M23 rebels was imminent in our area and on the day before we got there, five aid workers had been stopped at a road block and killed. We were housed near the Rwandan border so that if instructed we could immediately cross the border.

Again the many rebel armies used child soldiers, and I was desolate hearing the story of Frank, who had managed to escape. He told us that he had killed many people. He also told me that when the armies raided villages to capture future child soldiers, they often got them to shoot their parents to ensure that they could never return. Many of the rebel groups were Hutus who had fled Rwanda and had taken over the Cobalt Mines. They were able to finance their action because Western mobile firm companies would buy the cobalt directly from them despite knowing what the money would be used for. You may have noticed a bit of a theme here!

Many of the trips I went on were with Lynne Morris and Neil Warwick and we were also joined by Naomi Lewis in Chennai. These and the others who took me were very special and brave people. They, along with the localised teams, were inspirational in their bravery, their faith and their determination to help some of the most needy people on this earth.

I hope that these experiences helped to make me a slightly better person and to appreciate the life that I had. It was also life changing in that from their example I discovered a faith, which was not there when I first set off for Rwanda. Two quotes that I always used when giving talks were from Edmund Burke "No man made a greater mistake than he who did nothing because he could only do a little" and from Feargal Keane in Rwanda "This is not about charity, it is about humanity".

Chapter 23

BAD NEWS AND GOOD NEWS

At the beginning of 2005 Freda and I separated. We had been together for 23 years and had experienced some great times but my obsession with work and the life that I created with it undoubtedly damaged our relationship. At one stage I went to Relate explaining how our difficulties were all of my making but the very nice lady said that there are always faults on both sides so that was £50 well spent! But deep down I knew that I was responsible for the break up. Freda had made major sacrifices to enable us to be together and quite simply she deserved better.

As a result of the split I moved to our house in Thurlestone, which is a beautiful village but with 37% of the houses holiday homes (somebody in the pub told me so it must be true!) it was a very quiet place in January. The Village pub was my saviour, along with Roy, a great character and one of the very few locals. There would be times when we would be the only two in there. I have never been very good at remembering people's names, which I overcame in the Showbiz world by hugging and kissing everybody I thought I knew – male and female!

This show of affection normally worked although backfired a couple of times when used by mistake on people I had never met before! This tactic was obviously not going to work on the villagers of Thurlestone, so I kept a list of people's names and followed the tactic of using them as frequently as possible. So when Roy told me that the guy serving behind the bar was called Keith I went into overdrive. "Evening Keith – pint of lager please Keith – How's your day been Keith – Thank you Keith – Good Night Keith". This continued in similar vein for the next couple of months and I obviously got on so well with Keith that I got invited to his leaving do. I was chatting to Roy and said that it was sad that Keith was leaving and he looked at me quizzically and said 'Who?" and when I said Keith the guy who is leaving he informed me that he is not called Keith his name is Ian!

Roy was in his late 60's and always amused me. On one occasion I asked him what he had been doing all day and he replied "Shagging!" I assumed that I had misheard or misunderstood his local dialect but no he confirmed that I had heard right. He had first been to an Indian Restaurant and when I commented that it was nice of him to take the lady there he explained that he went on his own, met the lady afterwards and gave her a pastie! I was at a very low ebb and quite lonely so I was always pleased to see Roy in the pub and enjoy his many stories true and false!

Although this was undoubtedly the darkest period of my life, my golf benefited as I looked out at Thurlestone Golf Course and when it looked quiet I would nip out and have a round, I also got to play with Steve Hornbuckle, who, along with his wife Rita, were friends of mine and had a holiday home in the Village. I was also kept sane by 10 hour round trips to watch Southport (I know it does not sound sane!), the continuation of my Dunstable consultancy and finding them a great Manager in Jo Ditch, and planning for Wychwood. I was also a trustee for the charity CHYP (Cirencester Housing for Young People), which had been started by a great lady called Jane Gunner, and some other caring people and had four houses where they accommodated young homeless people between the ages of 16 and 24. They did great work and I tried to ensure I made all their meetings, which along with Wychwood meetings meant that I often had to stay in the area.

What I did learn was who were my real friends and who really cared about me. For whatever reason many people felt that they had to take sides in my marital dispute with the result that some people disappeared off my friendship radar. I will be forever grateful to those who went out of their way to visit or contact me. I continued to meet Stef for a round of golf at Cirencester, have a drink with Charles and John and Vivienne came down to stay and were a great support.

Colin and Claire were in a particularly difficult position, having known Freda from their youth, but they were brilliant in their attempts to be impartial and came and stayed a number of times as well as me visiting them. I also always enjoyed going to Torquay's Princess Theatre, where

Wendy was a great pal.

But despite these great friends, my brothers and sisters and all the other friends I had, who were automatically there for me from Apollo days, football and other areas of work I was still in a very dark place. I remember going to The Reel Cinema in Kingsbridge, which I did almost weekly, and watching Hotel Rwanda after which I just broke down in a flood of tears, not moving until a gentleman asked me to leave as they wanted to lock up!

It was during this period that I visited Sierra Leone, which was emotionally very draining and after nearly 24 hours travelling on the return journey arrived to find I could not get in the house. Luckily my friend Ian Potterton, whose Company looked after the house and garden, was contactable and arrived pretty quickly, as it turned out that having checked the house he had double locked it and I only had one key. At times like these I seriously worried that I was losing the plot.

That I didn't was down to all my friends who kept in contact, my sister Mary and her husband Tod and their children Quin and Lem who lived in Devon and who were in constant contact, including games of golf with Mary.

Above all though it was down to Ben. We spoke nearly every day and he regularly came down to stay with a combination of his lovely friends who would drink with me and kindly listen to all my stories without looking too bored! So Kit, Nasser, George, Phil, Will, Alex, Jamie, Sasha and others were always very welcome at Lower Furlong. I remember reading a newspaper article ridiculing parents who said that their child was their best friend, so I would not tell anybody else but you that Ben is my best mate.

I think my immaturity meant that we were able to go out drinking as equals at a very early age! When I moved to Thurlestone he was in his gap year, I should point out that in my day when you left school you celebrated with a wet weekend in Rhyl or if you wanted to go upmarket a couple of days in St Helens! Ben was due to go off to Laos, Thailand and Vietnam as one does and I was going to really miss him.

So I was very touched when a few days before he was due to leave he arrived with a computer and a table and insisted that he was not leaving until we could email each other as he would be in situations where he could not phone. He showed unusual perseverance as it took him two hours to put the table together before he got started on the computer and we were obviously losing valuable Village Inn time. He achieved his object and to this day if anybody would like to send me an email I will not only be able to read it but also to answer it, which although I say it myself is pretty impressive!

Ben obviously so enjoyed his trip that at the end of the year he invited me to join him, Kit and Naser on a boys' (obviously as none of us were girls!) trip to Thailand.

We had a fantastic time firstly in Bangkok where we were well entertained by Naser's dad, who had been the world poker champion and then on to Phuket and the Sheraton Hotel, which it turned out had been prepaid for by Naser's dad. So the holiday was wonderful although having just taken up the mouth organ, which Ben had bought me, I was a bit miffed to find that there was an elephant in the hotel, who could play it better than me! There are obviously lots of vices available in Thailand and I felt that I had to take advantage of this so I started smoking! I rather think that my three companions made better use of the opportunities. We would start each evening at a table on the water's edge with four Chiang Beers and Spring Rolls and I remember on the last night after more than one Chiang Beer, thanking them for making me feel young again and with that I smoked another cigarette!

After his gap year Ben went to Leeds to study Music technology, which, after nine months, he told me that he wanted to change courses and start again and study to be an accountant.

Nine months later he rang me to meet up for a drink and to tell me he didn't want to do that course, which was probably self-evident as he never attended a single lecture! On being asked what he would like to be, he said a pilot! I had loved visiting him, Alanta – his very nice girlfriend – and his friends and on one occasion they took me to The Elbow Rooms, where I was the oldest person there by at least 30 years!

Ben took me to an open day at Kidlington Airport, where the implications of training to be a pilot and the cost were fully explained. Freda and I agreed to fund it and Ben proved massively impressive having found out what he wanted to do. The exams kept coming and he kept passing them, which allowed him to go to Phoenix to put in the flying hours. It is probably not cool to be proud of your children but when he finally qualified as a pilot it was one of the best days of my life.

I ensured that I was on his first flight, when he flew with British Midland from Heathrow to Edinburgh. I told him to ignore me, which he did but when I was in the airport he texted me to say he had landed the plane and that he was thrilled that I had been there to share it with him. I felt so emotional that it called for a large glass of wine to celebrate and then another and, in the knowledge that I better eat something, ordered fish and chips. Another glass of wine later and I was in great form although slightly surprised that everybody else seemed to be having a coffee and egg and bacon – it was then I realised that it was not yet 10am!

Ben went to Easyjet next before not only getting a job with British Airways but even more important flying 747's on long haul. I still look at these Jumbo Jets and marvel at how my little boy can get them airborne.

Bit by bit life improved and with all the good things in my life the bit about being in a dark place was obviously nonsense, so please ignore it! In Thurlestone I reconnected with local friends Derek and Vanessa, had nights out with lan and Yanny including a trip to the Plymouth Casino, and met Mark and Caroline who were most entertaining. Mark was from Blackburn and was a director of the Hotel and Caroline had fronted a couple of TV programmes, was about to stand as an MP and was writing her second book. I was particularly impressed with the book part, as I knew that I would never be able to write a book of the slightest interest to anybody and am in the process of proving that! All these people were great fun and an evening in the Village Inn could prove most entertaining although I never deserted my friend Roy.

On top of this I was incredibly excited by the planning for our first Wychwood Festival. For the week before the Festival I stayed at Hunters Lodge, a pretty basic hotel, on the racecourse. As I watched the site being created I was enthralled by the massive main stage, the big top number 2 stage, two more stages, workshops, bars, caterers and traders. This was massive and all the love I had had for all the theatres was quickly transferred to Wychwood.

We opened Friday June 3rd 2005 and I was aware that of everybody involved I was the only one without a job. Pete had erected and then controlled the site, David had taken charge of the box office, Jerry was running the merchandising, Graeme was in charge of the whole thing and I was – well I was drinking! The first act due on was the Angel Brothers on stage two and just before that I got a call from Ben, who was working back stage and organising the bands to get to the No 2 stage, to say the compere had not arrived so would I come down and put them on. Would I ever!

What a joy to introduce the first ever act to play Wychwood, who had been organised by Ben. Perfect, I am obviously talentless but have always been ok at introducing others. Job done I returned to the beer only to receive another call from Ben to say the comperes for the Main Stage had also not turned up so would I introduce the first act ever on the main stage – I readily agreed and hurried over before finding out that they were called Candido Fabre Y Su Banda, which would have been a bit of a challenge sober, never mind after a few drinks.

The comperes for the main stage did not turn up until late on Saturday, by which time they were out of a job and I was loving it. The weather was mixed, the audience small but I was in my element. The Saturday headliner was Steve Earle, whose music I really enjoyed and on the Sunday night in the pouring rain we closed with Alabama 3 and an audience wearing bin liners to keep dry.

During the three days I drank with a Sony executive wearing wings, an 87 year-old man in a kaftan who danced for ever in front of the stage, family and friends, and a couple from Derbyshire, who explained that they had both just retired and on their list of things to do was to come to a Festival. It was Sunday now and pouring down and I tentatively asked if they had had a good day and the lady said that they had camped for all three days and that she had just had the best three days of her life. I was incredibly moved and just thought that for her to say that was priceless – which was just as well as we lost over £300,000!

By now I realised that Thurlestone, enjoyable though it was, geographically for what I was involved in was a problem so I decided to buy a flat in Cheltenham. Ben, as always, massively supportive, rang round the agents and came up with the details of the perfect house, cheaper and far better than an apartment, on Queens Road within walking distance of 56 bars and restaurants (at last count I have been to 39 of them) and six minutes from the station. We quickly met Anthony Bloomer who was the head prefect of the road, told us when to put our bins out and organised regular drinking sessions with Chris, Edgar, John, Max and Roger. Anthony is a great character and for some reason enjoys taking rhe mickey out of me!

Life was really looking up and sorry about being a bit pathetic earlier!

Then came one of life's magical moments when you know things are just meant to be. My phone rang and it was Linda, my first wife, telling me that her Mum, who I had been very fond of, had died and that she and Marcus after 14 years together had split up and that she was going back to St Helena to live.

I explained that I was also on my own and it would be fantastic to meet up for a drink in Colchester where she lived. Incidentally, if anybody is interested. Colchester is a very long way from Thurlestone! When we met it was though we had never been apart and I knew that I wanted to spend the rest of my life with her (if that sounds a bit slushy ignore it and leave it as we got on quite well!). The difficulty was that she was a home girl and she had set her heart on returning to St Helena. So I was thrilled when she agreed to postpone her plans to give our relationship a chance.

From my point of view and hopefully Linda's it was love at second sight!

In my wedding speech (yes we did go on to remarry and I knew that you could not wait to find out!) I said that Linda brought Love, Passion, Happiness and Inner Peace into my life. Well you can say these things at a wedding, although I am not sure why everybody laughed when I said Passion!

The next obstacle was to get Ben's approval and after we all met for a drink in Cirencester and then had a fabulous Christmas in Thurlestone, it became obvious that they would be great friends and that I was likely to be the odd one out! We have gone on holiday every year since following our first one to Maldives with Ben's girlfriend at the time, Alanta. During the time there a bloke and his wife came over when we were watching football in the bar and asked what the score was. He seemed an amiable enough chap and we got in a good old footie chat establishing that he supported Man City, his wife Arsenal, and of course Southport for us. He was telling us how he used to go to Southport for his holiday. We were obviously creating a real bond so it seemed only polite to ask them what they did for a living, which was a question that Liam Gallagher and Nicole Stapleton probably did not get asked very often!

We were also to go on some great holidays, organised by Ben to Dubai,

Thailand, Los Angeles and rather a lot of times to Las Vegas. Our later trips were with Georgina, who Ben was with for five years. Both Alanta and Georgina added enormously to the enjoyment of our holiday and we adored them both.

Another great benefit of being with Linda was reconnecting with her family, who having not seen me for 23 years, reacted as though I had just been away for a week with a bad cold, her brother Campbell even remembered that it was my round next!

Campbell and Ann were still living in the UK, which was great so we had lots of time together and when we went to the beautiful Island of St Helena, I got to know Colin who was married to Linda's sister Deborah. We got on brilliantly and he became a close friend and good drinking mate.

Colin and his son, Ian, owned a garage, had the Island's main car hire, ran all the school buses, and as he obviously had lots of spare time owned Colin's Bar in Sandy Bay as well.

Sadly Colin died frm a heart attack at the age of 61 as I was writing this book and I very much miss his friendship, St Helena has a special place in my heart and we went on to buy a house out there. We go every year, taking a week to get there via military flight from Brize Norton to Ascension Island, a couple of days there waiting for the RMS St Helena, the last mail ship in the world and then a three day sail. The time on the ship is great fun with deck cricket, skittles, pub nights and a BBQ on deck. Linda's friend Rodney Young – everybody from the Island has a nickname and his is School Bus – is one of the two captains. I should say "was" because sadly Rodney also died at the age of 53 as I was writing this and another bright light is extinguished.

On the Island my first best man Gilbert Legg, chosen for his long hair, is still there and is a good man to have a drink with, although he now has almost no hair. As people who I have known in the UK have returned to live on the Island, visiting has got even better. Campbell and Ann returned home as did Brian and June Yon, who are great company. Brian suffers me on the golf course and being a great sax player (him not me!) we formed a double act as Brian Yon the man with sax appeal, and Smiling Sam's Sounds of the 60's and 70's. Unfortunately the local paper misheard re: an advert and I became Smiling Fan!

We did the Golf Club Dinner Dance and of course, Colin's Bar. I would like to say that Smiling Fan was a big hit on the Island but obviously not and on one occasion nobody danced for my whole spot apart from when I put Creedence Clearwater Revival on (Don't ask!) and then applauded at the end probably out of relief! I was a bit of a novelty as I was the only talking DJ on the Island apart from Donny who had his own bar on the waterfront.

Apart from meeting up with all Linda's relations, too many to mention but all great company, there was the massive bonus of Ian and his wife and children. The oldest, Kieran is lovely and very keen on cricket and football. We take him to Rosemary Plain, where he seems to have established the rule that if he misses the ball he fetches it but if he hits it we go. The weak link in this arrangement is that he never misses it and also hits it a long way. The middle son is Kyle, who is a great talker and character. Age five he told us he wanted to be an archaeologist and discover fossilised dinosaur bones (a bit disconcerting when a 5 year-old wants to be something I cannot spell!) I suggested that he should be a Rock Star and I would be his manager. Asked to explain my role I told him I would take 20% of everything he earned so if he played Colin's Bar for £50 I would take £10 of it. He told me that he would not be playing Colin's Bar and that he would tour South America, Australia, Isle of Wight and Ascension, and at the end of the show he would jump into the crowd so they could get his autograph!

He decided that Uncle Ben would fly his plane and that the rest of the band and equipment would go in another plane. When Colin told him that he would have to sort out insurance he turned to me and said "Don't look at me, you are the manager, you sort it out!" The youngest is Kian and we look forward to finding out his character.

We found the perfect place and venue for our wedding, when we visited one of Linda's friends from St Helena, Peter Yon, who was in charge of the Deer Park Hotel in Honiton. The Hotel owned by the financier Nigel Wray, boasted an incredible collection of sporting memorabilia and, with its large grounds and great style, was the ideal venue. Even more crucial was Peter who took over all the arrangements including going with Linda to choose her dress.

I had a couple of ideas but these were quickly dismissed as Peter organised the wedding of our dreams. Good friend Pete Langford brought the Barron Knights to entertain us, Campbell made a great speech welcoming me into the family — again and Colin Brindle had everybody laughing at my expense. The Reverend Neil Warwick had done his bit during the marriage service with panache while Ben was my best man and did a brilliant speech ending with asking everybody to stand to toast the two most important people here – the bar staff!

There were 150 friends and family to share the day with us including Colin and Deborah and Campbell and Ann who had come over specially from St Helena, which made Linda's day – as well as a signed photo from Stevie Gerrard!

Chapter 24

WYCHWOOD......AND BEYOND!

This has probably proved to be a somewhat boring domestic interlude but work continued with the challenge of keeping Wychwood going and the joys of Theatrexperience.

After a financial disaster but artistic success, it got great reviews and feedback from customers, the challenge was how could we finance as second year of Wychwood. We ali agreed to put more money in but we needed further investment.

Our saviour turned out to be my friend Charlie. He and Mavis had popped in with their grandchildren, Scott and Adam, on the Saturday to see what Wychwood was all about, mainly out of support for me in the knowledge that it probably was not his thing. They were having such a good time that they booked in a hotel for the night to enable them to stay. Knowing that we needed further investment Charlie immediately offered to become involved. He was too good a friend for me to encourage this, but he insisted, put a substantial amount in the pot and ensured that Wychwood would survive for a second year and would be headlined by the Saw Doctors, Billy Bragg and Amadou and Marian.

The crowds turned up, the reviews were tremendous, we were nominated for the best Family Festival in the UK and lost considerably less money! Edward Gillespie as Chief Executive of the Racecourse was a massive supporter and to help us financially gave us the contract to provide the after-racing music at The Centaur at the Gold Cup meeting. This was some experience in a venue that housed 5,000 racegoers, who were 90% Irish, 95% male and 99% drunk! I had, of course, volunteered to compere the four days with two days of Doreen Doreen, already booked by the Racecourse and two days of Peatbog Fairies, a nine-piece Celtic Band including bagpipes.

The first night of Doreen Doreen went down brilliantly with popular covers enabling everyone to sing along leaving me to doubt our slightly more cultural approach to the gig. Following Doreen Doreen's show we were approached by the police who banned "Kung Fu Fighting" and "The Sex Pistols" version of "My Way" as likely to incite violence!

When I told Doreen Doreen (a lady) the news she was thrilled as she had obviously never been banned from singing anything in her life. She was so thrilled that she kept telling the audience, which resulted in them booing the police! I had to grab her at her first costume change and explain that if she mentioned the police again she would not get paid, which seemed to do the trick.

The two shows by the Peatbog Fairies were a worry and by now all my colleagues, who had shown great initial interest had disappeared. I need not have worried as loads of men took their shirts off and danced rigs and reels with each other! Obviously Edward was happy as we were invited to continue this until the Jockey Club decided to make cut backs of which we were one. In contrast, my friend Bob Sweet also used us to provide entertainment at Chelsea Flower Show.

For Wychwood to survive for a third year we all put some more money in, planned for Wychwood 2007. In the meantime I had Theatrexperience to work on. In reality I was obviously not a very good consultant. This was a result of me being self-opinionated and reluctant to write reports.

A leisure consultancy company brought me in to do the theatres on the Isle of Wight as part of their overall review of the Island's leisure facilities. I had been horrified by the ineptitude by just about everybody involved including their best theatre, which was attached to a school and could not have afternoon get-ins for shows as it was used for detention.

When I was asked to present my review to the Council I explained that they were the worse run theatres I had ever encountered with no co-operation between them and no coherent Arts policy. After the presentation the main guy from the consultancy company said, "Well, that went well" but as I was just about to bask in the glory of a job done well he explained that he was being sarcastic and that I had jeopardised their whole contract by ridiculing the person that had employed them and worse than that I had done it in front of his boss! Somewhat surprisingly I was never contacted by them again!

My role with Really Useful had come to an end once it was clear that Andrew's policy was not to add provincial theatres to their West End ones, and Ellen Kent and I agreed that I had outlived my usefulness with her company.

On top of that the Dunstable project came to an end with the opening of the Grove Theatre. I actually thought I had done a decent job for them by getting them an outstanding manager in Jo Ditch, and helping to programme the theatre by using my contacts. I had used my friend Barrie Stead to produce the pantomime and the opening show which included Brian Blessed and Tony Christie. There were a number of speeches after the show thanking everybody involved apart from me, and once I left the theatre that evening, apart from Jo I never heard from anybody again. So another satisfied customer!

The result of this was that the Theatrexperience, the world's leading theatre consultancy company now had not one single customer!

The truth was that the only thing that I really wanted to do was to run theatres and there was very little likelihood of that happening and just as I was coming to terms with this I got a call from John Gore head of Key Brand Theatres in America. John was English and our paths had crossed when he produced "Thunderbirds Ago Go".

I warmed to him immediately, when the telephone call was followed up by a meeting. Key Brand had bought some theatres from Clear Channel in the States and were looking to buy all their theatres in the UK. I was offered the role of being their British representative with the agreement that if their bid was successful I would get to be in charge of all my old theatres. I liked John enormously and he was a joy to work with as was the team he put in place to get the deal through.

I had the pleasure of going to a meeting at Clear Channel with 20 or so Key Brand members, and hosted by Paul Latham and, as he shook hands with each of them, he got to me, looked up and said, "Fucking hell, what are you doing here!"

He was incredibly kind to me throughout the meeting saying how much he had learnt from me and that I was the perfect person to run their theatres. After an hour he called for a break so that we could go to his office and catch up, particularly on how our respective boys were doing. He also took me in to see my old friend Barry Clayman, who was now Chairman of Clear Channels Music Division.

He had done my standing with my American colleagues no harm at all and by now I was getting very excited. The only two companies left in the bidding were Key Brand and Ambassadors Theatre Group. It was my view that ATG should not be allowed to buy the theatres as it would give them a monopoly of the provincial No 1 theatres. These were heady times for me and as word got round I started getting invited to opening nights again and receiving calls from people I had never heard from since the day I left.

John Gore asked me where I wanted to base myself and the main office and when I said I could use the existing Oxford office he asked me whether it would not be easier to buy offices in Cheltenham. This really was a perfect scenario and I was in no doubt that under John Gore the old Apollo theatre chain would get a massive boost and I could not wait to be back in the game.

It really seemed too good to be true and it was as Ambassadors got the theatres! It is one of my major regrets that I did not get the chance to work with John to create a Theatre Group run by theatre people with a real feel for the shows, the staff and the public.

I was to have one more opportunity to get involved with running theatres, when Nick Thomas, whose company I had always enjoyed, had built up a small chain of theatres, which had great scope for growth. We had a good chat and he asked me if I would like to be involved, and obviously I would but only if I was in charge of them and Nick did not see a problem with this. However there was a problem as he already had somebody running them!

In Nick style he said that he was sure that we could work together, but when we had lunch it was obvious that our views were so different that we very definitely could not work together so that was the end of that and my last chance to do what I loved best.

However, I was very lucky in that there was still Wychwood, which ticked all my boxes of only doing things that I really enjoyed and with people I really liked. Graeme and I had really bonded and were ambitious to grow the Festival and the Company, and with David, Charlie, Jerry and Pete we had great friends involved.

We had also involved all our friends and families to help particularly on the bars, where we worked on the principle that honest and incompetent was better than the alternative! Linda became in charge of Ice Cream before gaining promotion to run the Pimms Bus.

In our second year Graeme had managed to book both The Feeling and The Guillemots, who came to prominence by the time they appeared.

Graeme had a great eye for programming and we were helped by Steve Porter's vast music knowledge.

In the first year we had Gilles Peterson and he wanted to return for the second year but only if he could bring a Brazilian act called the Ed Motta Band with him. We were not in favour of doing this until we were told that they were sponsored by Brahma beer and that we could have as much stock as we wanted free of charge! That really swung it and we ordered many pallets of the bottles and sold them everywhere including the ice cream tent! As we organised year three we had all settled into our Festival roles. David ran the box office, and helped Charlie who ran the bars. Jerry ran the merchandising and information tent, Pete's Company ran the production for a fee so at least he was earning out of it, Graeme was the Festival Director and although they all worked incredibly hard I had the most arduous job of all, going on the stage to tell the audience who was about to appear and then returning at the end of the set to remind people who they had been listening to in case they had forgotten!

Our 3rd Festival saw a great increase in crowd numbers and revenue and had some great moments with the Fun Lovin Criminals, the Levellers and Badly Drawn Boy. However the highlight was a Mexican guitar playing duo Rodrigo Y Gabriela, who warmed up as I talked to them by strumming a Coke bottle. When they started there was about 700 in front of The Independent (who were fantastic new sponsors) Stage and by the end there were more than 6000 people, who were mesmerised by them. Rodrigo Y Gabriela were to go on and top the World Music Charts for more than a year as well as busk on the streets of Dublin!

It was about now that an experienced Festival promoter told us that it would take a new Festival about five years to reach break-even point. A shame that we did not meet him before we started! However the continued increase in audience numbers suggested that we were on course to do that and in 2010 we moved into profit with a show that included Happy Mondays, Lightning Seeds, Beautiful South (we had to call them The South because Paul Heaton had left), Seth Lakeman, Ade Edmondson and the Bad Shepherds, C Beebies' Justin Fletcher and our old friends The Levellers.

Justin Fletcher was a joy to work with and a real star. He opened on the Saturday morning when normally there would be a dozen or so hung over punters and I was astonished to be confronted by a few thousand youngsters with their Mums and Dads, who joined in as much as the children. Justin remains the only artiste that we have ever had to get security to move him to his meet and greet spot which shows his popularity. He went on to do many Wychwoods and was always a great pleasure to work with.

Wychwood 2010 was also helped by being sponsored by Waitrose as well as The Independent. We were also now well established in helping different charities and had World Vision as our partner of conscience, which was great for me with my involvement with them.

In the following two years we had continued to grow with acts such as The Proclaimers, Divine Comedy, Kate Rusby, Super Furry Animals, Supergrass, Bellowhead and The Wonder Stuff. We had also pulled off our greatest artiste coup when we booked an unknown young lady called Duffy, who by the time she played Wychwood was No 1 in both the singles and album charts.

In our very laid back and relaxed backstage she was kept away from everyone by her tour manager and stayed on the tour bus until she was due on stage. The tour manager listened to me introducing some of the bands and graciously decided that I was good enough to be allowed to introduce Duffy and I would also be the only person allowed to speak to her, which I did before she went on. She was shaking with nerves and I assured her that the audience would love her.

This little Welsh girl nervously went on stage (obviously after a wonderful introduction!) opened her mouth and mesmerised the crowd for one of my special Wychwood moments. The attempt to keep her away from everybody failed as a Sun photographer managed to get a picture of her bending over to pick something up on her way back to her tour bus with the result that Duffy's knickers at Wychwood appeared for all the world to see!

With all the great reviews, being nominated every year for the Best Family Festival and moving into profit, Wychwood was not only enormous fun but also fulfilling the original vision of giving people a fabulous three days with four stages of quality music plus lots more including a Headphone Disco until 3.00am.

For those never having experienced a Headphone Disco they are great fun with everybody being given headphones (there is a surprise!) on entry. There are two DJ's offering a choice of music to dance to, and of course, if you want just to chat you just removed the headphones. By now many of our friends were regulars including over half of the people who attended our wedding plus lots of our friends and family from St Helena.

I was particularly delighted that all my brothers and sisters plus their children treated it as a family reunion. Although I was busy it was great to spend some time with Mary and Tod, Stephen and Josephine, Simon and Michelle and Sarah and Donald. In a nutshell I was thrilled with Wychwood and loved every minute of the planning, marketing, ticket selling but above everything the event itself. We also had a wonderful band of helpers who were very loyal to what we were trying to achieve.

The stilt walking, juggling Jem Maynard Watts ran all the highly popular workshops and all the children's activities and spent three days cycling round the site with a never ending smile on his face. Backstage Gaynor and Emma looked after all the artistes and their requirements (normally telling them, no they could not have a bottle of brandy etc!) plus making a fuss of Ben and controlling my home of the main stage was Gary Newman, who did a brilliant job ensuring that everything ran to time, which is an incredibly difficult job when bands are having a great time and want to do loads of encores. On some occasions when artistes had run out of time the audience booed the compere for the lack of another song!

We have always had to work to the strictest of curfews imposed on us by the Council and on the one time when we asked the officer attending the Festival if he would be flexible and allow us an extra five minutes as James had gone up late, the answer was no and that we would be prosecuted if we went even one minute over!

All over the site we had fabulous people helping to make the event happen. Sue Torres was brilliant at amassing 200+ stewards, who all did it for the love of the event, there was Matt Stone who did a great job of ensuring that the site was a safe environment, Tamsin who ran the box office, Kim and Tim who were the long suffering merchandise stars.

Wychwood also brought Paul Gregg back into my life, when he attended as a guest of David Rogers who was now doing some projects with him. I was delighted to see Paul and when the main stage closed at 11 pm I assumed that he must have gone. However I found him working on the wine bar and bless him he was doing deals with customers to enable us to sell more – some things never change.

Paul kindly invited Linda and myself to the reopening of the Scarborough Open Air Festival, for which he was responsible. It was a fabulous occasion with Jose Carreras, Kiri Te Kanowa and of course Brian Blessed. As Wychwood we got involved with the second year of the venue but after a sell-out Elton John concert, business went downhill. Despite that we remained in regular contact and have had some very enjoyable times with him and his lovely wife Yoshiko.

The greatest joy of Wychwood was sharing it with the hard working Linda and not so hard working Ben! For one Festival Ben was based in Paris working for Easyjet and said that he would have to work and would not be able to make it. The thought of Wychwood without Ben was really disappointing and just before we opened the site he rang me to wish us all luck. The call was obviously made from our Car Park as he turned up with a big smile 20 minutes later. I felt it was better not to ask how he had managed to get the time off!

On one occasion Linda and I went to Paris and met up with Ben and on our night out I explained that Paris was based on Southport! This caused increased ridicule the longer the night went on and by the end I was not even sure why I said it and accepted that it was an absurd comment.

A week later I received a copy of a piece in a book from Angelika, Tim Parson's partner, which she explained was another connection with Napoleon to go with the one who spent his last years on St Helena. It would appear that Napoleon the Third escaped from prison in Paris, dressed in woman's clothing and went to the Lancashire seaside resort of Southport and he was so impressed by the beauty of the tree-lined Lords Street that when he returned as Emperor he decided to recreate Southport in Paris except larger! Not a lot of people know that!

Chapter 25

WYCHWOOD, TOYBOX AND THE NEVER ENDING STORY

Away from Wychwood and Theatrexperience life continued to be busy. As will be now be self-evident I enjoy standing up and talking. I had developed an after dinner, before dinner, before or after lunch, after breakfast talk called a "Backstage pass to (my age minus 21) years in Showbiz". This obviously proved very popular and was in such demand that I must have averaged almost two talks a year!

More importantly I was able to give talks on my travels and experiences with World Vision. The charity's main income came from child sponsorship but its strength was also its weakness as in the most volatile areas, for obvious reasons, they would not utilise child sponsorship. These countries were known as fragile states and they started a campaign entitled "Raw Hope" to encourage people to sponsor a project rather than a named child.

With my experience in some of the most desperate places on earth I was a massive supporter of the campaign. It was launched by Lynne Morris at the House of Lords, where Terry Waite and I were to be the guest speakers.

After his five years as a hostage I expected Terry to be a sombre kind of guy but nothing could have been further from the truth. As we chatted in advance of the lunch he explained that Macclesfield wanted him to be their Mayor as he had already spent five years wearing chains! It was at the time of the MP's expenses scandal and he told me that he could be in a lot of trouble as he had had five years free board and lodgings! It was an honour to be his partner in crime on this gig.

I did a good number of talks for World Vision including one in Edinburgh, which was attended by my sister Sarah and her husband Donald, a very definite bonus. Donald introduced me to a gentleman who had been Chief Provost of Edinburgh. He told me that he hoped that he was not going to be asked to sponsor another child and whilst he was on about it could I explain why he had never had a sponsored child, who could speak English?! These road shows were effective both in raising funds and awareness and I was delighted to be part of the team that delivered them.

I had also become Chairman of Cirencester Housing for Young People (Chyp) although Jane Gunner was still very much the leading light. These were difficult times with the Council attempting to take our supporting people funding off us to give to a company that worked in many other areas.

This culminated in a report, which I found offensive to the team of social workers, led by Millie, who ran the homes and to all the hardworking, caring souls on the committee. The report was factually incorrect and absurd in its complaints, such as we were teaching our residents how to cook and how to budget when they moved onto their own accommodation. This is apparently wrong and was not part of our remit!

Before the showdown meeting started I asked the Councillor sat next to me if he thought that it was a good idea for us to prepare our tenants for when they moved away by teaching them how to look after themselves. He said that he definitely agreed so I explained that he had obviously not bothered to read the report!

The meeting with nine people from the Council started badly when the lady chairing it said that the meeting which started at 6.00pm had to end at 7.30pm. I immediately made myself unpopular by querying this on the basis that nobody had another meeting to go to, so as we were talking about young people's lives we should stay here as long as required. I then insisted in going through their report line by line.

After an hour and a half we had been able to demonstrate that the report was flawed and basically incorrect but we still had more than half to go. I was determined to keep going to ensure that our team was supported but one of our trustees quite sensibly stopped the proceedings and asked the leading Council representative if they had already made the decision to withdraw our funding. On hearing that they had, I lost the plot, explained that they were a disgrace and had insulted some people who had done magnificent work with the homeless young people of the area. I stated that they were not the sort of people I could trust or work with, resigned as Chyp Chairman and stormed out of the room. This was very much out of character as I am normally a very pleasant and charming chap but I was extremely angry.

Having collected my possessions and walked out, I then came to my next problem which was how to get out of the building as the doors were locked. A return to the meeting to say "Excuse me could somebody let me out" was obviously out of the question and I toyed with ringing the Fire Brigade to report them for having locked exit doors but this seemed a bit dramatic. After about ten minutes I saw a very big sign telling me to press a green button to exit the building! Once out I was in such a dither I set my car alarm off right below the open window of the meeting! The moral of this experience was know how to get out before you storm out of meetings.

I would be a liar if I said that it gave me no pleasure when Jane told me a few years later that the Company that took over from us did such a lousy job that they lost the contract. Chyp, without me as Chairman, went from strength to strength utilising the houses that the Charity owned to make a real difference for many troubled and homeless 16–24 year olds. I assuage my conscience by running annual Sportsman's Dinners to raise money for Chyp.

I did 21 of these dinners with a sportsman and a comic and received great support from friends with Charles taking a table for every one. Nigel, Chris and others from Shrivenham Cricket Club never missed one and Stef and Graeme came to most of them. Some of the best speakers were John Conteh, Australian fast bowler Rodney Hogg, Willie Thorne, Welsh rugby legend Mervyn Davies and Ron 'Chopper' Harris.

We also had some great comics including Chris McGlade. Chris did a Southport gig for me and started by picking on the viocar who had just said grace, telling him that the Bible was all lies as it had said that Jesus was a carpenter and that he had got all their records and Jesus was not on any of them!

He is a very aggressive, political, funny man and he also became a friend.

My role was to run the event with help from Tom Watmore from Chyp and, of course, compere it including a raffle, an auction and just one joke. I can hear you shouting, 'I'm bored, tell me a joke!'

Well, I wasn't going to but if you insist – I went to visit an old actress friend of mine called Gloria, who was playing Cheltenham Everyman theatre. Gloria had just got married again and husband No 3 – Sebastian – was an actor and much younger than her. She enthused about his stud-like qualities saying, 'We went on honeymoon and on reaching our hotel room my clothes were off and we had a performance. After lunch we returned to our room and had another performance and then when I came out of the shower before dinner, Sebastian couldn't resist me and we had another performance and then after dinner we retired to our room and had a dress rehearsal.'

I had followed the performance but now I was a bit lost so I asked Gloria what a dress rehearsal was. She replied, 'Sam, it is the same as a performance but nobody comes!"

No wonder people bought tickets every year!

Cheltenham had proved to be an inspired choice for us to live as it is not only a fantastic town but it is also home for quite a few people from St Helena. I was worried that Linda, having foregone her dream of going home, would miss being amongst people from the Island. I need not have worried as on our first walk into Cheltenham centre I noticed a very attractive lady walking towards us. As she passed us, both she and Linda turned round as Linda asked if she was a Saint. She was and Jenny and her husband Gary Widdows became good friends with whom we enjoyed some great evenings before devastatingly Jenny died of a brain tumour.

Her close friend and ours Dan Yon had come over from Canada to see her and did a very moving eulogy at her funeral, which filled Cheltenham's Christ Church. Dan is a fascinating and lovely guy and as a film maker produced and directed "One Hundred Men" a moving and sometimes funny film about the men who left St Helena in 1949 to work on farms in England.

His latest film "Sathima's Windsong" based on the South African jazz singer Sathima Bea Benjamin, which covers her St Helena roots, her living in Cape Town's `pattern of brokeness' that marked South Africa's apartheid, recording with Duke Ellington in Paris to living for 30 years in New York. A remarkable story by a remarkable man. I will always be grateful to Dan, who when a guest lecturer at Cape Town University gave up a day of his life to show us the real Cape Town.

Within Cheltenham there is a really happy bunch of Saints who have become my friends as well as Linda's. There is a lady called Shirley Francis, who is the queen bee, and along with her friend Cynthia Bowers organise lots of get-togethers. I am always delighted to meet up with them all to share a drink or two and they are always great fun. When we need helpers to entertain the Southport footballers who we entertain every season after they have played Forest Green and Cheltenham, we are reliant on Christine and Kevin, Mashay, Evie and Andrew, Cynthia, all organised by Shirley, to provide the catering. Whilst they do all the work Linda seems to wander round kissing as many young footballers as she can! As she explains it is dirty work but somebody has got to do it!

Linda has another good Saint friend in Shirley Corker, whom she meets for lunch at 12.30pm and finishes lunch (drinks!) at 6.30pm. It is not home for her but at least she has been able, along with me, to enjoy the company of lots of her fellow countrymen in Cheltenham.

Our Cheltenham home is also very useful, due to its proximity to Brize Norton, for people to stay with us before travelling home. One of my favourite guests is Darren Plato along with his partner Lucille and his son Alex. Darren and I have put the world right on numerous occasions with a few pints in The Royal Union Pub. His sisters Helena and Tiffany with their partners Kurt and Chris have also been very welcome visitors.

Regardless of what is happening in our lives Ben and I have always ensured that we met up very regularly for a beer and a catch up. The venues have not always been glamorous, and have included the pub in Paddington Station and the Piano and Pitcher near Reading station. However these are some of the most precious times in my life as we sort all life's problems out but then wake up the next day and cannot remember what we agreed – at one stage we actually took notes!

Around this time we had a fabulous holiday in Dubai along with Ben and Georgina. The highlights for Ben was getting a birthday card from Ryan Giggs who was staying in the hotel and for Linda, a tennis fanatic, meeting and getting Roger Federer's autograph and for me ordering a draught pint of Heineken and having it served in an ice bucket — well as they say, little things.....etc!

I have obviously digressed yet again but in the world of Wychwood major progress had been made when Graeme met with Mark Makin, who has a very creative production company, and between them they decided that the one festival Cheltenham was lacking was a Comedy Festival. This resulted in Mark and his wife Penny, Graeme and I starting the Cheltenham Hobgoblin (thanks again to the lovely people at Wychwood Brewery) Comedy Festival.

Mark and Penny are a joy to be in partnership with even if Mark originally from the lovely Lancashire town of Todmorden thinks he is from Yorkshire! Our first festival was in 2011 and featured Miles Jupp, Arthur Smith and Stewart Francis, amongst others and was both great fun and successful.

Wychwood 2011 featured the Charletons, Waterboys and Ian Anderson from Jethro Tull and as always I loved every minute of it with loads of family and friends in attendance plus the nicest audience of all ages imaginable who just come to have a good time. The only slight weak link was that it reverted to a small loss mainly as a result of us losing the Waitrose sponsorship which had only ever been for one year.

Despite this neither Graeme and I could have anticipated that at one of our regular board meetings our colleagues decided that enough was enough and that they had all put a lot of time and effort into it and it was difficult to see how they would get any return out of it. I fully understood their stance and without their finance and expertise Wychwood would never have survived.

This obviously left Graeme and I in a dilemma as we still believed in the Festival. By now Graeme and I had become very close friends and Wychwood was our baby and we did not want to let it go. We agreed a deal in principle to buy the rights from the old company but desperately needed new investors to make this happen. I was very touched that the very first new invester was Ben, who just said that that we had all put too much into it to just let it go.

Graeme then set about finding others who could share our vision. He quite quickly met up with an old friend of his called Simon Collins who had been a major player in Foxy Bingo the online game. Simon, in his wonderful laid back way, wrote a cheque out and joined the gang. We were also lucky with another friend of Graeme's, Jonathan Clitheroe, who had been to Wychwood and enjoyed it, and he too put his hand up to be part of it.

Graeme and I then met up with a great guy called David Chilvers, who owned his own business involved in car stacking and was a Bristol Rovers fan which was obviously not his fault! After our second pint, David also wrote out a cheque and joined our merry band. He was then joined by Jamie Crick. the Classic FM presenter.

The board was later joined by Jesse Wood, Alex Mitchell and Sam Cunningham who ran Smashing Blouse Music, which had started programming our Big Top number 2 stage. Everybody who joined in fitted my mantra of only working with people I like, and as I was now the only old bugger on the Board I become the self-elected Chairman, which nobody either noticed or objected to. It was exciting times with a diverse group of young and talented people.

There was no doubt that 2012 was going to be a difficult year, particularly as our weekend clashed with the Jubilee celebrations. We were also faced with a change in Chief Executives at Cheltenham Racecourse with Edward Gillespie resigning. Edward had been our friend and had been massively supportive of Wychwood and it was hard to believe we would get the same support from Ian Renton the new Chief Executive.

As it hapened we struck lucky with Ian, a very different character from Edward, but every bit as supportive. Not only did Ian help us in every way he reasonably could he also ensured that his team at the Racecourse worked even more closely with us to our mutual benefit.

As we planned for the Festival we were very aware that David, Charlie and Jerry's departure left a massive gap in the areas in which they had worked so hard, We had already decided to change production companies and had brought in Chris Tarran's Company to be in charge of production and he had lots of new ideas and was a breath of fresh air and good to have involved.

David and Charlie had handled all the cash and so Graeme took over that roll. He was given a massive boost when he was contacted by Mary Young, a delightful lady who had worked with David on the cash in the first few years. She had been training as a lawyer at the time and she told Graeme that she had qualified and was now working for a Cheltenham law firm and that she would be very happy to come in and help him and as she was no longer an impoverished student she did not want paying. She is my sort of girl! So Mary joined the long list of fabulous people who did crucial jobs at Wychwood out of the goodness of their hearts. We knew that business was going to be difficult for our first show as Tribe Festivals but we had not reckoned on the weather making things even harder. It seemed to rain cvery day for the six weeks leading up to the event and despite another artistic and enjoyable success with James, Saw Doctors, The Damned and Hawkwind headlining, it was a baptism of fire for the new Tribe Festivals team. What was self-evident to all of us was that for Tribe to prosper we had to add more strings to our bow and not be at the mercy of the volatility of Wychwood. We made a major move in this direction when we did a deal with Stefan Edwards, who worked three months a year on Wychwood, to bring his Company Kiss My Face into Tribe enabling Stefan to work full time with us as well as becoming a director and shareholder.

Stefan brought Band Management and Services, Mega Roller Disco's, Rocky Horror Nights and the Walk the Line Festival into the fold. Along with the Comedy Festival this enabled Tribe to have four divisions and gave it crucial growth areas outside of Wychwood. It made for more exciting times and a proper long term future for the Company.

When Stefan left to pursue other interests while remaining in the Tribe crowd, we were equally lucky to get Nick Trevey to take over his role. Nick, too, was a breath of fresh air.

Time moved on and 2013 saw a massive improvement for Wychwood both in the numbers attending and Tribe's finances. Human League, Bill Bailey and Soul II Soul headlined. The audience had a ball, and I worked incredibly hard on a sweaty stage giving the crowd the very important information of what the people appearing were called, crucial work that not everybody fully appreciated!

As always, the reviews were wonderful, the social media comments heart-warming and as always we were nominated for the best Family Festival in the UK, as well as the best Medium Sized Festival and most impressive of all for the best Festival Toilets (known as the Shithouse Award!)

The following year Wychwood broke all records including its highest ever crowds. For me it was everything that Graeme and I had wanted to achieve. It was a dream weekend with all my brothers and sisters and their children there including sister Mary's son Quin who has never missed a single minute of the Festival.

My oldest friends Nick Hall and his partner Lucy and Martin Raybould and his wife Sue were there plus so many friends and Linda, having been released from working, had great fun with all our friends including the increasing numbers of Saints who had decided that it was a good way to spend a weekend. We also had Jemma, who was Linda's ex-partner Marcus's daughter and who Linda had helped to bring up, with her husband Matt. They were a lovely fun couple and I was always delighted to see them as I was Marcus' two boys Gavin and Dan and their partners Sarah and Sadie.

On top of all this, despite my heavy work load on stage, there was always Ben to have a beer with!

On stage if was also a dream year. We had labelled Friday as party night and we turned out to have the ideal line up. We had the perfect fun band in Thrill Collins, three great guys who we manage and they were followed by 10 CC's Graham Gouldman with an acoustic set of all the hits he had written. Graham is, of course, a prolific song writer and wrote hits for the Hollies, The Yardbirds and a number of others as well as his 10 CC catalogue. He was a lovely guy and wrote to us after the Festival to say how much he had enjoyed it and how unusual it was to be made so welcome with people backstage coming to say hello. His set went down a storm with a large audience singing along.

He was followed by The Real Thing, three guys that I had booked for £30 at The Vine Club many years ago. Astonishingly people of all ages seemed to know and love all their songs. It was great to look out from the stage and see everybody dancing and singing along.

Top of the Bill were the Stranglers, who all those years ago in Blackburn, I had to get the Council to unban them! They did a great set with all their hits and a perfect end to a perfect day. On the Saturday we had another great day with Bad Manners, insisting that I was part of a very long pre-gig hug, by the end of which I thought that Buster and I should have got engaged! They went down a storm and were followed by Reef, which was particularly special as they included our own Jesse Wood as their newest member and his first gig with them. They did a great set and were followed by Newton Faulkner who was simply superb.

Before his set we had been contacted by a terminally ill girl who asked if she could meet him and have a photo taken with him. Sadly she was too ill to make it and we were to later find out that the following Sunday he went unannounced to her house in Swindon and played for her in the garden. She sadly passed away on the Wednesday. It was a top gesture by a top guy.

Our Saturday headliner's were The Levellers, who every time we have a poll amongst our Wychwood family on which band they would like to play the Festival, always have more votes than all the others put together. This particular night they played a set that showed just why.

The Sunday simmered with the talents of Lee Thompson from Madness, Wolf Alice and Craig Charles but the headline act drew the biggest stage crowd I had ever seen on a Sunday. Forgetting everybody else I was excited when we booked The Boomtown Rats. However, when Bob Geldof's daughter Peaches died two months before the show, we wondered if they would cancel. Bob insisted though that he would carry out all his bookings.

When they arrived I checked with their tour manager on what I should say to Bob before going in to say hello. He just said that Bob was in his music zone and not to mention the tragedy. When I went into his dressing room (porta cabin!) we chatted about old times before I asked him if there was any particular introduction or was he happy for me to spout my usual rubbish. He was very specific and said "Sam you will stand back stage next to me and when I say go you will run on that stage and say, "Wychwood!...The greatest Rock n Roll band on the planet......The Boomtown Rats!" With a twinkle in his eye he added, ".....and you will do it with conviction"!

When the moment came he reminded me, "Sam – with conviction!" He was absolutely magnificent and played one of the greatest sets I have ever witnessed, not just at Wychwood but anywhere. It was one of those special moments that I will still remember even after I have forgotten my own name!

This Festival was also special as it involved the first appearance of the charity Toybox, who do magnificent work with street children in some of the toughest environments on earth. I had got involved in it when Lynne Morris, a very special friend going back to my trips with World Vision, became its Chief Executive.

I had also been asked to mentor Naomi Lewis, who had been on the World Vision trip that had been on to Chennai. She had followed Lynne to Spurgeons Charity when the mentoring request came. I obviously have not the slightest idea what mentoring is but if it means meeting an attractive lady for lunch, telling her your problems and listening to her advice I got it spot on!

Naomi also joined Toybox so after 26 years of supporting World Vision it was time for a change and I was delighted when David Lowbridge, Toybox's excellent Chairman asked me to join their Board.

Toybox was founded when two people watched on their TV while Police in Guatemala rounded up street children and shot them. It was to Guatemala that I was to go with Lynne and Naomi to witness Toybox's work first hand. Guatemala is a country that has suffered from massive American interference.

In 1948 after 125 years of different dictatorships, Guatemala had their first ever democratic election and voted in a socialist leader with a mandate to help the poor and to improve health and education. This arrangement did not suit the US so Eisenhower instructed the CIA to bring about a regime change which they did, bringing in a military dictator. The massive injustice of their involvement was to last more than 40 years.

In 1963 Guatemala's military junta, under pressure from intellectuals, students, workers and Mayan peasants decided to hold a free election. President Kennedy stopped this, got rid of the Junta and another military dictator was brought to power. He probably did this while signing the Civil Rights Bill in America!

Guatemala unsurprisingly is a screwed-up country with large areas controlled by gangs. Toybox's objectives are firstly to get children off the streets, secondly to help those who are on the streets and thirdly to get children birth certificates without which they do not officially exist.

On my first full day in the country we went in a minibus to the Ladies Prison in Guatemala City where two ladies had worked with Toybox and its representatives to get their children birth certificates. This was a major breakthrough as it was the first time that it had happened.

On the journey there our local guide explained that we were in Zone 18, an area controlled by the most vicious of all the gangs. She explained that when the Government had tried to get an influence in the area they replaced all the police, who were totally loyal to the Gang, with a new force and within seven days every single new policeman had been killed. It was also pointed out that a priest and an aid worker visited the area uninvited and they were both beheaded!

I was told not to worry as the gang had agreed us free passage into the prison. This was to prove not so as we were stopped a quarter of mile from the prison and told to get out of our vehicle and walk. I was frightened but I felt comforted to see the Army on the road with tanks and mentioned this to a guy who was walking next to me, but he took away my comfort by explaining that they too were totally controlled by the gang and then telling me to slow down as we were being watched.

Terror is a strange uncontrollable emotion. I have previously felt terror at a roadblock in Rwanda and when I heard gun shots in DRC Congo and I felt it again on this walk and I have never been so pleased to get into a prison!

The birth certificate ceremony was very moving and done with great compassion by four of the Governments registration officers. We were later to meet a very impressive man who was the Government's head of registration and he explained to us that he backed this campaign, not so the children could have a name on their grave, but rather so that they could live their dreams.

We were offered the opportunity to spend one night on the streets helping and talking to the street children and it gave me an experience that will stay with me forever. We spent time with young children, including a 14-year-old girl with her baby. Food and clothes were brought for them, plus colouring books.

One four- year-old girl latched on to me and she got an old bag filled with rubbish and we played catch. When the bag broke she disappeared and came back with another bag and the game continued, with me feeling truly blessed that she had chosen me.

We then went into an area where there was group of about 20 youngsters between the age of 12 and 20. One look at them sniffing glue and you would have walked a mile to avoid them. However our leader went up to them got them all to stand, to stop sniffing and to sing a hymn! This group was regularly attacked by the police and at one stage a number had died having been given poisoned sandwiches by the police. We had to keep one eye on our leader and if he took his hat off we were to get back quickly to the minibus as we were getting out pronto.

One of our team was a lady who had lived on the streets and had been to prison for delivering drugs for a gang. Whilst they were receiving food, drinks, clothes and medical help she came up to me and said one of the boys had asked if I would give him a hug. So for ten minutes I held 12-year-old Kevin. I was thrilled to be told a few months later that Kevin had agreed to come off the streets and he was eventually reunited with his mother and sister.

A year later Neil Warwick joined us on a visit to El Salvador. On this trip there were many sad similarities with Guatemala, but one really uplifting moment was when we met the members of the El Salvador ladies street football team, who had been funded by Toybox to go to the Street Children's World Cup in Brazil. Not only did they go but they beat Brazil in a play-off to be third.

Their testimonies were incredible, especially the goalkeeper who had saved the crucial penalty. Despite some horrific adversities they had stuck together and were going round the city holding coaching classes.

I mention these trips not because I take any credit from them but because firstly they matter to me and secondly for the incredibly brave team who do not just make one visit but go out night after night, week after week and month after month. On one of our visits our leader was confronted by a gang leader who told him that if he ever saw him there again he would personally chop him up into little bits. The next night he was back out on the streets.

Toybox and the local teams make a difference in some of the darkest places on earth and to that end I am immensely privileged to be a minute cog in what they achieve, be they driven by their faith or their overall concern for humanity.

On our trips to St Helena it had always been our plan that Ben would be the first visitor to go with us. However with the long journey by ship it was never going to work for him until the airport opened. So the first friends to ever travel with us to the Island were Bob (Rob to his friends) and Lyn Sweet. This came about following a boozy night in Malvern, where Linda and I traditionally met up with Rob on the night before his RHS show opened there. These were always fun nights for Rob and I whilst Linda as the driver stayed sober and listened to our rubbish. On this occasion we met in an Italian restaurant where Rob had told them it was my birthday (which it wasn't), which resulted in a great fuss plus Sambuca's on the house. During the evening Rob said that he had always wanted to go to St Helena and I told him he should do it before the Airport opened as the journey on the RMS St Helena was a special experience. So he rang Lyn and we all agreed to do it.

They were great companions and treasured every moment. When we arrived on Ascension we had arranged for the head of conservation, our friend Stedson Stroud to take Rob and Lyn up Green Mountain. Stedson and Rob bonded immediately as they looked at different plants, probably the only two people on earth that would know their names.

Ascension is a strange island owned by Britain but leased to the Americans for a military air base. Green mountain has an incredible array of vegetation but below it the Island was covered in volcanic ash and rocks. Its golf course is officially known as the worst in the world as wherever your ball lands you tee it up with sand and aim for the non green greens of rolled ash.

On previous visits we had always spent time with Ascension's leading musician, Colin "Mickey" who worked on the American Base. He had built a recording studio on the beach with BBQ facilities and a bar and it was his heaven on earth. His wife Valerie had been a bridesmaid at Linda and my first wedding and was thus 'family'.

Once we reached St Helena, Rob and Lyn loved every minute and fitted in brilliantly with our family and friends. On one occasion we went up Diana's Peak with Linda's cousin Wendy and her husband and my golfing friend Mocus.

The heavens opened and we were drenched to the skin but Rob kept stopping to take photographs. The next morning he showed me a photo that was incredibly exciting to him as it was a plant that you could not find anywhere else in the world. I explained to him that exciting to me was Southport scoring the winner in injury time – so we agreed to differ on this. On a previous visit Wendy's daughter Maria and her husband Richard had also insisted that we went on a long walk in the rain so it must be something in the family.

On the Island all the talk was about the new airport that was being built and our friend Pat Anderson, who was working on it, and his wife Vilma took us all on a guided tour. This was exciting progress for us and all other people on the Island as it would open it up for weekly flights and for me it would mean that Ben could come out and experience the special delights of St Helena.

In the end the British Government spent in the region of £290 million creating the Airport though there was one small weak link in that the plane that was commissioned by Comair the contracted Airline, would not land as a result of the windsheer (to you and me turbulence created by the Island's terrain)!

If you are a British Tax payer please do not think that your money is being wasted because that is not the case as your £290 million runway is being well used for go-carting! I haven't actually seen this myself but it was in the Daily Mail so it must be true.

Towards the end of Rob and Lyn's visit I arranged for Rob to go on the Tony Leo Radio Show. In advance of this they had both noticed that I featured on both the Island's radio stations as I had recorded lots of Links for one and had done some jingles on the other for Tony, for whom I had done the request programme after my very first visit. I was very moved when Rob during this interview said that St Helena was the most beautiful country he had ever visited.

Back in the UK life continued to be hectic but fun with some great friends. One of these was Jim Cumbes, who, as Chief Executive of Lancashire County Cricket Club had always invited us to the Old Trafford Test Match plus concerts such as Take That and Arctic Monkeys.

In my Apollo days I had always got tickets for the Lancashire players and had always been made to feel most welcome when I was there. The players were always very good at writing to say thank you for having them looked after in the theatres and the England fast bowler Peter Martin, a very talented artist, sent me a framed and signed print of his painting of the Old Trafford pavilion.

When Mike Atherton, as the current England Captain, agreed to be the sporting guest at a Southport Sportsman's Dinner, he arrived late, went to his place on the top table, saw me in the room and came all the way over to say hello. I was most impressed by this as was one of my guests, Jimmy Cricket, who insisted that the three of us had our photo taken. Mike's agent later told me that he had only agreed to do the gig as a favour to me, obviously a fine fellow as well as a great cricketer.

For all the great hospitality that Jim Cumbes offered me I was able to repay him by invitations to watch Southport games! When Jim eventually retired having overseen the incredible development of Old Trafford he was replaced by a lovely guy called Daniel Gidney, who had worked for Apollo and so far he has very kindly not crossed me off the list of invites. So Colin Brindle and I still get our very special Old Trafford day. It has also been special for Tribe to have been awarded the contract to provide the music and children's entertainers for Lancashire's T20 games.

Linda and I had also embarked on a European City a year campaign and after the joys of Paris, Budapest and Prague we went to Munich, to stay with my brother Simon, who was working out there. We had a fabulous three days, starting in a beer garden in the park where his apartment was.

He had planned every minute from the pain of Dachau Concentration Camp to the Olympic Centre, a great bier keller, and a fine restaurant near where he lived. He was a great organiser and obviously very popular with his neighbours, including his German neighbour who when we were leaving to go home at 7.00am was outside and presented Linda with a rose for the road! It was a massive joy to spend time with a younger brother who took control for the whole of our visit and was fantastic company.

Ben's friends also featured very much in our life including his school friend Kit, who is living in China and had raised multi-millions to launch his business. Linda and I are always touched that when he returns he always gets in touch and comes over for lunch. What he has achieved is incredible but over a beer he can still chat about the important things like how Forest Green, his local team, are doing.

I have obviously digressed yet again but back in the world of Wychwood we broke all crowd records again in 2015 with a show that was headlined by Ali Campbell, Micky Virtue, and Astro's UB 40, Boney M, Proclaimers and Ladysmith Black Mambazo. The following year with slightly lower numbers we had three gloriously sunny days in the great company of 10CC, Bill Bailey, The Waterboys, Idelwild, Peter Hook and of course our good friend Justin Fletcher.

To my incredible relief and no doubt even more to yours, if you have been able to follow the meandering route this book has taken the end is nigh!

At the start, which you will no doubt have long since forgotten I recalled a meeting when I explained that whatever little I had achieved was down to luck, more luck and even more luck and I am sure by now that this will have been more than obvious to you!

Top of the luck league was undoubtedly having Linda and Ben in my life.

Following my departure from Clear Channel I was determined not to do anything that I did not want and to do things only with people I liked, and in review I think that I achieved this. I spent nine years on the board of the Everyman Theatre where Geoffrey Rowe was Chief Executive and I enjoyed every minute spent with my colleagues on that Board. As well as being on the Board of Toybox, which is led by the inspiring Lynne Morris and has been an honour to be involved with, I also chaired the World Mission Group at my local church, Christ Church. I was asked to do this by our highly entertaining, thought provoking, West Brom supporting Vicar, Tim Mayfield.

It has been a pleasure to be part of a great team who take responsibility for distributing 8% of the Church's income to needy causes worldwide. It goes without saying that being Vice Chairman at Southport has been most enjoyable with Charlie as Chairman. Tribe Festivals and Wychwood has been very special to me and a great joy to work with both the new and the old team and of course more than anybody, Graeme. So overall object achieved and a gold star for Shrouder!

269

After the honour of being able to be part of the legendary Apollo story, I look at how theatres are run now with booking fees, handling fees, restoration fees yet, in most cases, none of the razzmatazz, friendliness and fun that I remember. Many years ago I went to visit a lady called Tamara Malcolm, who ran the Chipping Norton Theatre. She had obviously invited me with a view that we would have nothing in common, but we got on like a house on fire and an hour meeting moved on to a long lunch. As I was leaving she gave me a copy of the Howard & Wyndham 1935 handbook. I end with it as it has been my mantra for all places of entertainment.

"The audience is the most important factor in our life at Howard and Wyndham. There are good audiences and bad audiences, large audiences and small audiences, kind audiences and – getting the bird! No matter how good a manager or an actor becomes, no matter how large his salary, or how bright the electric sign which spells his name, there is always the audience. It is an old saying that no two audiences are ever alike, and an even more curious thing is that an audience is not necessarily a good thing because it is large. Generally speaking, people enjoy themselves more at a play when the audience is full, and actors enjoy playing far more to full houses than to empty ones, and yet it sometimes happens that an audience, though meagre, has a gift of `acting' (i.e. reacting to an artist's playing) that may give the people on stage that wonderful feeling of being in tune with them, which is the greatest compensation of our arduous task. On the other hand there are nights when the audience are more interested in the bars than the play, or have dined not wisely but too well. There are nights when they don't like the actors or the play, and there are sometimes, in Edinburgh, nights when they boo.

But – there comes sometimes in our theatrical life that one evening which we will never forget (and perhaps the audience will never forget either), when there is a breathless hush all over the theatre, when two thousand people, from the duchess in the gallery to the dustman in the stalls, sit, as it were, at the actor's feet, lost in the play. Forgotten is the business of the day, their individual cares, their grief's, their worries. No longer ordinary self-centred creatures, they sit watching a puppet-play and dream in an enchanted world. It may be a world of tinsel, unreal and make-believe. It may be our theatres are gaudy, palaces for only one evening, but there is magic that night which can never be beaten – magic that lasts a lifetime – that cannot be recorded on paper, that leaves nothing permanent behind but that lives in the hearts of the audiences and stays till the day that they die. It is a hard life for an actor or theatre manager, uphill and down dale, but it has its moments of greatness and its memories are paradise".

If you have read the whole book rather than just turned to the last page to see who done it, then you will be in need of a stiff drink whilst I must start work on volume two (only joking I promise!) An old comic used to end his act with, "If you give of your money you give of your wealth but if you give of your time you give of your life."

So many thanks for giving a bit of your life to read this rambling story – I hope that at least it helped you sleep!

COLIN WILLIAMS AND GERRY TAIT

Whilst writing this book two close friends of mine died. So Colin, my special friend on St Helena and Gerry, my pal for over 25 years at Apollo, Southport and in life, this book is also dedicated to you.

~ . ~

Oh yes.......

This book was written from memory with a little guidance from a few people along the way whom I thank. However it would never have happened if it was not for Bernard Bale, who in his role as editor and publisher persuaded me to do it, so it is his fault!

I wrote it in long hand and when I felt like giving up Bernard assured me that there would be somebody somewhere who might find it vaguely interesting! With such encouragement I bought another pen and kept going.

He also gave my musings a "haircut" and I have not got a clue what that means other than making some sort of sense of it, introducing punctuation, paragraphs, and chapters as well as correcting the spelling!

So a special thank you to Bernard for believing in the project and for entertaining me with many of his stories, including his talent for playing Subbuteo football!

Happy days at Wychwood…

...and Sam thanking the crowd